TEMPORARY ARCHIVES
POEMS BY WOMEN OF LATIN AMERICA

Temporary Archives
Poems by Women of Latin America

Edited by Juana Adcock
& Jèssica Pujol Duran

ArC
PUBLICATIONS

EDGE HILL
UNIVERSITY PRESS

2022

Published by Arc Publications
Nanholme Mill, Shaw Wood Road
Todmorden, OL14 6DA, UK
www.arcpublications.co.uk
and
Edge Hill University Press
Department of English History & Creative Writing
St Helens Road, Ormskirk L39 4QP, UK
www.edgehill.ac.uk/university-press/

Design by Tony Ward
Printed in Great Britain by
TJ Books, Padstow, Cornwall

Cover illustration:
'Conexiones-casuales' by Lucia Morán Giracca
reproduced by kind permission of the artist.

978 1908376 28 2 (pbk)

ACKNOWLEDGEMENTS
The publishers would like to thank:
Edge Hill University Press editorial assistant: Isabella Castaneda Godoy;
EHUP Interns Jade Ball, Lucy Barrett, Jack Bennett, Emma-Jo Coyle,
Lucy Duffell, Victoria Loftus and Sophie O'Neill; and the Department of
English, History and Creative Writing (Now English and Creative Arts).
Special thanks are also due to the Editors Juana Adcock
and Jèssica Pujol Duran and particualrly to James Byrne for conceiving
this project and making it possible.

Arc Publications
Anthologies in Translation
Series Editor: Jean Boase-Beier

CONTENTS

INTRODUCTION

This anthology brings together a wide range of contemporary Latin American women poets, some of whom might be known to English readers through individual publications, such as Sara Uribe's *Antígona González* (Les Figues Press, 2016) and Elvira Hernández's *The Chilean Flag* (Kenning Editions, 2019) in the US, and Gladys Mendía's *The Singing of the Mangroves* (Carnaval Press, 2019) and Virna Teixeira's *The Couple's Room* (Carnaval Press, 2018) in the UK, or through poems published in translation in numerous poetry magazines, e-zines, and anthologies. Despite having a wide readership in their own countries, and despite numerous translation efforts, their work continues to be absent from the shelves of the main bookshops and is mostly unknown to many English-language poetry readers. These were the first sparks that ignited the engine of this anthology: the will to gather in one book some of the scattered works published by poets and translators around the globe, and at the same time add some original commissions to the mix, in order to showcase the unique trajectories these authors have in their countries. The 24 poets included here are: Victoria Guerrero (Peru), Verónica Fisher (Argentina), Teresa Arijón (Argentina), Tania Favela (Mexico), Susana Villalba (Argentina), Sara Uribe (Mexico), Rosa Chávez (Guatemala), Neronessa (Dominican Republic), Maximiliano Sojo (Venezuela), Marcia Mogro (Bolivia), Mara Pastor (Puerto Rico), Luna Montenegro (Chile), Leonor Olmos (Chile), Katherine Bisquet (Cuba), Johanna Barraza (Colombia), Gladys Mendía (Venezuela), Érica Zíngano (Brazil), Elvira Hernández (Chile), Elvira Espejo (Bolivia), Josely Vianna Baptista (Brazil), Virna Teixeira (Brazil), Mikeas Sánchez (Mexico), Paula Ilabaca (Chile), and Fátima Vélez (Colombia).

Our decision as editors was not to use this publication to build up an idea of a generation, movement, or school that followed a particular poetics, but rather, to include writers from a wide selection of countries whose poetries are alive and widely read in Latin America and abroad today. Our intention is to provide a glimpse into the huge amount of diversity in styles, poetics, languages and experiences that exist throughout the continent. We do not subscribe to the idea of "world poetry" as it tends to designate poetry that crosses borders following a particular political urgency or poets caught in a global net that agrees with a particular sense of universality. It was our aim to use the most inclusive criteria possible during our selection process when it came to the categories that we wanted to represent. When we speak of 'women' in the subtitle of this anthology, we consider anyone with an experience of womanhood, be it as a cis woman, a non-binary person, or pre- or post-transition.

If the poets that we selected for this anthology have anything in common it is their shared capacity to capture, respond and signify issues that affect the everyday in a globalized world from a local perspective. There are poems that reflect on the intersections between nature and technology, that have this global / local sense in them, such as Luna Montenegro's 'let anything i see be something', where she pays attention to the impossible combination of the organic and the inorganic in their reception by our senses – "microscopic organisms in furious copulations / under each of your computer keys" – and Leonor Olmos' poem '11', where the poem is brought to a crisis like the body that writes it through a series of contradictions that involve the technological and the body, which are stuck onto each other, unable to be set apart by the individual – "a barcode / adhesive tape / packing tape on a body or on tissue or on a swollen abdomen". There are poems, like Elvira Hernández's 'Travel Letter', that reflect on how nature becomes privatised from a very local point of view, though our identities blur under their domain in a global situation:

> And you, on the other side of the world, beyond the Pillars of Hercules, easily located by ENTEL, by a ground-to-ground missile, by a communication satellite, by a Courier-Friend, where are you?

There are poems that lay bare the patterns of gender violence that takes place indoors but can happen anywhere, such as Verónica Fisher's 'Skimming Stones', in which the lyric 'I' is violated by the voice of her father that bursts, uninvitedly, into the poem:

> Daughter of mine
> and of a big
> bitch
> where did you bury
> the bones

that were still alive?

...

give me them, give me them now
daughter of
I buried them in my body
papa

Other poems focus on this same violence outside, like Maximiliano Sojo's 'Missvenezuela':

good evening, Caracas

on your right, the dead woman

raped
tossed on the side of a country road

lost without her passport,
budget boobjob
with her CADIVI allowance,
out of self respect

There is a lot of violence in these poems, as they tell us about different undigested realities that surround the poets, sometimes with broken or syncopated language as in Marcia Mogro's 'excavations', where the poet (un)writes an urbanised landscape while being told of the marvels of the natural world as in a dream:

last night
covered in rubbish I slept
I slept   c o v e r e d   i n   r u b b i s h

and

they say they have a formidable and defiant desert
they say the mountain range is reclining and in silence
they say the vision of the sea remains in the eye

or in Tania Favela's 'The March Towards Nowhere', where the dream has evaporated and only a naked, unequal and frayed reality remains:

(there) crashed and above the *open sky*   open for whom?
thought about that   as much   in everything
thought of the frayed   the ragged   the hungry
all the mouthless   (he thought about this) –the mouthless there
                                    on the ground –
                        – headless – crashed without knowing

Victoria Guerrero, in 'Urgent Poem', voices this violence and condemns the silence that surrounds it:

> Is this country my country?
>
> A dead country of dead girls?
>
> And who cares about this country?
> The owners of the country
> And who cares about this country?
> The owners of the country
> And who cares about this country?
> The owners of the country

and Rosa Chávez does something similar when she urges us to remember the violence committed upon the Americas in her prose poem 'Abya Yala':

> Abya Yala you were renamed and now they call you America
> Abya Yala of 1492 cacao, gold, feathers, stones
> so much weariness accumulated in the body of the earth

We find a violence in the word, and of the word: "The word is violence" states a line of Teresa Arijón – a very human violence:

> violence of the plummeting sun on the mountain,
> strange mountain of ferocious serpentine
> stones they say were carried here by men.

The destiny of the genders as a site of violence, and how trauma is held in the body, is also found in Johanna Barraza:

> Esteemed coroners,
> that body does not belong to you,
> it died in my arms,
> and since then
> I have given birth to it

and in Mikeas Sánchez, who writes in Zoque:

> I am woman and I celebrate every vein
> where I trap my ancestors' secrets
> all the Zoque men's words in my mouth
> all the Zoque women's wisdom in my spit

There are poems that speak to the idea of history and repetition as part of the structural violence present in our world. Gladys Mendía writes

> I walk through the streets of my neighbourhood and the
> oppressors have done an excellent job   all overcrowded
> all uniformed   all anaesthetised   objectified in traffic
> following the signs accelerating in the highways   star-filled
> without light   dreaming of disobedience

while Katherine Bisquet's

> History, we told it all so well
> that the others barely heard it.
> You could always shout

is countered in Paula Ilabaca by a speaker that says "i'm a voice i'm a little voice [...] that wants to begin to speak" and in Josely Vianna Baptista's

> bestow
> the
> ode
> the
> silence
> the
> name
> to
> despair
> tame
> the
> fear.

Both naming and non-naming, though, become entangled with the violence of the so-called historical truth. Sara Uribe asks, "What thing is the body when someone strips it of a name, a history, a family name?", and the violence of being stripped of a name is countered by Mara Pastor's renaming of the parts of a colonised body: "The day we erase those names / from women's bodies / another tongue will write their expansion."

There are poems that focus on remembering the past, some that dwell on reading the present and some that foresee a catastrophic future and sing for change, as Neronessa's 'Echoes', which works as a prayer and a voice that will resist amidst the destruction:

> I'll sing until my words leave bitemarks even if my soul gutters out:
> *Let eternity not spill upon our blood,*
> *when eternity succumbs let it not collapse upon our home.*
> *When eternity drowns let its muscles not drag us*
> *down to the lungs of the abyss.*

And we also find the violence of psychoses, our own mind, scarred and scattered, having lost touch with reality, hallucinating that violence, felt so close that it becomes real:

> her new lover comes to visit her daily
> he brings papaya he is upset
> she thought he wanted to kill her
> to steal her organs

– we read in Virna Teixeira's poems from 'Suite 136' a sort of violence that has been inserted into the body, has become part of our psyche, and is thus, a projection: reality is seen here as a threat to our survival.

The violence of politics and economics, the strains of exile, the redefinitions of gender and race, the violence inflicted on minorities and their languages, the violence of history and official narratives, but also the places reserved to love, happiness and celebration in these new contexts are present in these poems, as in Elvira Espejo's 'Hither and Heather', which tells us in Quechua: "Mallow root mallow root / my love roves the hills", and "Snatch you seize you / Cradle you in my heart", where despite all the sadness, the poet keeps a place of tenderness intact. In Susana Villalba there is rebellion and eroticism in the dismantling of conventional grammar to parody the traditional heteronormative ways in which desire is articulated:

i
i & me
my body & i went to that party
i danced
my body lovely rich & powerful – caressed
my betty boop my barefoot queen

an idea that is similar to what Fátima Vélez does, albeit with a completely different methodology, in her absurdist portraits of pleasure:

cannibals of feeling
devouring our capacity to enter
allowing us to graze pastures of sewers and toothbrushes

or in Érica Zíngano's poetry, that revolves around the absurdity of all of this with poignant humour, as in her poem 'Metaphysical Problems':

The Chicken is a step ahead
of the Egg
in the fight over who is leading
the race
of who came first
'The Egg has fallen behind
the Chicken again', an English study
from Sheffield University
announced.

Humour is a healthy resource when logic collapses into empty words and lies, and half-truths divert our attention from what really matters.

We can agree that all of these poets converge at one point, namely use of a language that awakens our senses and acts as both a depository of expression and as a vehicle to spread the unsaid. These are poetries that need to be read. This is indeed a diverse and rich anthology, and not only for the multiplicity of identities included in it, but also for their poetics, which branch out from a variety of traditions and contexts. We can read echoes of the Brazilian concrete poets in the work of Josely Vianna Baptista; the ephemeral materials of Fluxus in the work of Luna Montenegro; the rebellious words of the latest Berkley poets in Sara Uribe; the Spanish Neobaroque in Neronessa, and so on and so forth.

The title of the anthology, *Temporary Archives*, is taken from a line by Gladys Mendía, which resonated with the idea of the female body as a site of rebellion and memory, where the scars of the different violences inflicted upon it remain but are also healed by way of poetry, with a myriad of

> voices that call to the fertile fatherless voices of circumstances
> descriptive   arbitrary   eloquent achieve their non-purpose
> voices to the extreme   voices that rise

As editors we were particularly interested in linguistically innovative forms of naming these realities, with poetics that have been underrepresented in English. As with all the traditionally "female" crafts erased by history and time, the archives of female experience have often been lost and overlooked, and we felt that the idea of an archive, however temporary and provisional, could provide a framework within which to read this anthology.

It goes without saying that it would have been impossible to provide an exhaustive compendium of the poetries written by women throughout the continent of Latin America, and this kind of endeavour falls outside the scope of this book. Instead, this is a highly personal selection of voices reflecting a moment in time and are read within a particularly vital and convulsive historical context. The images and sounds of the "Green Wave" of the Latin American women's movement were never far from our minds as we made our selections. Chile's viral feminist anthem and dance steps 'El violador eres tú', devised by the collective Las Tesis and inspired by the works of Rita Segato, brought to the fore the structural violence and victim-blaming that too often pervades the discourse around women: "y la culpa no era mía ni dónde estaba ni cómo vestía" ("and I was not to blame, nor where I was, nor what I wore"), while Argentina saw the landmark legalization of abortion after five years of massive protest marches under the banner of #NiUnaMenos – a rallying call to end gender violence – and Mexico saw the barriers around the National Palace covered with the names of femicide victims. These moments inevitably affected what we felt drawn to as we made our selections.

The region of Latin America is of course one of overlapping definitions and geographies, and we opted for the most inclusive approach, not wanting to limit ourselves to Hispanic America, which would exclude the other languages spoken in the region, but instead looking at poets from the North, Central and South America as well as the Caribbean, including Puerto Rico, and poets writing in indigenous languages. Though the word "Latin" in the subtitle does not represent all the pre-Columbian languages and realities of the region, we take it for now as a provisional and imperfect designation for want of a better one. Equally, the idea of an anthology of "women" poets could prove problematic, as would the pronouns "she / her", for any poets identifying as non-binary or who simply do not feel fully represented in a "women's anthology". Still, we felt the need to compile this anthology, pointing at these issues and seeking new forms of representation, to push the poetries of these formidable authors to the frontlines of contemporary poetry.

Juana Adcock & Jèssica Pujol Duran

TEMPORARY ARCHIVES
POEMS BY WOMEN OF LATIN AMERICA

TERESA ARIJÓN (Argentina)

The poet, translator and playwright Teresa Arijón (b. 1969, Bueno Aires) has published 6 collections of poetry, most recently Os (2008) and Óstraca (collected poems, 2011). In 1995 she participated in the International Writing Program, University of Iowa and, from 1999 to 2001, ran the Poetry Workshop of the Antorchas Foundation with Diana Bellassi and Arturo Carrera. From 2001 to 2002 she worked on Puentes / Pontes (published 2003), the first bilingual anthology of contemporary Argentinian and Brazilian poetry.

ENGLISH TRANSLATIONS BY SAMUEL GRAY

If I were a man I would shave
with my grandfather's razor –
I would graze the cleft of my chin slowly,
I would trace the corners of my face with an aesthete's precision.
What a magnificent exercise of awareness and pulse,
to look into the mirror every morning,
blade in hand.

Si fuera hombre usaría
la navaja de mi abuelo para afeitarme –
rozaría lentamente el hueco del mentón,
trazaría los ángulos del rostro con precisión de esteta.
Ha de ser un magnífico ejercicio de conciencia y de pulso
mirarse cada día al espejo,
navaja en mano.

The word is violence –
violence of the plummeting sun on the mountain,
strange mountain of ferocious serpentine
stones they say were carried here by men.
Violence of the man on the dusty road
where violent dumptrucks pass –
on the greysilver of the highways
so black under this light so cutting
it defines everything
and leaves nothing to see.

La palabra es violencia –
violencia del sol que cae a pico sobre el monte,
curioso monte de piedras serpentinas y feroces
que dicen levantado por el hombre.
Violencia del hombre sobre el camino polvoriento
que violentos atraviesan camiones volcadores –
sobre las carreteras grisplata de tan negras
bajo esta luz cortante que todo lo define
y nada deja ver.

I

She says that, now,
when the wind shakes the branches
and the leaves trickle down over the tiles –
she says that now
her job is washing clothes at dawn –
a concert of buckets, water and soap and foam,
various fabrics and her hands –
small as mint and perfumed
with a scent I don't live in any more;
her hands, I mean,
hard at their unequivocal, familiar labours
still refusing the balm of forgetting.
At night, not so far from the house I live in now,
she washes clothes as if she were dreaming.
Later she writes – describes the colours,
the forest of silence and smoke,
the coursing of water through the grate
the red tiles –
as tame and delicate as the wind
that night after night blows on her hands
as if trying to revive the fire
between one and another heart.

II

We leave hour after hour behind,
the squandering of a world –
mute memory
of a past, passed
and smiling now from the photo
like it knew all along.

I

Dice que, ahora,
cuando el viento sacude las plantas
y hace caer hilillos de hojas
sobre las baldosas –
dice que ahora
su vocación es lavar ropa
de madrugada –
un concierto de baldes, agua y espuma de jabón,
telas varias y sus manos –
pequeñas como la menta
y perfumadas de un aire que ya no habito;
sus manos, digo,
en tareas rotundas, familiares
que aún se niegan al reparo del olvido.
De noche, no muy lejos
de la casa donde hoy vivo
ella lava su ropa como si soñara.
Luego escribe – describe los colores
la selva de humo y silencio
el correr del agua por la rejilla
y las baldosas rojas –
mansas y delicadas como el viento
que noche a noche roza sus manos
como queriendo avivar el fuego
entre uno y otro corazón.

II

Dejamos atrás horas y horas,
el derroche de un mundo –
muda memoria de
un pasado que pasó
y sonríe desde una foto,
como si supiera.

≋

I'm the one who was never born and waits, like the desirous one fleeing
for the destiny carved in their hand.
and the hand is just one more figure in the middle of the Pampas –
wilderness always,
palm out against the wind.

≋

soy el que no nació y espera, como quien deseoso huye,
el destino grabado en su mano.
y su mano no es sino una figura más en medio de la pampa –
para siempre agreste
de palma abierta contra el viento.

≋

I'm the one who was never born and searches
in the rock for their element,
the violence daring enough to cement them
to their little roadside shrine –
(while south of the world, an old farmer
leaves all he knows behind: the afternoons
on his wicker chair in the sun,
the tablecloth with green and white squares, his hat).

≋

soy el que no nació y busca
en la piedra su elemento,
la intrépida violencia que lo incruste
en su altarcito de santo popular –
(mientras al sur del mundo, un viejo campesino
deja atrás lo que conoce: las tardes
con la silla de paja al sol,
el mantel a cuadros blancos y verdes, su sombrero).

the one who was never born and recognizes
the borders of things: a continent exuberant
of opacities, where every once in a while
the tip of a spear is unearthed,
leather straps, rotten cords,
the curse from the bones of a foot.

el que no nació y reconoce
los bordes de las cosas: un continente de opacidades
exuberante, donde de tanto en tanto desentierran
una punta de lanza,
tientos, sogas podridas,
la luz mala en los huesos de un pie.

the wind is all lit up – with patience,
persistently, it carries sparks furious
to form bonfires –
to turn the grasslands into rivers of flame,
among the howls of small monkeys
and a pandemonium of parrots.
as if carrying a sandbag, a sack
voluminous enough to hide its trick,
the one who was never born arrives at the outskirts
of town, the furious limit
the barbed-wire, the water.
an animal in heat ranges the centaur's flanks
in the profound sky of the Pampas –
orbiting husks are revealed in rebellion
by the dreamt passion of an arrow
that never finds its mark.

❧

encendido está el viento – con paciencia
persistente lleva chispas furiosas
que formarán hogueras –
vueltos ríos de fuego arderán los pastizales,
entre los alaridos de los monos pequeños
y el vuelo de los loros en bandada.
como si cargara un costal de arena, una bolsa
que por su volumen esconde una trampa,
el no nacido llega al tope de las casas,
el límite furioso, el alambrado, el agua.
un animal en celo recorre los ijares del centauro
en el cielo profundo de la pampa –
revela en rebeldía los cascos orbitales
la ensoñada pasión de la flecha
que no dará en el blanco.

❧

slave hands
wove this basket –
pure red pierced, piercing osier
shot through with filigrees of light –
where in a brute
muddle, where without
innocence are kept
the fruits of the future.

❧

manos esclavas
han tejido esta cesta –
rojo puro punzó, punzante mimbre
atravesado por filigranas de luz –
donde se guardan
sin inocencia
en bruto embrollo
los frutos del porvenir.

❧

it appears in the brutal tragedy of thoughts
vacant like Maipu will be vacated,
land rolled flat, in whose presumed
monotony is embodied
the idea of a country
that builds by blood.

❧

aparece en la brutal tragedia de las meditaciones
vacías como vaciada será maipu,
esa tierra allanada que en presunta
monotonía encarna
la idea de un país
que a fuer de sangre forja.

❧

and the Pampas is only barren
extension
that is to contain the seed
of a people deaf to its voices –
domesticated.

❧

y la pampa no es sino baldía
extensión
que contendrá la siembra
de un pueblo sordo a sus voces –
domesticado.

≈

the one who was never born rests
their ear of ire against the plain –
feels the gallop, the hybrid
stampede –
and rises from their bones
on the first night.

≈

el que no nació apoya
el oído del odio contra el llano –
siente el galope, la híbrida
estampida –
se levanta de sus huesos
en la noche primera.

MUSEO DEL ORO – SAN JOSÉ DE COSTA RICA

the Indian's crown of feathers,
would it be safer on the body of the falcon?
the toucan? the black-chested-eagle?
would the animating venture of his voice
be better off in the wind?
the trees the ferocious poet chopped,
better off as mute stumps? constellations?
the metric scale, metallic,
imbalanced? in scraps?
rain on the rainforest doesn't redound,
is gold in these rocks,
ravaged gold, that took the form of animals,
before, in protohistory
but sits now on display in the museum –
bats, frogs with prodigious hind legs
spitting fire or water or seaweed,
a succession of butterflies caught in unexpected flight, serpents
injecting venom – their wisdom – into the shaman
who looks like a frog because he too
spits fire or water or seaweed.

the earth is two-faced,
one for the living, one for the dead.
there's more than one universe, someone says, so religions fail
because wouldn't that mean there's more than one heaven?
but paradise has no take-backs, no turn or return;
is fruit and spoils, given and
stolen away by the imagination.
and the flowers? savage red,
fabulous with the enormity of a lightning bolt,
they tempt monkeys as much as hummingbirds –
and no species triumphs over them
nor over the water.
the Caribbean sea,
which hides in its caves as much blood
as the bandit Mi Sangre hides in her breastplate,
and some day will carry this shore
and this jungle off
to the depths where unreachable and fantastic creatures
live in a singular blue and orange
phosphorescence that reflects the colour of sky
cut through with sun or an orange
still hanging unripe
from a tree while flowers,
which are orange blossoms,
perfume the warm air and
somebody – who? – passes
on a bicycle, leaving
tracks in the damp ground

MUSEO DEL ORO – SAN JOSÉ DE COSTA RICA

la corona de plumas del indio
¿se resguarda en el cuerpo del halcón,
del tucán, del águila mora?
la ventura animada de su voz
¿en el viento?
los árboles que el poeta feroz hachaba
¿tocones mudos, constelaciones?
la escala métrica, metálica
¿desmedida, destartalada?
la lluvia en el bosque lluvioso no redunda,
es oro en estas piedras,

oro arrasado que dibujó formas animales en la protohistoria
y hoy reposa en vitrinas de museo –
murciélagos, ranas de patas traseras
prodigiosas que largan fuego o agua o algas por sus bocas,
sucesión de mariposas atrapadas en vuelo inocurrido, serpientes
que inoculan su veneno – que es su sabiduría – al chamán
que se parece a una rana porque también
lanza fuego o agua o algas por la boca.
la tierra es una esfera de doble cara –
una para los vivos, otra para los muertos.
hay más de un universo, dice alguien, y las iglesias sucumben porque
¿habría entonces más de un cielo?
pero el paraíso no tiene retorno, ni contorno:
es fruto y hurto
de la imaginación.
¿y las flores? rojas, salvajes, fabulosas con la enormidad del rayo
tientan por igual a colibríes y monos –
y ninguna especie triunfa sobre ellas
ni sobre el agua.
el mar caribe, que esconde tanta sangre en sus fosas
como el bandido Mi Sangre en su pechera,
algún día se llevará esta orilla
y esta selva
hacia el fondo
donde habitan las criaturas fantásticas inaccesibles
las del azul único
y el naranja fosforescente
que reflejan
el color del cielo cruzado por el sol
o el de una naranja
que todavía cuelga
inmadura
de un árbol
mientras las flores
que son azahares
perfuman el aire caliente
y alguien —¿quién?— pasa en bicicleta
y deja la marca de las ruedas
en la tierra húmeda

JOHANNA BARRAZA TAFUR (Colombia)

The poet and photographer Johanna Barraza Tafur (b. 1995, Colombia) moved to Buenos Aires, Argentina in 2007 after the murder of her father. Her first book, Sembré nísperos en la tumba de mi padre *(I Sowed Loquats on My Father's Grave), won the 'German Vargas Cantillo' poetry prize in 2019 and, as well as being studied in an award-winning literary workshop in Colombia, her poetry has appeared online and in magazines in both Colombia and Argentina.*

ENGLISH TRANSLATION BY RAHUL BERY

from I SOWED LOQUATS ON MY FATHER'S GRAVE

A sharp-clawed creature.
As a good male specimen
it will have a big crest
and ample jowls.
Capable of delivering a knock-out blow
with its tail
and giving hell
to whoever dares cut him off.
Expert in courting rituals
and generally
on the solitary side
with an unaltering routine
because any change
exposes him to stress.
If you wanted to kill him
you'd know when
and where to find him.
An animal that wheezes unpleasantly,
a caporo*,
that's what my father was.

Whether a canary
is in a fit state to compete
is a question of instinct or luck;
Papá chose them by sight.
Once he took me to an aviary,

---

*The name used on the Colombian coast for the male iguana (author's note).

where there were more than fifty to a cage.
He watched them for half an hour
and when he settled on one
he wetted it with a syringe –
the canary didn't move
as if it knew what was happening.
The lady took it out of the cage
and put it in a paper bag
full of holes
so it could breathe.
We said goodbye
with Papá's words:
I hope it doesn't turn out weak and wily.

My father gave away the wily canaries
and took the best ones
to compete
at the Church of Santa Cruz.
I never attended a birdsong competition,
It's no place for young girls,
but he told me about them:
you pay your fee
at the bird supervisor's table,
where he will assign you a number.
More than a hundred take part.
When they're ready they're put into groups,
one challenges the other
and the battle of the feathers begins,
the canaries singing from their cages
as if it were their last day.
There are four judges for each round
whose job is to count the cheeps
in sets of three,
something like tweet-tweet-tweet,
with an extra point
for a colourful dotted ruff;
whoever has the most
at the end of a three-minute battle wins.
Bets are placed all around them,
spectators spur on the animals

and the owners lean on the judges.
The real business, he always insisted,
lies not in the competitions
but in the bird dealers who show up
ready to pay the going price
for the best birds of the day.

Gunshots ring out in the neighbourhood,
I rush to close the door
but someone I know pushes it open
and I let him enter.
They're shooting
at the people playing cards
on the corner, he says.
I run there
but a neighbour stops me
hugs me up against a fence,
asks me to stay still
and tries to stop me looking at the killer.
I decide to look at him
while he points the weapon at me,
my fear represents no danger.
The chairs and tables are full of holes,
I look for a wallet,
a shirt or a flip-flop,
something to hold onto.
Next to the loquat tree
I see my father's body,
I turn him over to cradle him
in my arms,
he opens his eyes
and his gaze penetrates me
like balm on a wound.

Ever since that day
death strolls through the neighbourhood,
right by the door to my house.
He's twenty years old,
with a name and surname,
always wears a cap

so that you can't see
his brown eyes,
which I liked
when I was little.
Now I'm being told I must pretend
I do not recognise them.

I spend hours out here,
worn out from watching bureaucracy
continue to pursue us beyond death.
Maybe this is why we become
part of a society?
Esteemed coroners,
that body does not belong to you,
it died in my arms,
and since then
I have given birth to it.
Every time those doors open,
in the background I see
men in white overalls
going into a room
and I feel like a bitch in labour
who doesn't want her creatures
to be touched by strange hands.
Gentlemen,
return him to me as I brought him to this world,
naked, bloodied,
don't touch him, don't open him up,
I want to be the one to see his cirrhotic liver,
and the trajectory of the bullets in his chest.
Maybe I'm asking too much,
maybe not,
but everyone should do
what they please
with their dead.

I killed my father
hundreds of times,
Mamá did too
though she won't admit it.

I wished him the worst luck in the game.
He'd vanish for days
and I'd poison him
whenever he was hungry.
I castrated him every time
he abandoned us
for other women
and I sunk a knife into him
when he came home drunk
smashing everything in his way.
They were perfect crimes,
in my mind.

In my family
there are almost no men left.
Jesús, Luis,
Enrique, Fernando, José.
Some died
in the internal armed conflict,
others from street violence,
and the ones that are left
are dying from the accumulated pain.
Their deaths rack up as I laugh,
as I love, as I sleep
or as I write this.
Death is a lesson
that I do not learn.

My father taught me to hate my grandfather,
his black sailor's hair
his sea smell.
Those attempts were in vain,
a few years ago I fell in love with him,
his wenge wood hair
in stark contrast to the greys showing through;
I surrendered before the dimples on his cheeks
which are now adorned with wrinkles.
Just like my grandmother
I forgot about his inability
to care for anyone,

bad father and bad husband,
I forgive him all this
and I forgive my father too
because he was his unknowing
apprentice.

The sun, the sea and the beating drums
have gone from me.
I'm a bunch of tangled rags
wandering down Callao,
washed-out like death.
A weeping woman, God help me!
Seeking permission
debating
between these people and my people,
a fugitive at sea.
If I return to my country I will be a prisoner
and every stay will be a transitory one.
Can somebody explain to me
the eagerness
we exiles feel
to belong to a land.

Back in Barranquilla
I recognise myself in that which doesn't change
or which changes so slowly
that I barely notice it.
Why should things change?
You were the one who went away,
my grandmother tells me.
The tree on my terrace
which my father believed was male
now bears chancleta mangoes.
Only in it do I see
a before and an after,
its shadow is my refuge
from the sun that beats
harder and harder.

The loquat tree
my father died next to
has been cut down.
My neighbour came by and brought me
its last fruits and a bullet
she found in its trunk.
We had two things in common,
we held his body
as he bled
and remained upright
paying no heed to the gunshots.

de SEMBRÉ NÍSPEROS EN LA TUMBA DE MI PADRE

Un ser con garras afiladas,
como buen macho
posee una gran cresta
y papada turgente.
Capaz de noquear a cualquiera
con su rabo
y mentarle la madre
a quien se atreva a cortárselo.
Experto en rituales de cortejo
y en general
de los más solitarios,
con una rutina inmutable
porque cualquier cambio
lo expone al estrés.
Si alguien quisiera matarlo
sabe en dónde
y a qué hora encontrarle.
Animal con desagradables resoplidos,
un caporo*,
eso era mi padre.

Que un canario
resulte bueno para competir
es cuestión de instinto o suerte,
papá los elegía a ojo.
Un día me llevó a una pajarera,
había más de cincuenta en una jaula.
Los observó durante media hora
y cuando se decidió por uno

* Se le llama a la iguana macho en la costa colombiana

lo mojó con una jeringa,
el canario no se movió
como si supiera lo que pasaba.
La dueña lo sacó de la jaula
y lo metió en una bolsa de papel
llena de agujeros
para que respirara.
Nos despedimos
con esta frase de papá:
Espero que no salga flojo y con mañas.

Mi padre regalaba los canarios con mañas
mientras que a los mejores
los llevaba a competir
a la Iglesia de la Santa Cruz.
Nunca presencié una competencia de trino,
No es un lugar para niñas,
pero me la relataba:
la inscripción se paga
pasando por la mesa
del supervisor de pájaros,
quien le asignará un número.
Compiten más de cien.
Cuando están listos son agrupados,
uno reta al otro
y empieza *la batalla de plumas,*
los canarios cantan desde sus jaulas
como si fuera su último día.
Hay cuatro jurados por ronda
encargados de contar los trinos,
por cada tres seguidos,
algo así como tri-tri-tri,
marcan un punto a favor
con un collar de bolitas de colores,
gana el que más acumule
al final de una batalla de tres minutos.
Alrededor corren las apuestas,
aficionados alientan a las criaturas
y los dueños presionan al jurado.
El negocio, esto lo repetía fervorosamente,
no está en la competencia
sino en los pajareros que asisten
dispuestos a pagar lo que sea
por los mejores del día.

En el barrio suenan disparos,
me apresuro a cerrar la puerta

pero un conocido la empuja
y lo dejo entrar.
Les disparan
a los que juegan cartas
en la esquina, dice.
Corro hacia el lugar
pero un vecino me detiene,
me abraza contra una reja,
pide que no me mueva
e intenta que no mire al sicario.
Decido mirarlo
mientras me apunta con el arma,
mi miedo no representa un peligro.
Las sillas y las mesas están agujereadas,
yo busco una billetera,
una camisa o una chancleta,
algo a lo que aferrarme.
Junto al árbol de níspero
veo el cuerpo de mi padre,
lo volteo para acunarlo
en mis brazos,
abre sus ojos
y su mirada penetra en mí
como bálsamo sobre una herida.

Desde aquel día
la muerte se pasea por el barrio,
junto a la puerta de mi casa.
Tiene 20 años,
nombre y apellido,
siempre usa una gorra
que no permite ver
sus ojos cafés,
esos que me gustaron
cuando era chica.
Ahora me obligan a jugar
a que no les conozco.

Llevo horas aquí afuera,
abrumada de ver como la burocracia
nos persigue más allá de la muerte.
¿Acaso nos volvemos parte
de una sociedad para esto?
Señores forenses,
ese cuerpo no les pertenece,
murió en mis brazos
y desde entonces

yo lo parí.
Cada vez que esas puertas se abren
veo en el fondo
hombres con overoles blancos
entrar a una sala
y me siento como perra en labor
que no quiere que sus criaturas
sean tocadas por manos extrañas.
Señores,
devuélvanmelo como lo traje a este mundo,
desnudo, ensangrentado,
no lo toquen, no lo abran,
quiero ser yo quien vea su hígado cirrótico
y la trayectoria de las balas en su pecho.
Quizás pido mucho,
quizás no,
cada quién debería
hacer con sus muertos
lo que le plazca.

Maté a mi padre
cientos de veces,
mamá también lo hizo
aunque no lo admita.
Le deseé la peor suerte en el juego.
Se marchaba durante días
y yo lo envenenaba
cada vez que sentía hambre.
Lo castré todas las veces
que nos abandonó
por otras mujeres
y le clavé un cuchillo
cuando volvía borracho
rompiendo todo a su alrededor.
Fueron crímenes perfectos,
en mis pensamientos.

En mi familia
casi no quedan hombres:
Jesús, Luis,
Enrique, Fernando, José.
Algunos murieron
por el conflicto armado interno,
otros por la violencia urbana
y los que quedan
mueren por el dolor acumulado.
Sus muertes llegan mientras río,

mientras amo, duermo
o escribo esto.
La muerte es una lección
y yo no la aprendo.

Mi padre me enseñó a odiar a mi abuelo,
su piel negra de marinero
y su olor a mar.
Ese esfuerzo fue en vano,
hace unos años me enamoré de él,
de su pelo color wengué
que se opone rotundamente a las canas,
caí rendida ante los hoyuelos de sus mejillas
que ahora se adornan con arrugas.
Al igual que mi abuela
olvidé su incapacidad
de cuidar a alguien,
mal padre y mal marido,
todo eso le perdono
y también perdono a mi padre
porque fue su aprendiz
sin saberlo.

De mí se han ido el sol,
el mar y los tambores.
Soy greñas y harapos
vagando por Callao,
desvaída como la muerte,
¡ay de mí, llorona!
pidiendo permiso,
debatiéndome
entre esta gente y la mía,
una fugitiva en altamar.
Si vuelvo a mi país seré prisionera
y cada morada transitoria.
Que alguien me explique
el afán que sentimos
los expatriados
por pertenecer a una tierra.

Vuelvo a Barranquilla,
me reconozco en lo que no cambia
o cambia tan lentamente
que casi no lo percibo.
¿Por qué cambiarían las cosas?
Fuiste tú quien se fue,
me dice mi abuela.

El árbol de mi terraza,
al que mi padre creía macho,
ya da mangos de chancleta.
Solo en él veo
un antes y un después,
su sombra es mi refugio
al sol que pega
cada vez más fuerte.

El árbol de níspero
junto al que murió mi padre
ha sido cortado.
Mi vecina vino a traerme
sus últimos frutos y una bala
que encontró en su tronco.
Teníamos dos cosas en común,
haber sostenido su cuerpo
mientras sangraba
y mantenernos en pie
sin importar los disparos.

KATHERINE BISQUET (Cuba)

Katherine Bisquet (b. 1992) is a writer and editor. Her poetry collection Algo aquí se descompone *(Colección Sur Editoriales) was published in 2014 and* Uranio empobrecido *(Rialta Ediciones, Querétaro, México) appeared in 2021. She organised and curated the first biennial of independent art in Cuba in 2018, and is the co-creator of Cinema in Quarantine (CCC) 2020, an initiative to research, rescue and promote Cuban cinema. Currently resident in Berlin, she writes the column* Putas Presas.

ENGLISH TRANSLATIONS BY JAMES WOMACK

from DEPLETED URANIUM / *de* URANIO EMPOBRECIDO

1992

I was born in December
In neither the month nor the city of disillusionment
For my mother clenched her guts tight
And then released them there in the city

The oracles disposed of my body
In the same place my mother had thought
To see if this fixed destiny would give way
To the desolation of her ancestors
But I was born in December
What business of mine are these uncompleted things

AÑO 92

Yo nací en el mes de diciembre
No en el mes ni en la ciudad del desencanto
Porque mi madre aguantó sus intestinos
Y los botó allá por el centro

Dispusieron los oráculos mi cuerpo
Donde mismo había creído mi madre
Para ver si este destino rígido sucumbiría
A la desolación de sus ancestros
Pero yo nací en el mes de diciembre
Qué tengo que ver yo con lo inconcluso

PROJECT OF THE CENTURY

To my fleeting mother

I guess it's time which hardens these metal bodies
or corrodes them.
I guess it must be that when they meet with sea-salt
they really do all rust,
and they fear navigating these hulks that are clad
in the iron of the 1980s.
It must also be that once upon a time they fled
to other lands where they could educate themselves,
where they could build the iron robot utopia,
and stopped still, halfway along the road.
Must be that they were forged in the crucible of the impossible
at the flexion point of all possibilities,
and after a few, so few years the immense wall collapsed.
We hung; are still hanging.
And then the hope fell away, the hope of living from energy,
the hope of living with energy fell away,
in an unfinished city,

in a generation unfinished,
though young and ingenious still.
And all were caught in the shipwreck,
for they were made of uranium,
for they did not pull the lever,
for they had seen the robot, which is still there, still asleep,
in a separate world that no one now knows.

EL PROYECTO DEL SIGLO

A mi madre fugitiva

Será el tiempo el que endurece los cuerpos de metal
o el que los corroe.
Será que cuando tocan la sal del océano
efectivamente se oxidan,
y temen navegar esos mastodontes armados
con los hierros del 80.
Será además que ya una vez huyeron
a otras tierras para formarse,
para armar la utopía *del robot de hierro*
y quedaron en la mitad del camino.
Será que en esas tierras se forjaron con lo imposible
en el momento de lo posible,
y después de tan pocos años cayó el colosal paredón.
Pendimos, aún pendemos.
Entonces cayó la esperanza de vivir de la energía,
cayó la esperanza de vivir con energía,
en una ciudad inconclusa,
en una generación inconclusa,
joven e ingeniosa aún.
Y el naufragio alcanzó a todos,
por estar hechos de uranio,
por no haber empujado la palanca,
por ver al robot que aún duerme,
en un apartado mundo que todos desconocen.

NUCLEAR CITY MON AMOUR

You saw nothing in Nuclear City.
Nothing.
I saw it all,
everything.
I saw the hospital,
I'm sure I did.

There's definitely a hospital in Nuclear City.
You can't see it?
You did not see the hospital in Nuclear City.
You saw nothing in Nuclear City.
Four times, I saw the reactor four times.
What reactor? In Nuclear City?
I saw the Nuclear City reactor four times.
I saw the engineers come and go.
The engineers, coming and going, thoughtful,
through the iron walls,
dismantling them,
because there was no other option.
The walls,
the walls,
dismantling them,
no other option.
Official justifications,
no other option.
I saw the reactor four times.
I saw the engineers,
I even, I even
looked thoughtfully at the iron,
the iron, tender as flesh.
I saw the great dome of the reactor.
Who could imagine it?
Young skin, sacrificed skin,
surviving skin,
still suffering, the pain of suffering.
Buildings, empty buildings,
unfinished buildings.
Blonde-haired
foreign women.
I stood in the square;
I felt too hot.
Forty degrees out on the square.
I knew this.
The temperature, the sun on the square.
How could I not see it?
The ocean… it's simple.
You saw nothing in Nuclear City.
Nothing.

The dismantling took place with the utmost seriousness.
History took place with the utmost seriousness.
History, we told it all so well
that the others barely heard it.
You could always shout.
But what could someone do,
if they know nothing?
I've always thought about the fate
of Nuclear City.
Always.
No.
Why on earth would you have thought of it?
I've met people.
In '91,
I haven't made it up,
from '91 onwards,
thousands of people appeared, leaving the electro-nuclear station
walking free from failure as well.
And those people live… here. I've seen them.
People have told me things.
I've seen them.
After '91,
'92,
'93.
You saw nothing.
Nothing.
After '94.
Nuclear City was filled with its failures.
Failures everywhere, radiochemical failures, electro-nuclear ones,
thermophysical failures…-
I haven't made anything up.
You've made it all up.
I've made up nothing.
Like life itself,
this fantasy existed,
this fantasy of bringing a dream to life.
My fantasy has been that they'll never forget this.
Just as in real life.
I've seen their descendants as well,
the children who were in the womb.
I have seen conformity,

innocence,
the apparent ignorance
of all the inheritors of Nuclear City,
those who accommodate themselves to such an unfair fate;
the imagination,
normally so fertile, closes down when faced with this.
Listen, I know all this.
I know everything; I know how it goes on.
Nothing.
You know nothing.
Women raise their children.
It all goes on.
Men take risks.
It all goes on.
Empty locales.
The coast scrapes it all.
Scraped all these people.
Hunger.
There's no land anywhere in the city.
The fury of a city.
The fury of a whole city.
Who's it aimed at, the fury of a whole city?
The fury of a whole city...
aimed at what?
Hey, listen to me.
Like you, I know oblivion.
No.
You do not know oblivion.
Like you, I am endowed with memory.
I know forgetfulness.
No.
You are not endowed with memory.
Like you, I too have tried to fight with all my strength against oblivion.
Like you, I have forgotten things.
Like you, I have desired to have an inconsolable memory,
a memory made of shadows and rock.
I have fought on my own behalf,
with all my strength,
against the horror of losing
the need for remembrance.
Like you, I have forgotten things.

Why deny the obvious need for memory?
Listen to me.
I still know it all.
It will begin again.
Thousands of young people.
Official figures.
It will start again.
The earth will be hot again.
That's Cuba for you, they'll say.
The tarmac will burn.
Disorder will reign.
A whole city will be destroyed and turned into ash.

CIUDAD NUCLEAR MON AMOUR

– No has visto nada en La Ciudad Nuclear.
Nada.
– Lo he visto todo,
todo.
He visto el policlínico,
estoy segura.
Existe un policlínico en La Ciudad Nuclear.
¿Cómo podría no verlo?
– No has visto el policlínico en La Ciudad Nuclear.
No has visto nada en La Ciudad Nuclear.
– Cuatro veces al reactor.
– ¿Qué reactor en La Ciudad Nuclear?
– Cuatro veces al reactor en La Ciudad Nuclear.
He visto a los ingenieros pasearse.
Los ingenieros se pasean, pensativos,
a través de las paredes de hierro,
el desmantelamiento,
a falta de otra cosa.
Las paredes,
las paredes,
el desmantelamiento,
a falta de otra cosa.
Las justificaciones,
a falta de otra cosa.
Cuatro veces al reactor.
He mirado a los ingenieros,
he mirado, incluso yo,
pensativa, el hierro,
el hierro vulnerable como la carne.
He visto la gran cúpula.
¿Quién lo habría dicho?

Pieles jóvenes, sacrificadas,
sobrevivientes,
todavía en la pena del sufrimiento.
Edificios, edificios vacíos,
edificios inacabados.
Cabelleras rubias
de mujeres extranjeras.
He tenido calor
en la plaza.
Cuarenta grados en la plaza.
Yo lo sé.
La temperatura del sol en la plaza.
¿Cómo ignorarlo?
El mar… muy sencillo.
– No has visto nada en La Ciudad Nuclear.
Nada.
– El desmantelamiento se ha hecho con la mayor seriedad posible.
La historia se ha hecho con la mayor seriedad posible.
La historia es tan bien contada
que los otros apenas saben.
Siempre uno puede gritar.
¿Pero qué puede hacer el otro,
si no sabe nada?
Siempre he pensado en el destino
de la Ciudad Nuclear.
Siempre.
– No.
¿Por qué habrías pensado?
– He conocido gente.
En el 91,
no me lo he inventado,
desde el 91,
miles de personas aparecieron desde la electronuclear,
y el fracaso.
Y esas personas viven…aquí. Los he visto.
Me lo ha contado la gente.
Los he visto.
Desde el 91,
desde el 92,
desde el 93.
– No has visto nada.
Nada.
– Desde el 94.
La Ciudad Nuclear se llenó de sus fracasos.
Por todas partes, radioquímicos y electronucleares,
y termofísicos…
No me he inventado nada.

– Lo has inventado todo.
– Nada.
Igual que en la vida,
esta ilusión existió,
esa ilusión de lograr un sueño.
He tenido la ilusión de que jamás olvidarán.
Igual que en la vida.
También he visto a los descendientes,
a los que estaban en el vientre.
He visto la conformidad,
la inocencia,
el desconocimiento aparente
de los herederos de La Ciudad Nuclear,
que se acomodan a un destino tan injusto,
que la imaginación,
habitualmente tan fecunda,
ante ellos, se cierra.
Escucha, lo sé.
Lo sé todo. Cómo continúa.
– Nada.
No sabes nada.
– Las mujeres crían a sus hijos.
Pero continúa.
Los hombres corren el riesgo.
Pero continúa.
Situaciones desiertas.
La costa araña.
Ha arañado a esta gente.
El hambre.
No hay tierra en la ciudad entera.
La furia de una ciudad entera.
La furia de una ciudad entera.
¿Contra quién la furia de una ciudad entera?
La furia de una ciudad entera...
contra qué?
Escúchame.
Como tú, conozco el olvido.
– No.
No conoces el olvido.
– Como tú, estoy dotada de memoria.
Conozco el olvido.
– No.
No estás dotada de memoria.
– Como tú, yo también he intentado luchar con todas mis
                                        fuerzas contra el olvido.
Como tú, he olvidado.
Como tú, he deseado tener una memoria inconsolable,
una memoria de sombras y piedras.

He luchado por mi cuenta,
con todas mis fuerzas,
contra el horror de ya no entender
la necesidad de acordarse.
Como tú, he olvidado.
¿Por qué negar la necesidad evidente de la memoria?
Escúchame.
Todavía sé.
Volverá a empezar.
Miles de jóvenes.
Son cifras oficiales.
Volverá a empezar.
Habrá calor sobre la tierra.
Así es Cuba, dirán.
El asfalto arderá.
Un profundo desorden reinará.
Una ciudad entera será destruida y se convertirá en cenizas.

EXHUMATION

To Maricela Arcelú, of course

Maricela, the black
Chemical Production Technician (CPT)
University of Las Villas
Only six went to Hungary
Radiochemist
Beloved of everyone
A new project
1987
The promise
Special training in corrosion
Didn't get to use it
Protests
Deactivation and radioactive waste
Connected to this
With her thunderous laugh
1992
Economic paralysis
She remains
Chemical technician
Conservation processes
She still remains

Governmental Measures
Redeployment of technical staff
A daughter
Ministerio de la Industria Básica
Strengthening Our Industrial Base
Unmarried
Nuclear Electric Plant staff
Higher degrees
Building No. 27, Apartment 12
Polytechnic
Lecturer
One dog
One sewing machine
Certificates on the wall
Staff transfer.

EXHUMACIÓN

A Maricela Arcelú, por supuesto

Maricela, la negra
Tecnóloga de las Producciones Químicas (TPQ)
Universidad de Las Villas
Solo seis para Hungría
Radioquímica
La querida por todos,
Un nuevo proyecto
Año 87
La promesa
Especialidad de corrosión
No la aplica
Protesta
Desactivación y desechos radiactivos
Se vincula
La de la risa estruendosa
Año 92
Parálisis
Se queda
Tecnóloga química
Proceso de conservación
Aún permanece
Medidas del Gobierno
Reubicación de técnicos
Una hija
MINBAS
Fortalecimiento de la Industria

Soltera
Personal de la CEN
Alta preparación
Edificio 27, apartamento 12
Politécnico
Profesora
Un perro
Una máquina de coser
Títulos en la pared
La permuta.

THE MOTHER

A woman clings hard to the calm
perpetual blackout
where I live.
The necessary machinery
for power to return
is deaf
deaf too the inclusion
of this crusade
the overwhelming taste of those who say

                      responsibility.

A woman
dissolves herself
contaminates herself
offers herself
stabs herself with the symbol
                chews it
                spits it out.
For those who don't know
a woman
believes she does
whatever the hell she wants.

LA MADRE

Una mujer se aferra a la quietud
del apagón
constante de donde vivo.
Sorda
la maquinaria necesaria

para el arranque
la inclusión
de esta cruzada
el sabor apabullante de los que dicen
> responsabilidad.

Una mujer
se disuelve
se contamina
se ofrece
se clava el símbolo
> lo mastica
> lo escupe.

Para los que no lo sepan
una mujer
cree hacer
lo que le da la gana.

UNNATURAL

Humans howl like wild beasts,
and wild beasts seem human.
> OSIP MANDELSTAM

One always thinks one's time is behind the times.
The belly no longer can contain the heavy urine.
Breasts lie in the sweat of the earth.
Boots kick rage to silence.

Your own ideals slip out of sight.
The voice not history's but next to history does not reply.
The echo no longer resonates in the arteries.
Light will not come.
Someone,
Viciously,
mutilates himself
dissolves into the motionless
sanity
that lies over the fateful stain of morning.
Enters the day
like a wild beast blown apart by a hunter.

FUERA DE LUGAR

> *Los humanos aúllan como fieras,*
> *y las fieras parecen humanas.*
> OSIP MANDELSTAM

Uno toma por desfasado el tiempo de su tiempo.
El vientre no aguanta más la orina espesa.
Bajo el sudor de la tierra los senos yacen.
Las botas acallan la furia.

Uno pierde de vista los ideales.
No responde la voz adyacente a la historia.
El eco no retumba más en las arterias.
La luz no llegará.
Uno,
Severamente,
se mutila
se deshace en la cordura
inmóvil
sobre el rastro aciago de las madrugadas.
Se introduce en el día
como se abre una fiera en la pólvora.

THE WIND SCATTERS

The gentlemen out on the seafront
are all enthusiasts
and carefully
announce
their arrival.

Forward, my comrades!
Forward my faithful soldiers!

Can you smell the jungle?
Can you smell the jungle?
Can you smell the pus in the sores?
Can you smell the horses' fierce sores?
They have black eyes
lost in the hillside
they
know the pain of the fallen

they
know
far more than the weapons know
they, the outcasts of class, know the chafing sores
they, the fallen
know the smell of blood.

But the wind on the seafront
will not bring the greasy stench of the dead
and they,
the enthusiasts,
sense nothing but the fervour of the masses.

DONDE EL VIENTO SE DISEMINA

Los señores del promontorio
son los entusiastas,
anuncian
cuidadosamente
la llegada.

¡Adelante compañeros!
¡Adelante mis fieles soldados!

Sientes el olor de la manigua?
Sientes el olor de la manigua?
Siente el sudor de las llagas?
Sientes el ardor de las llagas de los caballos?
Ellos tienen ojos negros
que se pierden en el monte
ellos
saben del dolor de los caídos
ellos
saben
mucho más que las armas
ellos, los desclasados, saben de las llagas de las sogas
ellos, los caídos
saben del olor de la sangre.

Pero donde sopla el viento en el promontorio
no llega el grasiento hedor de los muertos
ellos,
los entusiastas,
solo sienten el fervor de las masas.

EBB TIDE

All the years of hindrance are now quiet
in the mind almost
in reason's unbearable harmony almost
in the fatalism of conscience almost.

They grow dust, the years do,
and the dust is always silent
and is terrible
terrible indeed
consuming itself
consuming itself
forgetting itself
over and again.

This is a chaos of construction
for all time of all time
and the dead always appear
from where you least expect it
and never give you any peace
because they themselves are never still.

And there will be another time within time
and that which was silent will remain silent
in any crack in history's bland kindness
in the evocation of one who has died
in a poet's inexact paraphrase.

EN RETIRADA

Han quedado en silencio los años de estorbo
casi en la mente
casi en la insoportable armonía de la razón
casi en el fatalismo de la conciencia.

Han quedado en el polvo
y el polvo que siempre calla
es terrible
efectivamente terrible
que se consuma
y que se consuma
y que se olvide
otra vez.

Es un caos de construcciones
por los siglos de los siglos
y que siempre salen los muertos
de donde menos te imaginas
y que nunca te dejan tranquilo
porque nunca reposan.

Ya será en el tiempo otro lapso
entonces lo que quedó en silencio seguirá en silencio
en cualquier resquicio de la amabilidad histórica
en la evocación de un muerto
en el reducto inexacto de un poeta.

ROSA CHÁVEZ (Guatemala)

Rosa Chávez (b. 1980) is a poet of Mayan K'iche' Kaqchiquel origin. She has published six collections of poetry, the most recent of which is Abaya Yala *(Fanzine, Sincronía Editorial, 2016). She has acted in plays, performances in public spaces and cultural centres and has been a part of numerous collectives of urban art, community and the Mayan movement in Guatemala. Her work has appeared in magazines, plays and festivals and in anthologies of Latin American poetry in Europe and the USA and has been translated into Mayan K'iche, English, French, Norwegian and German.*

ENGLISH TRANSLATIONS BY JUANA ADCOCK

ABYA YALA

1

Abya Yala you were renamed and now they call you America
Abya Yala of 1492 cacao, gold, feathers, stones
so much weariness accumulated in the body of the earth
Abya Yala the cycles of dying badly are endless
America begone with your legacy of fear and venom
I am as exhausted as you are
my letters are sick like your body
America when will you return to your origin?
it is time to remove the veil that shrouds your history
when will you be reflected in your dead?
when will you sing the names of the rebellions and battles for
                                                    your dignity?

Abya Yala your holy books were burned in smouldering tears
America when will you cease sending your spawn to the pits
your intentions nauseate me
I pass myself off as another to wander your labyrinths
America you sowed sin, guilt and shame, you drew this world
                                                with your finger
your burden weighs me down
you made me want to close my eyes and levitate
but there is no way to reconcile with this reality
sombre poets try to escape their own evil, they are frightening
they are so frightening or is this mockery
I am trying to get to the root
I will not renounce my delirium
America stop jolting me, I don't know what I'm doing but I
                                                believe in it

America the kernels are falling off the cob
I don't read the news for months, I fall every day with each murder
America I am moved by the pamphlets and protest songs
America I am still a carefree child and I have no regrets
I smoke sacred herbs and swallow stars at every chance
I am lost and I find myself for days on end at home gazing at the
                                                flowers that are born in me
I drink in the Chinese cafés and I don't take anyone to my bed
it was decided that there would be trouble here
you should have seen me reading the Chilam Balam
the Ajq'ij priest can see I'm fine
I will never again repeat the Lord's prayer
I feel the vibrations of the universe and I travel to other dimensions
America I still haven't told you what you did to my uncle
when as a wetback he crossed the desert to find you
listen to me I'm talking to you
how can you let the internet govern your emotional life?
I am obsessed with the internet
I go online every day
the internet beams at me from all its networks every time I walk
                                                through its eyes
I look at it when all the lights have gone out
they keep telling me about what I should be, good women are serious
women activists are serious, they are all serious women except me
it occurs to me that I am Abya Yala

too much pretension and I wind up speaking to myself
the indigenous peoples rise up against me
I don't have the chance to rebel
I must consider my ephemeral possessions in a country that has
                                              dispossessed me
my natural resources are reduced to a few doses of psilocybin,
                         millions of bodies that preceded my history
unpublishable poems that travel at the speed of silence
and countless deaths and mental rebirths
I will not speak of my clandestine prisons nor of the millions who
                                            have been extinguished
in the damp of darker times
I don't want to be president nor return to any religion
America how to write a ceremonial discourse
with your mediocre knowledge of the spirit
I will continue my verses outside your control and your domestication
each one of its tentacles has bodies and desires that are offensive in
                                                      your eyes
America new hymns will be sung that begin to crack your old carapace
Abya Yala liberate the bound names
Abya Yala save the movements that make the empire tremble
Abya Yala may they not fade from our memory: Mama Maquin,
     Tupac Amaru, Atanasio Tzul, Bartolina Sisa, Guaicaipuro
Abya Yala I am the survivor of slavery and genocide
Abya Yala when I was 13 years old my mother told me that in the year
     1982 my uncle was abducted by a death squad, he belonged to the
                                       guerrilla army of the poor
he was a loving tailor, in those days to be an insurgent was a courageous
                                        and heartfelt decision
life on the edge of death begot beings resplendent with bravery
I wept when I learned my uncle was one more of the thousands of
                                  disappeared and massacred souls
he was accused by people dressed up as stones
Abya Yala you never wanted war
America everyone else is the bad guy
those who are not scared of you, illegal migrants, warrior women,
                                       the anti-America outbreaks
America this is the reality
America it's what I see when I turn on the television
America is this good?

I cannot turn my back on history
I don't want to deliver my body to the mechanism that will use me
against my own people
and besides my bones are numb and my eyes are alight
Abya Yala here I grant you my expanded consciousness, my fierce
intellect
here is my body for ever rebelling and thrilled.

ABYA YALA

1

Abya Yala fuiste renombrada y ahora te llaman América
Abya Yala de 1492 cacao, oro, plumas, piedras,
tanto cansancio acumulado en el cuerpo de la tierra
Abya Yala los ciclos de la mala muerte no terminan
América vete lejos con tu herencia de miedo y veneno
estoy tan cansada como tú
mis letras están enfermas como tu cuerpo
América ¿cuándo volverás a tu origen?
es tiempo de destapar el velo que cubre tu historia
¿cuándo te reflejarás en tus muertos?
¿cuándo cantarás los nombres de las rebeliones por tu dignidad?
Abya Yala fueron quemados tus libros sagrados ardiendo en llanto
América ¿cuándo cesara el envió de tus engendros a la tierra?
tus intensiones me provocan nauseas
me disfrazo para pasearme por tus laberintos
América sembraste el pecado, la culpa y la vergüenza, trazaste
con tu dedo este mundo
tu peso recae sobre mi espalda y me dobla
me hiciste querer cerrar los ojos y levitar
pero no hay manera de reconciliarse con esta realidad
oscuros poetas intentan escapar de su propia maldad, asustan
asustan tanto o acaso esto es solo una burla
estoy tratando de llegar a la raíz
no voy a renunciar a mi delirio
América deja de sacudirme, no sé lo que hago pero creo en ello
América los dientes del maíz se están cayendo
no leo periódicos en meses, cada día caigo con cada asesinato
América me conmueven los panfletos y las canciones de protesta
América sigo siendo una niña libre y no me arrepiento
fumo plantas sagradas y trago estrellas cada vez que puedo
me pierdo y me encuentro días enteros en mi casa mirando las
flores que me nacen
bebo en las cafeterías chinas y no me llevo a nadie a mi cama
decidido aquí habrán problemas

me hubieras visto leyendo el Chilam Balam
el ajquij mira que estoy bien
no rezaré nunca más el padre nuestro
siento las vibraciones del universo y viajo a otras dimensiones
América aún no te cuento lo que le hiciste a mi tío
cuando de mojado cruzó el desierto para encontrarte
escúchame te estoy hablando
¿cómo vas a permitir que internet decida tu vida emocional?
estoy obsesionada con internet
todos los días me conecto
internet me mira desde todas las redes cada vez que paso por sus ojos
lo veo a escondidas cuando se han apagado todas las luces
siempre me hablan de lo que debo ser, las mujeres buenas son serias,
las activistas son serias, todas son serias menos yo
se me ocurre que yo soy Abya Yala
demasiada pretensión me deja hablando sola
se levantan contra mí los pueblos originarios
no tengo la oportunidad de la rebeldía
debo considerar mis efímeras posesiones en un país que me ha despojado
mis bienes naturales se reducen a unas dosis de psilocibina, millones
                de cuerpos que antecedieron mi historia
poemas impublicables que viajan a la velocidad del silencio
e incontables muertes y renacimientos mentales
no hablaré de mis cárceles clandestinas ni de los millones que se han
                          apagado
en la humedad de los tiempos más oscuros
no quiero ser presidente ni volver a religión alguna
América cómo escribir un discurso ceremonial
con tu mediocre conocimiento del espíritu
continuaré mis versos fuera de tu control y tu domesticación
cada uno de sus tentáculos tienen cuerpos y deseos que ofenden tu mirada
América se cantarán nuevos himnos que resquiebren tu vieja coraza
Abya Yala libera los nombres amarrados
Abya Yala salva a los movimientos que hacen temblar al imperio
Abya Yala que no mueran de nuestra memoria Mama Maquin, Tupac
        Amaru, Atanasio Tzul, Bartolina Sisa, Guaicaipuro,
Abya Yala yo soy la sobreviviente de la esclavitud y el genocidio
Abya Yala cuando tenía 13 años mi mamá me contó que en el año 1982
        mi tío fue secuestrado por un escuadrón de la muerte, él pertenecía
                    al ejército guerrillero de los pobres
era un sastre amoroso, en ese tiempo ser insurgente era una salvaje
                    y sincera decisión
la vida al borde la muerte criaba entes resplandecientes de valentía
lloré al saber que mi tío fue uno más de miles de almas desaparecidas
                    y masacradas
lo acusaron personas disfrazadas de piedras

Abya Yala nunca quisiste la guerra
América todos los otros son los malos
los que no te tienen miedo, los migrantes ilegales, las mujeres guerreras,
                              los brotes antiamérica
América ésta es la realidad
América es lo que veo al encender la televisión
América ¿esto es bueno?
no puedo darle la espalda a la historia
no quiero entregar mi cuerpo al mecanismo que me usará en
                              contra de los míos
además tengo los huesos entumecidos y la mirada encendida
Abya Yala aquí te entrego mi conciencia expandida, mi salvaje intelecto
aquí mi cuerpo siempre rebelde y complacido.

4

A month ago I moved to the capital
my granddad abandoned us and the hunger at home was sore,
I work at a house
(the lady says as a maid)
though I don't quite understand what that is,
they gave me a uniform,
that day I cried and cried
I was ashamed to wear it and show my legs,
the lady says in my village we are all unwashed shucos
that's why I shower every day
my long hair was cut
she says because of lice,
I can't speak good Castilla and people make fun of me
my heart grows sad
yesterday I went to see my cousin, I was in a good mood as I was
                              wearing my handwoven skirt
the bus driver couldn't be bothered to stop and when I was about to step
                              off he sped up
"hurry up stupid Indian" he said
I fell and scraped my knee
people were in stitches
my heart became sad
my cousin says I'll get used to it
that on Sundays we'll go to the central park
that there are dance halls

with groups from back home that come to the fair
I'm in my tiny room counting the money I was paid
minus the soap and two glasses I broke
the lady says I'm really thick
I don't understand why they treat me badly
am I not a person too?

4

Hace un mes vine a la capital
mi tata nos abandonó y en la casa el hambre dolía,
yo trabajo en una casa
(la señora dice que de doméstica)
aunque no entiendo muy bien qué es eso,
me dieron un disfraz de tela,
ese día lloré mucho, lloré mucho
me daba vergüenza ponerlo y enseñar las piernas,
la señora dice que en mi pueblo todos somos shucos
por eso me baño todos los días
mi pelo largo lo cortaron
dice que por los piojos,
no puedo hablar bien castilla y la gente se ríe de mí
mi corazón se pone triste,
ayer fui a ver a mi prima voy contenta porque puse mi corte,
el chofer no quería parar y cuando iba a bajar, rápido arrancó,
– apurate india burra – me dijo
yo me caí y me raspé la rodilla
risa y risa estaba la gente
mi corazón se puso trise
dice mi prima que ya me voy a acostumbrar
que el domingo vamos al parque central
que hay salones para bailar
con los grupos que llegan a la feria de allá, de mi pueblo
estoy en mi cuartito contando el dinero que me pagaron
menos el jabón y dos vasos que quebré
la señora dice que soy bien bruta
no entiendo porque me tratan mal
¿acaso no soy gente pues?

17

I shed this skin that no longer belongs to me
this abandoned skin that bore witness to another death
someone will find my scales stiff in the heart of darkness

someone will pull out three of my canine teeth for their medicine.
I will return then to give birth to myself with open eyes
I will return to scar over like a bearded fire-worm
I will return to stretch out my tongue to tickle the past
I am no longer this abandoned skin
I tense my muscles in pain
I am being born.

17

Dejo tirada esta piel que ya no me pertenece
esta piel abandonada testiga de otra muerte
alguien encontrará mis escamas tiesas en el corazón de las sombras
alguien me quitará tres colmillos para su medicina.
Volveré entonces a parirme con los ojos abiertos
volveré a cicatrizar como gusano de fuego
volveré a estirar mi lengua para hacerle cosquillas al pasado
ya no soy esta piel abandonada
contraigo los músculos con dolor
estoy naciendo.

21

I am a brown woman
I am not afraid of the word that was ransacked from me by the war
I walk trusting that so many deaths will bring me back to life
my thirteen senses have offered themselves up to the hands of time
because I look them in the eye they called me insolent Indian
because I'm finding myself in the truths that have been buried
because I name what has burned in my throat
they called me resentful Indian
I will not forget the words said to me by a playmate in early childhood:
Indian girls can't skip
I take leaps that crack thunder
they shatter, they let out sparks in that crude bigotry
because my brown skin has decided to feel the touch of freedom
I've been called rancid blood, a bad example,
I don't want to be an example,
I am hot blood that tends to my spirit's call
I am a spirit from whom are born desires, thorns
roots, tree trunks, callings from this and other times

brown, sweaty, shameless, big-mouthed brown flesh
flesh that dances, that dances with open and closed eyes
that recovers movement
flesh and bones that dance for all the joy and the dancing
that were denied to my ancestors
mouth that chews mushrooms in the winter of the future
childish mouth that was plundered by brutality
mouth that reclaims its song, its roar, its saliva.

21

Soy una mujer morena
no le tengo miedo a la palabra que me arrebató la guerra
camino confiando en que tantas muertes me regresarán a la vida
mis trece sentidos se han ofrecido jugosos a las manos del tiempo
por mirar de frente me han dicho india creída
por buscarme en las verdades enterradas
por nombrar lo que me apretaba la garganta
me han dicho india resentida
no olvido que un compañero de juegos en mi primera infancia
me dijo:
las indias no pueden saltar
y yo pego brincos que truenan
que revientan, que le sacan chispas a la rudeza de aquel desprecio
porque mi piel morena ha decidido sentir el tacto de la libertad
me han dicho sangre rancia, mal ejemplo,
no quiero ser ejemplo,
soy sangre caliente que atiende el llamado de mi voluntad
soy espíritu al que le nacen deseos, espinas,
raíces, troncos, llamados de éste y otros tiempos
morena, sudorosa, sinvergüenza, apalabrada carne morena
carne que baila, que baila con los ojos abiertos y cerrados
que recupera su movimiento
carne y huesos que danzan por toda la alegría y el baile
que le fueron negados a mis ancestros
boca que mastica hongos en el invierno del futuro
boca infantil que fue saqueada por la brutalidad
boca que recupera su canto, su grito, su saliva.

22

I'm an old lady in a park
the future dissolves in my wrinkles
nourishment of my hand are the illusions that shatter the sky's ceiling

my smile subtle and permanent basks in the sun
my memories are children that braid my hair
my vacant gaze finds itself facing inwards
I'm an old lady in a park
a hag who reveals her name to the strange world
I walk with an empty belly
and the enormous desire to turn the world around
each day I become smaller
each day my bones shrink
each day my moth-eaten memory fades
I no longer recognise the hands of my loved ones
I spend the afternoon threading the needle of silence
I return to the ingenuity of small footwear
and luckily I have lost the capacity to die for someone
I'm an old lady in a park
a woman hunchedbacked by life
a sinister gaze free of guilt
I have two legs made of flesh
and one made of wood carved with my beloved's face
I am all the women of my species
and I cry out for each of my lives and my deaths
I pretend I have no fear and in reality I have no fear
I'm an old lady in a park
the years only confirm the age of my secret
I heedlessly surrender to my fate
I am no longer tormented by the past
I have been awake a long time.

22

Soy una anciana en un parque
el futuro se deshace en mis arrugas
alimento de mi mano las ilusiones que destruyen el techo del cielo
mi sonrisa leve y permanente toma el sol
los recuerdos son niños que me trenzan el cabello
mi mirada perdida se encuentra hacia adentro
soy una anciana en un parque
una vieja que revela su nombre al mundo extraño
camino con el vientre vacío
y las enormes ganas de voltear al mundo
cada día me vuelvo más pequeña
cada día mis huesos disminuyen
cada día mi memoria se apolilla

ya no reconozco el gesto de las manos
paso la tarde enhebrando la aguja del silencio
vuelvo a la ingenuidad del calzado pequeño
y afortunadamente he perdido la capacidad de morir por alguien
soy una anciana en un parque
una mujer con la vida jorobada
una siniestra mirada libre de culpa
tengo dos piernas de carne
y una de madera tallada con el rostro de mi amor
soy todas las de mi especie
y clamo por cada una de mis vidas y mis muertes
finjo que no tengo miedo y en realidad no tengo miedo
Soy una anciana en un parque
los años solo confirman la edad de mi secreto
me entrego sin reparo al destino
ya no me atormenta el pasado
estoy despierta hace mucho tiempo.

23

They tear off our head and the heart keeps beating
they rip off our hide and the heart keeps beating
they cut us in half and the heart keeps beating
they drink our blood and the heart keeps beating
we were made to beat without respite.

23

Nos quitan la cabeza y el corazón sigue latiendo
nos arrancan el pellejo y el corazón sigue latiendo
nos parten a la mitad y el corazón sigue latiendo
beben nuestra sangre y el corazón sigue latiendo
estamos criados para latir sin descanso.

24

Elena Kame is a spell, she bites with her little canine mouth, her saliva leads to the great river, she digs deep caves and tall mountains, her love is an incantation that blinds the road numbing the mind's reason, her voice breaks the bones of melancholy returning in a murmuration and a peal of laughter, her nails taste of chilli and cacao, she drinks liquid lava, she seals with beeswax, she dedicates her tears to the archaic symbols of sadness, body of invisible rain, she draws colourful little graves and paints her cheeks with achiote, indecipherable stars of shiny paper adorn her temples, her face is the caustic and derisive mask of memory, she wraps their hearts in a corn husk delicately perforating the nipples of sound, she threads heartbeats like beads onto an ancient necklace, she makes thorns blush loving with the tenacity of someone who has descended barefoot and vanishing the nine levels of the underworld, Elena Kame overflows like at the beginning of time at the great end of time, her spirit is at once a spell and incantation.

24

Elena Kame es un hechizo, muerde con su boquita canina, su saliva conduce al gran río, hacia profundas cuevas y altos cerros, su amor es un encanto que ciega el camino adormeciendo las razones de la cabeza, su voz quebranta los huesos de la melancolía devolviéndose en murmullo y carcajada, sus uñas saben a chile y a cacao, traga en fluido de lava, sella con cera de abeja, dedica sus lágrimas a los símbolos arcaicos de la tristeza, cuerpo de lluvia invisible, dibuja tumbitas de colores y pinta sus mejillas con achiote, indescifrables estrellas de papel brillante le adornan la sien, su rostro es la máscara cáustica y burlona de la memoria, envuelve sus corazones con hoja de tusa perforando delicadamente los pezones del sonido, enhebra latidos que lucen como cuentas de collar antiguo, hace sonrojar a las espinas amando con la tenacidad de quien ha bajado descalza y desvanecida los nueve niveles del inframundo, Elena Kame se desborda como al principio de los tiempos en el gran final de los tiempos, su espíritu es hechizo y encanto a la vez.

from the theatrical performance **AWAS**

V

THE DISSOCIATION
(Video)

Dissociated Being makes a journey through the same places but in different directions: Body Being carries the three stones tied to it as in the previous scene, Spirit Being drags the stones tied to a sash. Each journey has a different energy. The energy of Spirit Being is contained, neutral, fluid, one walk in a state of abstraction, does not react to what is around it. The energy of Body Being is robotic in tension, its energy observes, searches, though it does not interact with its surroundings.

VI

MOURNING

Being appears seated facing away from the audience on the pounding stone, its feet move the pestle. The stones tied to the sashes, and the coffer, are left behind on the stage.

Off-stage Voice:

> Pick it up
> take what belongs to you
> grab it, it's yours
> don't allow them to take it away
> pick it up
> let it dry out in the sun
> pick out the weevils
> pull out teeth
> one by one
> crush its body
> grind its body
> mould its body
> cook its body
> don't leave it lying
> don't pull bad faces at it
> pick it up with care
> speak to it, it's yours
> it's your inheritance
> it's what I'm leaving to you.

Being stands up and walks towards the stones, drags them until reaching the coffer. One by one it places them inside the coffer manipulating them in different ways, treating it as if it were a coffin, tying it with the sash and carrying it on its shoulder. It walks to the pounding stone.

Being:

> I deliver this name dug up at the root, I deliver it fresh, newly washed with my blood, a pyre of howls goes with it, I deliver these remains in the bowl of my heart, I have too many dregs of disgrace, the dregs of shame, the dregs

of eternal waiting.
Being positions the coffer next to the pounding stone, forming the image
of a grave. She sits beside it.
Being *(slowly exiting the scene):*
>   I was devoured, crushed, beaten
>   I was all the women of my species
>   and I call out for each of my lives and my deaths
>   I pretend I have no fear and in reality I have no fear
>   I heedlessly surrender to my fate
>   I am no longer tormented by the past
>   I have been asleep a long time.
I am an old lady who lives like in the old times in the new times
>   I spend the afternoon threading the needle of silence.
>   Luckily I have lost the ability to die for someone.
>   I heedlessly surrender to my fate.
>   I am no longer tormented by the past.
The stage remains empty for a few seconds.

de la obra teatral AWAS

V

EL DESDOBLAMIENTO
(Video)
Ser desdoblado hace un recorrido por los mismos lugares pero en
diferentes direcciones: Ser cuerpo carga las tres piedras amarradas
sobre sí como en la escena anterior, Ser espíritu jala las piedras
atadas a una faja. Cada recorrido tiene una energía diferente.
La energía del Ser espíritu es contenida, neutral, fluida, una
caminata en un estado de abstracción, no reacciona a lo que hay
a su alrededor. La energía del Ser cuerpo es autómata en tensión,
su mirada observa, busca, aunque no interactúa con su alrededor.

VI

EL DUELO
Ser aparece sentada de espaldas al público sobre la piedra de
moler, sus pies mueven la mano de piedra. Las piedras amarradas
a las fajas y el cofre se encuentran abandonados en el escenario.
Voz en off:
>   Pepenalo
>   tomá lo que te pertenece
>   agarralo que es tuyo
>   no dejés que te lo quiten
>   pepenalo
>   ponelo a secar al sol

quitale los gorgojos
quitale uno por uno los dientes
machacá su cuerpo
molé su cuerpo
moldeá su cuerpo
cocé su cuerpo
no lo dejés tirado
no le hagás malas caras
pepenalo con cuidado
hablale, es tuyo
es tu herencia
es lo que te estoy dejando.
Ser se levanta y se dirige hacia las piedras, las jala hasta
llegar al cofre. Una por una las pone dentro del cofre ma-
nipulándolas de manera diferente, manipulándolo como si fuera
un ataúd, atándolo con la faja y cargándolo sobre su hombro. Se
dirige hacia la piedra de moler.

Ser:
Entrego este nombre arrancado de raíz, lo entrego
fresco, recién lavado con mi sangre, una pira de aullidos
le acompañan, entrego estos restos en la vasija de mi
corazón, me sobran los restos de la desgracia, los restos
de la vergüenza, los restos de la eterna espera.
Ser posiciona el cajón junto a la piedra de moler, formando la
imagen de una tumba. Se sienta a la par de ella.
Ser (*saliendo poco a poco de escena*):
Fui devorada, machacada, aporreada
fui todas las de mi especie,
y clamo por cada una de mis vidas y mis
muertes,
finjo que no tengo miedo, y en realidad no
tengo miedo,
estoy dormida hace mucho tiempo.
Soy una anciana que vive como en los viejos tiempos en los
nuevos tiempos
Me paso la tarde enhebrando la aguja del
silencio.
Afortunadamente he perdido la capacidad de morir por
alguien.
Me entrego sin reparo al destino.
Ya no me atormenta el pasado.
Queda por unos segundos el escenario vacío.

ELVIRA ESPEJO AYCA (Bolivia)

Elvira Espejo Ayca (b. 1981) is a poet, visual artist, weaver and narrator of the oral tradition from her place of origin, Qaqachaka, in Avoroa Province, Oruro. She speaks Aymara and Quechua, and is director of the Museo Nacional de Etnografía & Folklore, La Paz. She has published 3 poetry collections, the second of which Phaqar kirki-t'ikha takiy takiy / Canto a las Flores *(Song to the Flowers, 2006) was awarded the international poetry prize in Venezuela's global festival of poetry 2007. Co-author of several books on Andean textiles, she has also produced DVDs in collaboration with the Bolivian musician Álvaro Montenegro.*

ENGLISH TRANSLATIONS BY JUANA ADCOCK

from HITHER AND THITHER / de KAYPI JAQHAYPI

Translator's note: In translating these poems, I was struck by the form, and I have tried to achieve a similar effect in English. I relied greatly on José Navarro's help with the Quechua, as well as the author's self-translations into Spanish. The author's surname translates as 'Mirror'; this wordplay shows up in one of her poems.

Mallow root mallow root
my love roves the hills

> Malwa saphi malwa saphi
> munasqay luma wasapi

When I was a child
the sun would soar
now that I've grown
the sun lies low

> Juch'uy nuqa kaxti
> intipis phawarin
> kunan wiñapuxtin
> intipis pakaykun

Clouds brew, the wind blows
crowds come through, weighed down by their woes

> Phuyu phuyu mushan wayrawan jamushan
> runa jamushan kuyay kuyay jamushan

Bringing the rain and gusts of wind
doing as you do, they come after you

> Parawan suxrawan jamushani
> qanrayku jina jamushan

Across the river blue, resolute as the fortress on the plains
I walk in search of you

> Silisti mayu pukara pampa
> noqa purimuni qanta maskaspa

Around here you'll become
yonder you'll never be gone

> Kay chikaymanta chikaylla purinki
> kay karumanta ama munankichu

Why come after me? Why pursue?
When I'm in search of you

> Ima munaspa qhipay purinki
> nuqata qanta maskaspa

I will follow the river downstream, so they say
I will follow the river upstream
Where will I find you?

> Uraymayuntachus risax
> wichay mayuntachus risax
> mayllapichus taripallasqayki

Round the Pampass of Oruro
in search of Bolivia
gathering dahlia flowers
I roam in tears

Ururu pampa rishaspa
Bolivia maskaspa
Dalias t'ikasta pallaspa
Waqaspa purini

I'm leaving Oruro
Having lost my aguayo
why should I stay

Llijllitayta chinkachikurqani
Ururumanta kunan ripushani

Condor of mine soaring the heights
your white scarf tied tight
grazing the Illimani ridge
where must you go?

Kuntursituy altu phawa
Yurax chalinita wataykusqa
illimani limantachus phawashanki
Mayllapitax purishanki

You will be mine
I will be yours, together
may we always be so – crying

Qanllachu nuqapax
Nuqachu qanllapax
Kayjina waqanaypax

Snatch you seize you
Cradle you in my heart

Suwasqayki pusasqayki
Sunqa ukunta pusasqayki

Blustery hills and hills bone-dry
Ranging them all – I'll be whirring by

> Ichhu ichhu luma wayra wayra luma
> Nuqa ripunaypa chikay karu luma

A parrot on the tree top can never be caught
What we have lived cannot be untaught

> Sach'api luritu ni jap'iy atina
> Recuerdos ninchispi ni qunqay atina

For my shucked white corn and how far I have flown
I'm the thorn in their side

> Yurax saramanta pilasqaypis tiyan
> Purisqallaymanta invidiapis tiyan

Calf of vicuña, calf of a deer
I'm forever the yearling of my other half

> Vicuña uñita taruka uñita
> Jina puni kani munasqan uñita

Village of Chapare, glimmering village beyond
There's no holding me down

> Chapari llaxtita naranja llaxtita
> Astawan purisax imanawanqatax

Is this truly my village?
Stony silent place
I inhabit

> Akasu nuqaqa kaypunichu llaxtay
> rumi rumi wasa achay nuqax llaxtay

Up and down roads I'll go high and go low
on his arm always or maybe alone

> Uray kallintachus risax
> wichay callintachus risax
> mayqin supayllapis payllawanpunichu

If I were an apple tree I'd be dressed in white
If you truly loved me you'd be here by my side

> Mansana kaspaqa yurax t'ikhanayki
> nuqata munaspa laduypi kanayki

Ulupika tree budding in and of itself
In my native land I come into my own

> Ulupika sach'a kikin puquymanta
> nuqa tarishani kikin llaxtaymanta

Peach tree in bloom – green, violet and blush
forever loving – only by force

> Durasnu t'ikita qumir muradita
> inamurashanki alafuersallata

Sowing corn
for the new harvest
my desire for you
quickens my step

> Sarata tarpuni
> musux puqunaypa
> munakusharqayki
> musux purinaypax

Gathering flowers from my loam
My mother may taunt me but it's him I will marry

Alfa canchaymanta
t'ikha pallamusax
mamaypis rimachun
jina kasarasax

I'm weaving a sash of three colours
for my three lovers
from three places

Chumpita awani
kinsa kulurmanta
nuqax munay kashan
kinsa luwarmanta

This aguayo –
from all you have gathered
woven by me alone
from all you have gathered

Nuqax llijllitay
sapan junt'asqita
nuqata munaspa
sapan junt'asqita

Your petals plucked
In a pleasurable way
Oh, poor flower!
Whiling your hours away

Chhalla chhallarasqa
wiru wirurasqa
ay puyri t'ikita
timpun pasarasqa

Plains and mountain highs
I've traversed
in search of butterflies

Lumasta wayqusta
nuqa putimuni
pìlpintusta maskarispa

Because I am mirror my light has shone long
When I was alone I got further along

Ispijitu kaspa
karusta k'anchani
sapitay kashaspa
karusta purini

Tower on the craggy cliffs
facing the village of Wari –
wicked people
staring at me

Challapata torre
wari qawarisqa
supay runas
nuqa qhawarisqa

Am I the Ilisu river
to meander through valleys?
Am I married
to spend all day crying

Ilisuchu kani
wallipi kanaypax
casadachu kani
waqas purinaypax

my visions and point of view
are the source of contempt
say what they may
I'll keep looking ahead

qawarisqaymanta
invidiapis tiyan
astawan qawasax
imanawanqatax

saying city I've come
treading the cement of sorrow

> Siudad nispa
> jamuni
> semento patapi
> llakiy purishani

Sun blazing on the mountain peak
while I'm in the village of the wretched

> Intiqay luma patapi
> nuqaqay runax llaxtampi

Dear weeping willow
giving me shade
when my heart aches
take me away – loving

> Sawsi llurun pacha
> llanthuy llanthumuwan
> sunquyki nanaxtin
> munaspa pùsaway

The tree blossoms
in all sorts of colours
and all they can ask about
is my grey sorrow

> Sach'apis t'ikhasqa
> tukuy kulurmanta
> tukuypis tapusqa
> nuqa supaymanta

Seer of all flowers
I like their sweet scent
bewitched by my lover
I dreamt of his heart

Tukuy t'ikas pata
q'apaysitunta gustariwan
supay munasqanta
sunqitunta gustawan

The frost, frost will be
the dew, dew will be
the puna, grassland will be
the valley, valley will be

Siwi siwipuni
chhulla chhullapuni
puna punapuni
walli wallipuni

TANIA FAVELA BUSTILLO (Mexico)

Tania Favela Bustillo (b. 1970) is a poet and essayist. From 2000 to 2011 she was part of the Editorial Board of the magazine El poeta y su trabajo *directed by the Argentinian poet Hugo Gola. Her first book of poetry,* Materia del camino *(2006) was published when she was 35, and this was followed in 2013 by her second collection,* Pequeños resquicios. *Her third collection,* La marcha hacia ninguna parte, *appeared in 2017 from Komorebi Ediciones, an independent Chilean publisher. Her most recent book,* La imagen rueda *was published in 2022 in the editorial Libros de la resistencia of Madrid. She is currently a full-time academic at the Universidad Iberoamericana.*

ENGLISH TRANSLATIONS BY JÈSSICA PUJOL DURAN

from THE MARCH TOWARDS NOWHERE / de LA MARCHA HACIA NINGUNA PARTE

≈

The dreamer bites the word's nails (he says) the dreamer is an empty box
a tunnel that awakens is the dreamer (says)   a tunnel awakening
      with a broken mouth spits out chunks of dream the dreamer with a
                                        [broken mouth sings
                                              hums (says)
the dreamer bites his fingernails – delicious – (she says)
      the hands he eats the dreamer   empty box that sings voicelessly
            the dreamer slides between newborn words

slides – says, thinks, sees –: *the earth is a cold planet* (the dreamer says to himself)
　　　　drumming, drum (the earth is) (the dreamer says to himself)
the earth is elastic
　　　　descends to the flesh and from there to the dream
　　　　　　descends (drum, drumming) to the beat of her
　　　　　　　　　　　　　　　　　　　　or him.

　　　　≈

　　El soñador se come las uñas de las palabras (dice él)　el soñador es una caja vacía
　　un túnel que despierta es el soñador (dice)　　un túnel despertando
　　　　con la boca rota escupe pedazos de sueño el soñador　con la boca rota canta
　　　　　　　　　　　　　　　　　　　　canturrea (dice)
　　el soñador se come las uñas　　los dedos – deliciosos – (dice ella)
　　　　　las manos se come el soñador　　caja vacía que canta sin voz
　　　　　　　　el soñador se desliza entre palabras recién nacidas
　　　　　se desliza – dice, piensa, ve – : *la tierra es un planeta frío* (se dice el soñador)
　　　　　　　tamborileo, tambor (la tierra es) (se dice el soñador)
　　　　la tierra es elástica
　　　　　　desciende hasta la carne y de ahí hasta el sueño
　　　　　　　　desciende (tambor, tamborileo) al ritmo de ella
　　　　　　　　　　　　　　　　　　o de él.

　≈

(for Dad)

as strange as it sounds, they are all you *without I*
a trait　a deviation　(the difference that arises from the sameness)
　　or the other way round, they are all I *without you* – but nothing is resolved there
　at most everything stirs up
　　　everything is a blind spot there where so much seeing resounds
the stranger crosses from side to side
　　　　　similar to you *without me*　(similar to so many)
　or the other way round (they say)　　rootless
the stranger crosses from stretch to plot – making himself up –
　　　　　blind spot again　　voice or song?
they sound, crossing the air, the aria (remember) the opera always sounding
　(interwoven voices) – or a choral drama – already without a Dionysian sense
nothing is resolved, at most it is a bit stirred　– to fishing –　they say –
　　　to fishing　– in troubled waters the fisherman wins –
　　　　　as strange as it sounds (I say): *I am the fish*

≋

(para papá)

por extraño que suene todos son tú *sin yo*
un rasgo   un desvío   (la diferencia que surge de la semejanza)
                    o al revés todos son yo *sin ti* – pero ahí nada se resuelve –
            a lo más todo se revuelve
                        todo es punto ciego ahí donde tanto ver resuena
el extraño atraviesa de lado a lado
                    semejante a *ti sin mí*   (semejante a tantos)
            o al revés (dicen)   sin raíz
el extraño atraviesa de tramo a trama – inventándose –
                            punto ciego otra vez   ¿la voz o el canto?
suenan, atraviesan el aire, el aria (recuerdas) la ópera sonando siempre
        (voces entretejidas) – o un drama coral – ya sin sentido dionisíaco
nada se resuelve, a lo más todo se revuelve un poco – a la pesca – dicen –
        a la pesca – a río revuelto gana el pescador –
                        por extraño que suene (digo): *yo soy el pez*

≋

he "ragged" the "frayed" little poems (his) – he said –
            he heard himself say – almost whispering   almost silently –
        as fraying one's own voice – one's own impoverished voice –
ɪndressed (or almost) almost *that was what I was looking for and escaped* all attire – he said –
                                        all attire
    hence exposed   hence the starry sky – overhead – (he thought)
ɪɪs own head seeing flashes too   against what or who? against himself
    herself   until hitting the ground   – until making it sound like a hollow calabash –
                                    (maté for brewing)
    (there) crashed and above the *open sky*   open for whom?
ʰought about that   as much   in everything
        thought of the frayed   the ragged   the hungry
ɪll the mouthless   (he thought about this) – the mouthless there on the ground –
                            – headless – crashed without knowing
ʰere – cracking their heads open – as it were
                (he thought) as if meaning   as knowing the muteness of it
        the fraying of that song that does not
        of that saying, which barely (barely walks) – he said – he heard
    himself say

as if repeating the voice of another
repeating the voice of others
– he heard – (now) (before) the frayed
and above the *open sky*

≈

los "harapientos" los "deshilachados" poemillas (suyos) – dijo –
se oyó decir – casi murmurando   casi en silencio –
como deshilachando la propia voz – la propia voz empobrecida –
desvestida (o casi)   casi *eso era lo que buscaba y escapaba* a todo ropaje – dijo –
a todo ropaje
de ahí la intemperie de ahí el cielo estrellado – sobre la cabeza – (pensó)
estrellada también la propia cabeza ¿contra qué o quién? contra sí mismo
sí misma   hasta dar en el suelo – hasta hacerla sonar como una calabaz hueca –
(mate para cebar)
(ahí) estrellada y arriba *cielo abierto*   ¿abierto para quién?
pensó en eso   en tanto   en todo
pensó en los deshilachados los harapientos los hambrientos
todos los sin boca (en eso pensó) – los sin boca ahí sobre el suelo –
– descabezados – estrellados sin saber
ahí – rompiéndose las bruces –   como quien dice
(pensó) como queriendo decir   como sabiendo lo mudo de eso
lo deshilachado de ese canto que no
de ese decir que apenas   (a penas anda) – dijo – se oyó decir
como repitiendo la voz de otro
repitiendo la voz de otros
– se oyó – (ahora) (antes) los deshilachados
y arriba *el cielo abierto*

≈

It sounded still   (in there) hardened   floating out
(there) said the voice: there was and no longer   stayed and no longer
again (they say the voice said): don't let it cease   – don't let it break –
that thread of man (it said)
fear sounded still   sounded river   sounded stones falling from on high
sounded flowers *flowers for the ear* (they say the voice said)
drilling inwards
don't let those flowers break (it said) those mouths that float in there hardened
delay yes delay (said) the world – all – eyes and ears
roughness also   what is missing is that (said)
la mare és tot – go figure – without detour or anything.

(18th December 2015)

❦

Sonaba quieto (ahí adentro) endurecido flotando afuera
(ahí) dijo la voz: ahí hubo y ya no estuvo y ya no
otra vez (dicen que dijo la voz): que no cese   – que no se rompa –
　　　　　　　　　　　ese hilo del hombre (dijo)
el miedo sonaba quieto sonaba río sonaba piedras cayendo desde lo alto
sonaba flores   *flores para el oído* (dicen que dijo la voz)
　　　　　　　　　　　　　　　taladrando hacia adentro
que no se rompan (dijo) esas flores esas bocas que flotan ahí adentro endurecidas
　　　　　　　　demora sí demora (dijo) el mundo – todo – ojos y oídos
aspereza también lo que falta es eso (dijo)
　　　　　　　　　　la mare és tot – figúrate – sin desvío ni nada.

(18 diciembre 2015)

❦

the woman used to say   the woman used to (you think) the woman used to go out
– bag in hand –　　　　　a huge bulge　　　　filled
filling the space　　　　　　　　– the empty space – (I say) (she says)
the woman used to go out – bag in hand –   ten dogs circling her
surrounding her   – saturated space –   a pack (they say) a pack
no murmur can be heard there   *no voice*
　　　　　　　ten dogs, sign of helplessness

❦

la mujer solía decir la mujer solía (piensas) la mujer solía salir
– bolsa en mano – un bulto enorme   lleno
llenando el espacio   – el espacio vacío – (digo) (dice)
la mujer solía salir   – bolsa en mano –   diez perros rondándola
rodeándola   – saturado el espacio –   una jauría (dicen) una jauría
ningún murmullo puede oírse ahí   *ninguna voz*
　　　　　　diez perros, señal de desamparo

from LITTLE LOOPHOLES / *de* PEQUEÑOS RESQUICIOS

SOMETHING ABOUT BEES

honey drops
like the air's dew
(thought Aristotle)
when the stars appear
                or the rainbow is drawn
honey drops
drop
by drop

favourite food
of the gods

Kama
        the love of god
carries a bow of bees

honey metaphors

the bees
  are also
    Ra's tears

                    '''' '' ''
                    '' ' ' ''
                    '' '' ' '
                    ' ''

  so believed the Egyptians
  1400 years ago

  *

  saffron gorse willow
  coltsfoot almond tree
  plum tree wallflower
  raspberry bush

hawthorn mustard
broom besom
thyme
clover
blackberry

honey sources

a bee remembers and recognises the position of the sun in the
sky,
the angle between the direction of flight and the horizontal
line
drawn from the hive toward the sun. If when flying
in that direction it finds pollen and nectar, it will perform
her dance upon her return

        oscillating
    her abdomen
    over the surface
    of the honeycomb
    dances
       forming
          eights
    888
    88
    888
that trace
the direction of the flight
the direction of the sun

the nourishment
is there
ready

  *

honey is good
honey is sweet
so shall the knowledge of wisdom be unto thy soul

King Solomon said

did he think
            perhaps
like Plato
or Saint Ambrose
that his wisdom
came from
            the kiss
                        of a bee?

countless myths
countless stories

Achilles
Homer accounts
was placed in the robes of the gods
in rich ointments
and in sweet honey

Herod
King of Judea
after killing his wife
kept
her body
preserved in honey
for 7 years
'because I loved her
even after death'

love and death
tears   dew   honey
the kiss
            of a bee

(the logical train
of thought
doesn't work
for the meeting

only
the free
stripped
word
     awakes
those relationships
precise and distanced
of which Reverdy
spoke)

isn't this poetry?

the dance
of the bee
looking for
its food?

all dance
encloses
an encrypted language

Salome
asking for the head
of the Baptist

the dance
of the dervishes
the dance of words
the dance
of the bees
circles
that reveal
life
     or death

ecstasy
at last

ALGO SOBRE LAS ABEJAS

la miel cae
como el rocío del aire
(pensaba Aristóteles)
cuando aparecen las estrellas
              o se dibuja el arco iris
la miel cae
gota
a gota

alimento favorito
de los dioses

Kama
   dios del amor
lleva un arco de abejas

metáforas de la miel

las abejas
   son también
      las lágrimas de Ra

               '''' '' ''
               '' ' ' ''
               '' '' ' '
               ' ''

creyeron los egipcios
1400 años atrás

     *

azafrán tojo sauce
fárfara almendro
ciruelo alhelí
frambueso
mostaza espino
escobetilla
tomillo
trébol
zarzamora

fuentes de miel

una abeja recuerda y reconoce la posición del sol en el
cielo, el ángulo que hay entre la dirección del vuelo y la
línea horizontal trazada desde la colmena en dirección
al sol. Si al volar en esa dirección encuentra polen y
néctar, al regresar realizará su danza

    oscilando
su abdomen
sobre la superficie
del panal
danza
    formando
      ochos

    888
    88
    888

que trazan
la dirección del vuelo
la dirección del sol

el alimento
está ahí
a punto

     *

la miel es buena
la miel es dulce
así será la sabiduría para tu alma
dijo el Rey Salomón

¿creería
     quizá
como Platón
o San Ambrosio
que su sabiduría
provenía
   del beso
      de una abeja?

innumerables mitos
innumerables historias

Aquiles
cuenta Homero

fue colocado en el ropaje de los dioses
en ricos ungüentos
y en dulce miel

Herodes
Rey de Judea
tras matar a su esposa
mantuvo
7 años
su cuerpo
conservado en miel
"porque la amaba
aún después de muerta"

el amor y la muerte
lágrimas   rocío   miel
el beso
    de una abeja

(la línea lógica
del pensamiento
no sirve
para el encuentro
sólo
la palabra
libre
despojada

      despierta
esas relaciones
precisas y lejanas
de las que hablaba
Reverdy)

¿no es esto poesía?

¿la danza
de la abeja
buscando
su alimento?

toda danza
encierra
un lenguaje cifrado

Salomé
pidiendo la cabeza
del Bautista

la danza
de los derviches
la danza de las palabras
la danza
de las abejas
círculos
que revelan
la vida
    o la muerte

éxtasis
al fin

from ROAD MATTER / *de la* MATERIA DEL CAMINO

a handful of soil
is what fits in the hand

a handful of soil
is what happens

a handful / a fist
a dagger

where to sow it?

in full hands
there is no separation

a handful of soil
is what we are trying

❧

un puñado de tierra
es lo que cabe en la mano

un puñado de tierra
es lo que sucede

un puñado/ un puño
un puñal

¿dónde sembrarlo?

a manos llenas
no hay separación

un puñado de tierra
es lo que intentamos

❧

to Rodolfo Zanabria

cactus
the sea owes you nothing
orca of the past
underwater
black cactus
head of the desert

cactus
the miracle
of the abandoned
is called
resignation

black cactus
head of silence

≈

a Rodolfo Zanabria

biznaga
nada te debe el mar
orca de antes
submarina
biznaga negra
cabeza del desierto

biznaga
el milagro
de los abandonados
se llama
resignación

biznaga negra
cabeza del silencio

≈

clear
the forest

know how to rough down
the trunk

sketch out the leaves

put in the forest
other forests

voice
sketch

moan?

water eye
spring
flower bud
sprouting

resisting

          ❧

        desbrozar
        el bosque

        saber desbastar
        el tronco

        bosquejar las hojas

        meter en el bosque
        otros bosques

        bosquejo
        de voz

        ¿quejido?

        ojo de agua
        manantial
        brotas
        botón de flor

        resistes

❧

blackberry
fruit of the black mulberry

marabout

you eat the white fruit
the red fruit

pleasure
     bud?

marabout / blackberry
black fruit

mature

you enjoy the field

without dwelling
or morals

        ≈

     mora
     fruto del moral

     morabito

     comes el fruto blanco
     el fruto rojo

     ¿botón
       de placer?

     morabito / zarzamora
     fruto negro

     maduro

     disfrutas del campo

     sin morada
     ni moral

VERÓNICA VIOLA FISHER (Argentina)

V. V. Fisher (b. 1974, Buenos Aires) has published: Hacer sapito *(Editorial Nusud, Buenos Aires, 1995 / 2005 by Gog y Magog),* A boca de jarro *(Edición A Secas, Buenos Aires, 2003),* Arveja Negra *(Vox, Bahía Blanca, 2005),* Notas para un agitador *(La calabaza del diablo, Santiago de Chile, 2008),* Boomerang *(27 pulqui, Buenos Aires, 2015),* Pavadas *(el autor, Buenos Aires, 2017 / Liberteca , 2021),* Había una vez *(Caleta Olivia, Buenos Aires, 2019) and* Pavadas Platónicas *(Liberteca, Buenos Aires, 2021). She is trans feminist and works as a librarian at a public school.*

ENGLISH TRANSLATIONS BY MARTHA SPRACKLAND

from SKIMMING STONES / de HACER SAPITO

My house is one
whole house a holy union
I'm lying
it is broken and black
like the eyes of
God made it
split in four
eyes two children
keep watch

Mi casa es una
entera casa miento
está rota y negra
como los ojos de
Dios la hizo
partida en cuatro
ojos dos hijos
velan

I am never going
to forgive her
for saying
mami

first I go first
never
second, said
papi

     ≋

       Nunca voy
       a perdonarla
       por decir
       mamá
       primero voy
       nunca
       segundo- dijo
       papá

≋

My house is one whole
hull a holy union
I'm lying because when it split
it was full of rancid
juice and peel
it is husk
just skin
of grapes makes
the wine of my house –
it is blood

     ≋

       Mi casa es una entera
       casca
       miento porque al quebrarse
       estaba llena de jugo
       podrido y casca
       es hollejo
       solamente corteza
       de las uvas se hace
       el vino de mi casa
       es sangre

≈

From mami I had an umbilical cord
and from papi I also
had a cerebral
cord
that the doctor tied
innumerable times with a
vast and fearsome force
From navel to anus
a baby poop white
like mami's hands
but my brain doesn't know how
to do digestion
its navel is my mouth
and my mouth is a slash
to the huge
knot
a gash and blood
like papi's hands
trying to tie
his cord again

≈

De mamá tuve un cordón umbilical
y de papá también
tuve un cordón
cerebral
que el médico anudó
innumerables veces con una
fuerza descomunal y atroz
Desde el ombligo al ano
un bebé caquita blanca
como las manos de mamá
pero mi cerebro no sabe
hacer la digestión
su ombligo es mi boca
y mi boca es un tajo
al nudo
atroz un tajo y sangre
como las manos de papá
intentando anudar
otra vez su cordón

≋

Daughter of mine
and of a big
bitch
where did you bury
the bones
that were still alive?
you are man's best friend
and I am your father
give me them
I want my bones
landless I feel
that look like ivory
daughter of mine
under sand
or delved in a shaft
in the ocean are you?
give me them, give me them now
daughter of
I buried them in my body
papi

≋

Hija mía
y de una gran
perra
¿dónde enterraste
los huesos
que todavía, estaban vivos?
sos el mejor amigo del hombre
y soy tu padre
dámelos
quiero mis huesos
sin tierra
que parezcan marfil
hija mía
¿bajo arena
o cavaste un pozo
en el océano?
dámelos, dámelos ya
hija de
-los enterré en mi cuerpo
papá

My daughter makes fun
of me
look how she sticks out
her tongue at me and I
her own and only
scorned father?
insolent brat stop
writing now and what
the little devil
with the rhyme pushes
her tongue out and pushes
my buttons
look she repents
late I too
put out my tongue at her and here
end the poem.

Mi hija se burla
de mí
miren cómo me saca
la lengua y yo
su propio y único
padre burlado?
mocosa insolente dejá
ya de escribir y qué
cosa la mocosa
con la rima me saca
la lengua y me saca
de quicio
mírenla se arrepiente
tarde yo también
le saqué la lengua y aquí
termino el poema.

≈

They drank in the empire
to bursting ate
everything vomited and everything
from the first
to the last
mouthful shot
all over some proud
god the roman
had a right to
his chick and could
eat the young birds
of prey their
profile resembling my old
portrait with laurels
on my little bald head
give me the savour
the scent of laurel and the
umbilical cord for a necklace
of gold golden-browned
over a low flame a little
delicacy a Roman balance
is the red crown
of my family tree
laden I say
full stuffed
with hatchlings like me
rookie birds of praise
Caesar
fucked my old lady
once one afternoon
in the empire

≈

Bebían en el imperio
hasta reventar comían
de todo vomitaban y todos
desde el primero
hasta el último
bocado se disparaba

sobre algún dios
erguido el romano
tenía derecho sobre
su mina y podía
comerse las crías Ave
de rapiña sus narices
de perfil se parecen a mi viejo
retrato con laureles
sobre mi cabecita
pelada darme el gusto
el aroma del laurel y el cordón
umbilical como collar
de oro doradito
a fuego lento una pequeña
exquisitez romana
es la copa roja
de mi árbol genealógico
llena qué digo
llena rellena
de crías como yo
alumnas de Ave
César
se cogió a mi vieja
una vez una tarde
en el imperio

There are special stones for throwing in a lake.
They snag on the level water, bounding over its surface.
Every touch spawns a small circle that
spreads into other larger ones, little by little.
Finally the pebble sinks.
Skipping stones is a game the old
pass on to the young.
No one ever stops playing. At the sight of a lake, that
sheet empty of signs, I hear again the chime of
rings arising in a chain to
at last drown myself in the depths.

≈

Hay piedritas especiales para lanzar a un lago.
Pican a ras del agua dando saltitos en su superficie.
Cada roce genera un círculo pequeño que se
extiende en otros más grandes, vez a vez.
Finalmente esa piedrita se hunde.
Hacer sapito es un juego que los mayores
transmiten a los niños.
Nadie deja nunca de jugar. Al ver un lago, esa
lámina ausente de signos, vuelvo a oír el tintineo de
los anillos sucediéndose en una cadena para
finalmente ahogarme en lo más hondo.

from NOTES FOR AN AGITATOR / *de* NOTAS PARA UN AGITADOR

≈

On a vertical stave the notes
tumble on top of each other
dangle, sustained
and in lengthening try to reach
the heavens but
when they sound
avid and vulnerable they are

a complete contradiction:
if I brandish that staff
it rains black grapes

≈

En un pentagrama vertical las notas
caen unas sobre otras
cuelgan sostenidas
y en la duración intentan alcanzar
el cielo pero
solo cuando toca
ávido y vulnerable son

contradicción plena:
si blandeo el pentagrama
llueven uvas negras

M   A   R   C   H   O   R   R   E   C   I   T   A   L

¡¡!!   I searched for your face in the crowd   ringed by horses of horsepower

    four days before Christmas   drums with fanfare rhythm

      denied your name   in the centre

        it was unnecessary   such a concentration

horsepower ringing

     a rhythm of drums   ¡¡!!

         centre

     fanfare   ¡¡!!

¡¡!!   listen   but set up camp on the grass

        against the usual music   no

       camping on the grass   if the heads look like balls

it's not enough   red-card tongues

     to get me excited   I got a pass to the pitch

         ¡¡!!

        without the heads   and listen to us speak

             ¡¡·!!

    tongues   lashing a dead horse

     on the playing field   I searched for your face   ¡¡!!

and listen to us flogging   days before

dead   dead   dead

        ¿¡!?   ¿¡!?

horses   horses   horses

in   b   a   t   t   l   e   s   t   a   n   c   e

M A R C H A O R E C I T A L

¡¡!!   busqué tu cara en la multitud   cercada por caballos de fuerza
    cuatro días antes de navidad   baterías de ritmo alharaca
        negaron tu nombre   en el centro
                    fue innecesaria   tanta concentración
    caballos de fuerza cercada
            ritmo de baterías   ¡¡!!
                centro   ¡¡!!
    alharaca
¡¡!!   atenta   pero sentar plaza sobre el césped
                    contra la música de siempre   no
    sobre el césped sentarse   si las cabezas parecen pelotas
no alcanza   lenguas de tarjeta roja
    a emocionarme   saqué entrada en el campo de juego
            ¡¡!!
        sin las cabezas   y nos escucho hablar
                        ¡¡!!
    lenguas   de bueyes perdidos

    en el campo de juego   busqué tu cara   ¡¡!!

y nos escucho hablar   días antes

de bueyes   de bueyes   de bueyes

            ¿¡!?   ¿¡!?

        perdidos   perdidos   perdidos

en   p   o   s   e   de   c   o   m   b   a   t   e

TOCCATA

he has no signature, hasn't invented one – yet – scrawls on the dotted line
anaesthetised in oranges and yellows
behind the gauze   colours of the end of night   little light
showing that loose thread AN ARM that corroded edge THE TEETH an icy breeze that warns
– The Knuckles Drill The Centre Of The Meniscus –
                    TOCK_TOCK   TACK_TICK
                              TACK_TOCCATA_TICK
                                        TOCK_TICK_TACK
                                        ATTACK_TOCK
          he signs with a fist, embedded against the page and sinks – again – brown
                                                                  the swamp
                                             TOCK

                                    REFLECT

                              TICK_TACK

          TICK_TACK
          ATTACK

KICK
BELIEVE
that the swamp is solid ground   do politics of the body
TOCK_TOCK   the foot is the latch
the crank that creaks
the handle of the PUMP that we shove to fill the TANK
of the nameless, of spirits
          on the dotted line – now – the thread is biodegradable and
                                        disappears
          into the wound – rinds of sapped fruit – the skin
                    – rusted tin cans – the heads
he signs with five knuckles five notes at the same pitch   scrrrapescrrrapescrrrape   germs of
sound labile claws

TOCATA

no tiene firma, no la inventó –todavía– garabatea sobre la línea de puntos
anestesiada entre naranjas y amarillos
detrás de la gasa   colores del fin de la noche   pequeña luz
mostrando esa hilacha UN BRAZO ese borde corroído LOS DIENTES una brisa helada que avisa
            – Los Nudillos Taladran El Centro El Menisco –
                        TOC_TOC   TAC_ TIC
                                TAC_TOCATA_TIC
                                    TOC_TIC_TAC
                                        ATACA_TOC
                                            el pantano

firma dando el puño, embebido contra la hoja y se hunde – otra vez – marrón

                                        TOC
                        REFLEJA

PATEA
CREE
que el pantano es tierra firme   hace política del cuerpo
TOC_TOC   el pie es el picaporte
la manivela que cruje
el mango de la BOMBA que empujamos con fuerza para llenar el TANQUE
de anónimos, de ánimos
            TIC_TAC   TIC_TAC
            ATACA
            sobre la línea de puntos – ahora– el hilo es biodegradable y
                        desaparece
            al fondo de la herida –cáscaras de fruta extinguida – la piel
                – latas de conserva oxidadas – las cabezas
firma con cinco nudillos cinco notas a la misma altura   garrapeasgarrapeasgarrapeas
                            bacterias del sonido garras lábiles

VICTORIA GUERRERO PEIRANO (PERU)

Victoria Guerrero Peirano (1971) is a poet, teacher, and feminist activist. Her recent publication of her Y la muerte no tendrá dominio (And death will not have dominion, *2019) won the 2020 National Literature Prize. She is the author of five poetry collections, including a compilation of her poetry,* Documents of Barbarie (Poetry 2002-2012) (2013), *which won ProART in 2015. She cares for her dog and cat and survives by teaching at the university.*

ENGLISH TRANSLATIONS BY ANNA ROSENWONG & MARÍA JOSÉ GIMÉNEZ

URGENT POEM

Like a beggar
I feed my dead

Little girls who die locked away
Trapped in covert factories
Electrocuted doing overt work
Tossed out like garbage or found in sacks

Is this country my country?

A dead country of dead girls?

And who cares about this country?
The owners of the country
And who cares about this country?
The owners of the country
And who cares about this country?
The owners of the country

They love this country
They run banks churches universities
They cut deals with politicians
They sign pacts with transnationals
They invite them in
Welcome Welcome

They nod their heads They pat their backs

And they are not sated

But when all those little girls
Electrocuted
Raped
Burned
Locked away
in secret factories
in malls and movie theatres
in fast food restaurants
Escape from their sacks and rise
When all of them become one single fist

You
Fathers of the fatherland
You
Murderers
You will know what fear is
And this country will no longer be foreign to us

And at last I will be able to feed my dead
In peace

POEMA URGENTE

Como una mendiga
Doy de comer a mis muertas

Muchachitas que mueren encerradas
Atrapadas en fábricas clandestinas
Electrocutadas en trabajos no clandestinos
Arrojadas a descampados o encontradas en costales

¿Este país es mi país?

¿Un país muerto de muchachas muertas?

¿Y a quién le importa este país?
A los dueños del país
¿Y a quién le importa este país?
A los dueños del país
¿Y a quién le importa este país?
A los dueños del país

Ellos aman este país
Dirigen bancos iglesias universidades
Hacen tratos con políticos
Firman alianzas con transnacionales
Les dan la bienvenida
Welcome Welcome
Mueven las cabezas Se palmean las espaldas

Y no se sacian

Pero cuando todas esas muchachitas
Electrocutadas
Violadas
Quemadas
Encerradas
en fábricas clandestinas
en malls y cines
en restaurantes de comida rápida
Salgan de sus costales y se levanten
Cuando todas ellas sean un solo puño

Ustedes
Padres de la patria
Ustedes
Asesinos
Sabrán lo que es el miedo
Y este país ya no nos será ajeno

Y al fin podré dar de comer a mis muertas
Con tranquilidad

1-02

Today I cut my sister's hair
the locks fell like huge tears on the baseboards
I swept it up and tossed it in the trash
All that dead hair used to fill my dreams
One day I dreamt of the dead hair   The strands joined back together
Each hair reconnected and demanded I account for my sad deed
I was dumbstruck
The dead hair insisted: Are you there? Why did you mutilate me?
I gathered up the hair and my sister's face appeared floating in the distance
Why did you throw my hair in the rubbish bin?

The head of hair demanded food and also water lots of water

But my hands were sewn together   I couldn't offer water
My legs did not hop to   I couldn't go looking
My breasts were dry   I couldn't offer milk
I was stiffer than that dead hair I cut
Or I was deader or maybe I had died and didn't know it

My sister took pity on me on my silence
She calmed the head of hair
She spoke to it sweetly like it was a little girl
She insisted it rest   that it sleep in my dream
Basically   that it stop fucking with me
After all what is a mother if she doesn't say those things

I must learn from her what a mother does
I must imitate my sister in order to mother

Am I a mother or imitating a mother?
Maybe I just play at motherhood like a parody practically a joke
Anyway I have no child to legitimize my being in labour

What should I do?
Everything I write boils down to two or three words
Mother Daughter Sister
A trinity Psychoanalysis failed to foresee

My sister-daughter
My daughter-sister
She appears in my dreams
She's real and looks at me with plaintive eyes:

Why did you throw my hair away?

1-02

Hoy le corté el pelo a mi hermana
Su cabello caía como grandes lágrimas sobre el zócalo frío
Lo barrí y lo tiré a la basura
Tanto pelo muerto cubría mis sueños
Soñé un día con el pelo muerto   Otra vez unía sus hebras
Cada una se juntaba y me demandaba respuestas a mi triste hazaña
Yo permanecía muda-quieta
El pelo muerto insistía: ¿Estás allí? ¿Por qué me mutilaste?
Recogía el cabello y el rostro de mi hermana aparecía flotando a la distancia
¿Por qué arrojaste mis cabellos a la bolsa de basura?

La cabellera me exigía alimento también agua abundante agua

Pero mis manos estaban cosidas   No podía dar de beber
Mis piernas no daban un brinco   No podía buscar
Y mis senos estaban secos   No podía dar de lactar
Yo estaba más tiesa que aquel pelo muerto que corté
O yo estaba más muerta o quizá ya había muerto y no lo sabía

Mi hermana sintió piedad de mí de mi silencio
Calmó a la cabellera
Le habló con voz dulce como si fuera una hija pequeña
Le exigió que descansara   que durmiera en mi sueño
En suma   que no jodiera
Después de todo qué es una madre si no dice estas cosas

Yo he de aprender por ella lo que hace una madre
Yo he de imitar a mi hermana para poder ser su madre

¿Soy la madre o imito a la madre?
Quizá solo ejerzo la maternidad como un remedo casi un chiste
Pues no tengo ningún hijo que legitime mi condición de parturienta

¿Qué hacer?
Todo lo que escribo se reduce a dos o tres palabras
Madre Hija Hermana
Es una trilogía no prevista por el Psicoanálisis

Mi hermana-hija
Mi hija-hermana
Aparece en mis sueños
Es real y me mira con ojos lastimeros:

¿Por qué botaste mis cabellos al tacho de basura?

from THE CHEMOTHERAPY NOTEBOOKS (AGAINST POETRY) / *de*
CUADERNOS DE QUIMIOTERAPIA (CONTRA LA POESÍA)

TESTIMONY ON BEHALF (VICTORIALAND)

> *How shall I speak of the not-I without screaming?*
> VALLEJO

I wonder at what moment my name became a dagger shot
                                through with eight letters
8 round letters with its vowels and its consonants choppy
biting into the I
grating on the you

Today I saw you poison yourself with
pretentious confession and being
                the life of
                the Party
Making a spectacle of yourself dancing a disgraceful cumbia in
                                front of your dead

Did they not bring me here
teaching me
        lech-er-ous-
                ly
to desire everything for sale?

I have no feelings – they say
Yet everything inside me shivers nervously
And how I have felt the pull of doubt

                          but

my feelings were futile because they came from deep down
and you couldn't see them
You were no chiromancer – as you claimed
(or chiro*practor*)
and in your eyes submission was the only form of Love

Is this not *the time of burning reason*?

I know what the critics want from me
            the affectation of going around with my heart in my throat

But the I can do no such thing

The lone I chases ice cream carts and cheap lunch specials
whereby it survives the daily foray of being:
            fat / small / naive / hairy / see-through
            runty / uncouth / haggard…

Lined up outside the banks I sing songs by josé josé
And embroider futuristic images onto old denim jackets
                  to frighten away debts and meals at odd hours

                  This wounds me deeply

And again you wonder at what moment each consonant
and each i
and each o
and each a
began to transform into dead letters
letters printed on faded electric water and telephone bills
Washed-out vowels that once burned
                              a noir
                                    o bleu
                                          i rouge

Now my name is a testament to barbarity
                              Entrenched in its I
                   Purring insolently in its you

Never more!
Never more!
– I say

So be it

TESTIMONIO DE PARTE (VICTORIALAND)

¿Cómo hablar del no-yó sin dar un grito?
                              VALLEJO

Me pregunto en qué momento mi nombre fue un puñal
                              atravesado por ocho letras
8 letras redondas con sus vocales y sus consonantes agitadas
mordiéndose en el yo
crispándose en el tú

Hoy te he visto envenenarte con confesiones pretenciosas y ser
                              el centro de
                              la Fiesta
Exhibirte con un vergonzoso baile cumbiambero delante de tus
                              muertos

¿Acaso no me trajeron aquí
enseñándome
        im-pú-di-ca-
                    mente
a desear todo lo que se vende?

No tengo sentimientos – dicen
Mas todo se agita en mi interior nerviosamente
Y cómo he sentido la duda jalonearme

                    pero

mis sentimientos eran vanos porque venían del fondo
y no los podías ver
No eras quiromántico – según decías
(o quiro*práctico*)
y ante tus ojos solo la sumisión era una forma de Amor

¿No *es este el tiempo de la razón ardiente?*

Yo sé que los críticos piden de mí
        la cursilería de andar con el corazón en la boca

Mas Yo no puede hacer eso

Yo solo corre tras heladeros o restaurantes de menú baratos
a través de las cuales sobrevive la incursión diaria de ser:
        gorda / pequeña / imberbe / velluda / transparente
        raquítica / potona / ojerosa…

En la cola de los bancos canto canciones de josé josé
Y bordo imágenes futuristas en viejas casacas de *yin*
            para espantar las deudas y la comida
                     a deshora

           Esto me hiere tremendamente

Y otra vez te preguntas en qué momento cada consonante
 y cada i
 y cada o
 y cada a
empezaron a convertirse en letras muertas
letras impresas en pálidos recibos de luz agua y teléfono
Vocales descoloridas que alguna vez ardieron
                a noir
                   o bleu
                      i rouge

Mi nombre es ahora un documento de barbarie
               Atrincherado en su yo
          Ronroneando insolente en su tú

Never more!
Never more!
– me digo

DANCE

1

He smokes
She spins her rings
GOTTFRIED BENN

Watching my corpse   *This Peruvian corpse*
            floating downriver
                    dragged
                            toward Peru's dirty desert seas
I remembered my mad grandmother
        and her strange song
                the odd echo of her voice through adobe walls
            blue eyes looking at me peering into the heart of a fleshless fruit

Sáenz Peña 450   Where my bewildering dance was born

        In the middle of a gothic celebration sparkling in shades of chicha
            Lit by a Lima church of middling lineage
                they celebrated the wedding feast of Madness

        One ring subsumed into the other to covenant the new Alliance
                    Husbands & Wives
                recited the old madhouse poem

                one vinyl record followed another
            like my mother followed hers and I her

Hence, the origin of this corpse displaced from its dirty native land

Therefore, Husband
        give me two old rings so we can reach an understanding

Now that you know the past
It's your turn to shake up the future

The dice in the centre of the table bellow their ballad:

6   6

As the poet said:

> *A roll of the dice will never abolish chance*

BAILE

1

> *Él fuma*
> *Ella hace rodar sus anillos*
>   GOTTFRIED BENN

Viendo mi cadáver   *Este cadáver peruano*
           flotando río abajo
              arrastrado
                       hacia sucios mares del desierto del Perú
recordé a mi abuela loca
       y su extraño canto
              el eco atravesado de su voz en paredes de adobe
       ojos azules que me miran observan el corazón de una fruta
descarnada

Sáenz Peña 450   Allí nació mi desatinado baile

       En medio de una fiesta gótica chispeante de tonos chicha
          Alumbrada por una iglesia limeña de mediana alcurnia
             se celebraron las bodas de la Locura

       Un anillo se hundió en el otro para pactar la nueva Alianza
               Esposos & Esposas
          recitaron el viejo poema del manicomio

          un disco de vinilo siguió a otro
       como mi madre siguió a la suya y yo a ella

He ahí el origen de este cadáver desplazado de su sucia tierra natal

Entonces Esposo
       dame dos anillos viejos para entendernos

Ahora que conoces el pasado
Es tu turno de agitar el futuro

Los dados al centro de la mesa mugen su balada:

6   6

Lo dicho:

Un golpe de dados nunca abolirá el azar

English translations of the following poems by
Anastatia Spicer & Honora Spicer

from DIARY OF A PROLETARIAN SEAMSTRESS / de DIARIO DE UNA COSTURERA PROLETARIA

≋

I leave words   I forget
I thread needles red black blue fuchsia green
Tired of Public Competitions for Teaching Positions
I began to embroider each garment in my wardrobe
I arranged my doctoral diplomas and stowed them near the bookshelf
So they wouldn't feel inferior
CV back to "0"
I file it
bury it
The market wants professionals at record speed
Titles and master's degrees,
etc. in bulk

But we seamstresses are timeless

≋

Dejo la palabra   La olvido
Ensarto hilos rojos negros azules fucsias verdes
Harta ya de los Concursos Públicos para Plazas Docentes
Empecé a bordar cada prenda de mi ropero

Arreglé mis títulos doctorales y los guardé junto a la estantería de libro
Para que no se sintieran menos
CV a foja «0»
Lo archivo
lo fondeo
El mercado quiere profesionales en tiempo récord
Títulos y masters,
etc. a granel

Pero las costureras somos para siempre

TABLECLOTH

My mother made a tablecloth
She crocheted
At the time I didn't know anything
She took it everywhere
I wondered at how she crocheted in the darkness of a theatre
But she did
And the next day there hadn't been a single stitch added or dropped
That was my mother in those days
A strange woman
She worked during the day and on the weekends stitched
She took me to the theatre
I didn't understand her then
My friends' mothers stayed home
Cooking   Picking them up from school   Packing lunch boxes
When the tablecloth was finished
She put it on the table
It was magnificent
But at that time I didn't understand
It was complicated
I was tangled in her delicate weft
I saw my mother through the pane of thread
She kept being different from the rest:
She worked during the day
Embroidered on the weekends
And couldn't really stand being at home
I never understood her
Maybe I didn't know enough
She also never taught me

Thought it was too much for me – or too little
Now my mother says she can't do anything with her hands
The tablecloth is tucked away in the kitchen cabinet
I got myself knee-deep in diplomas
And I don't know how to embroider

MANTEL

Mi madre tejió un mantel
A croché
En ese tiempo yo no sabía nada
Lo llevaba a todos lados
Me asombraba que tejiera en la oscuridad de un cine
Pero ella lo hacía
Y al día siguiente no sobraba ni faltaba una sola pastilla
Así era mi madre en aquellos tiempos
Una mujer extraña
Trabajaba de día y los fines de semana tejía
Me llevaba al teatro
Yo no la entendía en ese entonces
Las madres de mis amigas permanecían en casa
Cocinaban   Las recogían de la escuela   Les preparaban la lonchera
Cuando el mantel estuvo terminado
Lo puso en la mesa
Era magnífico
Pero yo en ese tiempo no lo entendí
Era complicado
Me enredaba en su delicada trama
Veía a mi madre a través de esos anteojos de hilo
Ella seguía siendo diferente a las otras:
Trabajaba de día
Bordaba los fines de semana
Y no soportaba demasiado estar en casa
Yo nunca la entendí
Quizá no supe lo suficiente
Tampoco ella me enseñó
Pensó que era demasiado para mí –o muy poco
Ahora mi madre dice que no puede hacer nada con sus manos
El mantel permanece guardado en el cajón de la cocina
Yo me llené de diplomas
Y no sé bordar

NN2

I lock myself in
I lock myself in with the same key with which they locked me in
I take hold of the master key and turn the lock twice
The machine is old
Moth wings blanket everything

By force I sit and learn the alphabet
By force I count the days until I can leave here
By force I press the pedal   Accelerating rage
By force they put me in here

I see light once a day
One day I will return the master key
By that day I hope the boss is dead

NN2

Me encierro
Me encierro con la misma llave con que me encerraron ellos
Tomo la llave del patrón y le doy dos vueltas a la cerradura
La máquina está vieja
Las alas de las polillas lo cubren todo

A fuerza me siento y aprendo el alfabeto
A fuerza cuento los días en que he de salir de aquí
A fuerza acelero el pedal   Acelero la rabia
A fuerza me metieron aquí

Veo la luz una vez al día
Un día le devolveré las llaves al patrón

Ese día espero que ya esté muerto

ELVIRA HERNÁNDEZ (Chile)

Elvira Hernández (1951, pseudonym of Rosa María Teresa Adriasola Olave) is a poet, essayist, and literary critic. In 1979, during the Pinochet dictatorship, she was mistakenly arrested as a terrorist and even, after her release, was regarded with suspicion. This gave rise to her book, La bandera de Chile, *a diary of poetic reflections on Chile during the dictatorship, which became symbolic of the resistance. Her collection* ¡Arre! Halley ¡Arre! *was published in 1986, and since then Hernández has continued to publish both poetry books and essays, the latter under her real name, Teresa Adriasola.*

'THE CHILEAN FLAG' IS TRANSLATED BY ALEC SCHUMACHER
ALL OTHER ENGLISH TRANSLATIONS BY JÈSSICA PUJOL DURAN

from GIDDY-UP, HALLEY! GIDDY-UP / de ¡ARRE! HALLEY ¡ARRE!

AUSTRAL CELESTIAL HUNT

grains of sugar mixed with grains of sand, motoring jams mo-
bilising, buses rented at a reasonable price: God only knows
if I will come back. Tour-offers, high fidelity German binocu-
lars, disposable Taiwanese binoculars, sleeping-bags, hot water
bottles, tea and coffee in sachets, the equipax, strong wind, bags
that fly like kites, nylons that billow like tulle, cans that roll like
thunder, bottles that crack like skulls, camp beds, two-in-one,
one for all, CONFORT toilet paper, the stars in the distance, last
quarter, room out in the open, blah, blah, blah, blah, honey-
moon, with you bread and butter, the daily crumb of diazepam,
eternal breakfasts, clouds, clouds of flies, jars of preserves, fruit
peelings, pure peel, battery-operated radio, battery-operated TV,
camping stove, inextinguishable campfire, cigarettes, butts, the
left out, the tail, pissing outdoors

following the line, peaks, sand dunes, sand, rocks, an entire
sidereal map assonated with hiccups and farts, one-two-three,
Grandmother's Footsteps! guitar solo, quena solo, English eau
de cologne, acqua mirage, green bird mirage, eye drops, can-
nabis sativa, laughter, detergents, the Devil's Chupilca, smoked
eye-glasses, the Three Marys, cassettes, smoke gets in your eyes,
packaged smoke for the great writing art in the sky, streamers,

feather dusters, etc. mixed with etc. protos und spaghettis, reins
of runaway horse, laughing in who's face?, fans to death of the
shooting comets with the digitised photo in hand

the furnishing of this time

ah! tremendous desire to print the cosmos
with the cerebral eye camera, that full colour
astral mystery printing off with starring
the film roll without reaching the END
is repeated, the desire to touch with our
eye's hands the small portion of the
unknown world –great– put the
eyes over, seize…, yes, evil eye,
keep in the memory, in the saliva of the
tongue, in the most mucous edge of the skin,
go on for a while, the extraordinary experience
of the celestial body (José Maximiliano will focus on
the star) in the firm concavity of the
firmament of a hand, in the tearful
opacity of a screen, the shooting star
cartwheeling through the sky, showing off,
on the odd seats of expectation.

CACERÍA CELESTE AUSTRAL

granos de azúcar mezclados con granos de arena, caravanas
movilísticas movilizándose, buses arrendados a precio
módico: sólo Dios sabe si regreso. Tour-ofertas, binoculares
alemanes de alta fidelidad, larga vistas taiwaneses desechables,
sacos de dormir, saquitos para el agua caliente, té y café en
saquets, el equipax, viento fuerte, bolsas que vuelan como
volantines, nilones que ondean como tules, latas que ruedan
como truenos, botellas que se quiebran como cráneos, catres
de campaña, dos-en-uno, uno para todos, papel CONFORT,
los astros a lo lejos, cuarto menguante, cuarto a la intemperie,
blá, blá, blá, blá, luna de miel, contigo pan y cebolla, el pan
diario de díazeacepam, desayunos eternos, nubes, nubes de
moscas, tarros en conserva, cáscaras de frutas, pura cáscara,
radio a pilas, TV con batería, cocinilla de camping, fogata
inextinguible, puchos, colillas, la corta, la cola, meadas al
aire libre

siguiendo la línea, picos, médanos, arena, rocas, todo un
mapa sideral asonantado de hipos y peos, un-dos-tres
¡momia!, solo de guitarra, solo de quena, eau de cologne
inglesa, espejismo de acqua, espejismo de pájaro verde,
colirios, cannabis sativa, risas, detergentes, chupilca del
diablo, lentes ahumados, las Tres Marías, casettes, smoke
gets in your eyes, humo envasado para el gran writing art en
el cielo, serpentinas, plumeros, etc. mezclado con etc. protos
und spaghettis, riendas de caballo desbocado, riéndose
en las barbas de ¿quién?, hinchas a muerte de los fugaces
cometas con la foto digitalizada en la mano

el amoblado de este tiempo

¡ah! deseo tremebundo de imprimir el cosmos
con la cámara ocular cerebral, ese misterio
astral full color imprimiéndose de starring
el rollo de la película sin llegar al END
se repite, el deseo de ir tocando con las
manos de los ojos esa pequeña porción de
mundo desconocido –grande – poner los
ojos encima, apoderarse…, sí, mal de ojo,
retener en la memoria, en la saliva de la
lengua, en el borde más mucoso de la piel,
rollo para rato, la experiencia extraordinaria
del astro (José Maximiliano se fijará en
la estrella) en la firme concavidad del
firmamento de una mano, en la opacidad
lagrimosa de una pantalla, el astro fugaz
haciendo cabriolas por el cielo, luciéndose,
sobre las butacas impares de la expectación.

from TRAVEL LETTER / de CARTAS DE VIAJE

Look at the dogfish I ride
  – the figurative beast –
novice up there
in my fishing endeavours
  countertop there

astride that fish of mine
  flap and flap
coupled touching land

       him maimed
       me barren

the dogfish I ride
like meteor or hail
perching on the colossal slab
  my magnificent insect
places its legs in the aeroplane parking lot
silences the control tower
and I roll down the ladder of his teeth
  all vomit and miracle

      &

Robinson Crusoe accompanied his days with Friday. He played his
game all week. No one will accompany me through this white land
where dust is flour that falls from the sky.
     My wagon will crawl in vain.
     The compass is asleep.

    It is the hour of the wolf.
In black and white the panorama of space and time.

        Me barren
          crippled
        South American Indian

I am not crossing the Bering Strait again to return my hand to anyone.
In that white boreal cake you will not find the imprint of my limbs.
I won't attempt a new record with the tiny wheels of my butt.

       I am not Captain Avalos
       I am not the Contreras Shark
       I am a tongue blistered by
           electricity

I will never be a teardrop hanging from Mount Everest
I'm sitting and swinging on the ashlar of my pelvis
                              the edge of the world.

                    &

I come from the Land of the Eternal Landfills, from the Temperate
Aerosol, from the Piety Highlands making cream. Transvestite
flora and fauna slipping off the long ripped-off land. Thrown off the
Roller Coaster our brains cry Eden and Land, Heaven and Earth.
          And, here I am in the Old World lobby!

Gone are the Little Blue Feet at the Persian and Korean Fair.

                    &

        "In good weather, the 12th of October of 1987
              I have crossed the border"

Patagonian, I raise the Indian huts of my infertility.
New Zealand albatross breakfasts and whatever falls into my pot.
                    Buzzard or Chincol sparrow
                  that's the impasse
            the horizon of a deserted morning.

I come from the Land of the Flower Clocks, from Three
and Four Poplars. I come back from "Faust" and I have
searched all these years for Juan Alacalufe Disappeared.

In my *sentimental journey*, the search of the Impossible
Love. It's my mutilations that take their seat in the grave
of the dappled mare and like a screeching centaur I
rush tumbling through the rectitude of the tundra.

          It's hard to hit the mark.

  The steppe page does not give way to the handling of
              calluses.

The page is not handrail or pastime
    nor railing for children.
The page of apparent emptiness is written,
    you just have to feel for it.

And you, on the other side of the world, beyond the Pillars of
Hercules, easily located by ENTEL, by a ground-to-ground
missile, by a communication satellite, by a Courier-Friend,
where are you?

(...)

DIE KUNST ZU REISEN, brother
the act and art of leaving
    of blending in with white.

To cross the insurmountable boundary of things
    jump through the hoop, the trapeze
        jump into the void
and the suitcase loaded with nothing that accompanies.

The night hood has a double depth
    an incommunicable secret passage.

We live in a circus box
    suddenly doves and rabbits fly
    suddenly fills with worms.

I can't agree with anyone but
    myself, brother.
I can't raise my hand but to drink
    my own blood that halts.

The landscape is one
    tired and methodical and
        raises her arms to say goodbye,
            barren.

Vean el escualo que monto
   -la fiera figurada-
principianta ahí arriba
en mis faenas de pesca
    encimera ahí
a horcajadas sobre ese pez mío
   aletazo y aletazo
mancornados tocando tierra

              él manco
              yo herma

el escualo que monto
como meteoro o granizo
posándose en la colosal losa
   mi magnífico insecto
pone sus patas en el parking de aviones
silencia la torre de control
y ruedo por la escalerilla de sus dientes
   hecha vómito y milagro

        &

Robinson Crusoe se acompañó de Viernes sus días. Hizo su juego toda la semana. A mí nadie me acompañará por esta tierra blanca donde el polvo es harina que cae del cielo.
   Mi carromato se arrastrará en vano.
   La brújula está dormida.

   Es la hora del lobo.
En blanco y negro el panorama de espacio y tiempo.

             Yo herma
                cuchepa
                india sudamericana

No vuelvo a cruzar el Estrecho de Behring para devolverle la mano a nadie. En esa blanca torta boreal no encontrarán la huella de mis extremidades. No intento una plusmarca con las ruedecitas de mi trasero.

             No soy el Capitán Avalos
             No soy el Tiburón Contreras
             Soy lengua ampollada por la
                  electricidad

Nunca estaré colgando de una lágrima del Everest
Estoy sentada y me columpio en el sillar de mi pelvis
el filo del mundo.

&

Vengo del País de los Vertederos Eternos, del Aerosol Templado,
de los Montes de Piedad haciendo nata. Flora y Fauna Travesti
largándose por el larguero de tierra sableada. Despeñados por la
Montaña Rusa nuestros sesos lloran Edén y Landia, Cielo y Tierra.
Y, ¡héme aquí en el lobby del Viejo Mundo!

Atrás quedaron los Piececitos Azules en la Feria Persa y Coreana.

&

"Con buen tiempo, el 12 de octubre de 1987
he cruzado la frontera"

Patagona levanto las tolderías de mi esterilidad.
Desayunos albatros de Nueva Zelandia y lo que caiga a mi olla.
Chincol o jote
ese es el impasse
el horizonte de una mañana desierta.

Vengo del País del Reloj de Flores, de Tres y
Cuatro Álamos. Vengo de vuelta del "Fausto"
y he buscado todos estos años a Juan Alacalufe
Desaparecido.

En mi *sentimental journey*, la búsqueda del Amor
Imposible. Son mis mutilaciones las que toman
asiento en la yacija del rodado y como un centauro
chirriante me precipito dando tumbos por la
rectitud de la tundra.

Cuesta dar en el blanco.

La página esteparia no cede al manoseo de
la callosidad.
La página no es pasamano ni pasatiempo
ni baranda para niños.
La página del vacío aparente viene escrita
sólo hay que tactar.

Y tú, al otro lado del mundo, más allá de las Columnas de Hércules, fácilmente ubicable por ENTEL, por un misil tierra-a-tierra, por un satélite de comunicación, por un Correo Amigo ¿dónde estás?

(…)

DIE KUNST ZU REISEN, hermano
el acto y el arte de partir
        de confundirse con el blanco.

Pasar el límite infranqueable de las cosas
        pasar por el aro, el trapecio
                saltar al vacío
y la maleta cargada de nada que acompaña.

La capota de la noche tiene un doble fondo
        un pasaje secreto incomunicable.

Vivimos en un cajón de circo
        de pronto vuelan palomas y conejos
                de pronto se llena de gusanos.

No puedo pactar con nadie sino es
        conmigo misma, hermano.
No puedo alzar la mano sino para beber
        mi propia sangre que se detiene.

El paisaje es uno solo
        cansado y metódico y
                levanta los brazos para despedirse
                        herma.

from THE CHILEAN FLAG / de LA BANDERA DE CHILE

No one has said a word about the Chilean Flag
        in its bearing   in the fabric
        throughout the entire oblong desert
                it has not been named
                The Chilean Flag
                        absent

The Chilean Flag says nothing about herself
she reads herself in her mirror small and round
glinting delayed in time like an echo
there is much broken glass
shattered like the lines of an open hand
read
in search of stones for her desires

≈

Lifting a curtain of smoke the Chilean Flag
asphyxiates and expires not able to do more
the flag is incredible
she will never see the burning subsoil of her holy

fields
the lost treasures in the crooks of the air
the marine burials that are a jewel

we will see the marvellous mountain range sinking in the
penumbra

fictitious she laughs
the Chilean Flag

≈

The Chilean Flag is a foreigner in her own country
she doesn't have ID
she isn't majority
she is no longer recognized
the prolonged fasting has put death's thumb upon her
the churches administer her last rites
the Legations' party horn and sound of the trumpets

The Chilean Flag forces herself to be more than a flag

≈

48 hours is the day of the Chilean Flag
the salutes of hundreds of salvos

the discourses of fifty sheets of paper
the processions of two or three regiments
the ribbons the standards the banners ad infinitum
    at the speed of light the toasts and honours

The Chilean Flag knows that its day is the day of judgement

≈

The Chilean Flag is used as a gag

and that's why surely that's why

no one says anything

Nadie ha dicho una palabra sobre la Bandera de Chile
        en el porte   en la tela
            en todo su desierto cuadrilongo
                no la han nombrado
                La Bandera de Chile
                    ausente

La Bandera de Chile no dice nada sobre sí misma
    se lee en su espejo de bolsillo redondo
espejea retardada en el tiempo como un eco
        hay muchos vidrios rotos
    trizados como las líneas de una mano abierta
            se lee
    en busca de piedras para sus ganas

≈

Levanta una cortina de humo la Bandera de Chile
asfixia y da aire a más no poder
                        es increíble la bandera
no verá nunca el subsuelo encendido de sus campos
                            santos
        los tesoros perdidos en los recodos del aire
        los entierros marinos que son joya

veremos la cordillera maravillosa sumiéndose en la penumbra

ficticia ríe

la Bandera de Chile

≈

La Bandera de Chile es extranjera en su propio país
no tiene carta ciudadana
no es mayoría
ya no se la reconoce
los ayunos prolongados le ponen el pulgar de la muerte
las iglesias le ponen la extremaunción
las Legaciones serpentina y sonido de trompetas

La Bandera de Chile fuerza ser más que una bandera

≈

De 48 horas es el día de la Bandera de Chile
los saludos de centenas de salvas
de cincuenta carillas los discursos
de dos y tres regimientos las procesiones
las escarapelas los estandartes los pendones al infinito
a la velocidad de la luz los brindis y honores

La Bandera de Chile sabe que su día es el del juicio

≈

La Bandera de Chile es usada de mordaza

y por eso seguramente por eso

nadie dice nada

PAULA ILABACA NÚÑEZ (Chile)

Paula Ilabaca Núñez (1979, Santiago) is a writer, editor, and lecturer. She received the Pablo Neruda Prize, 2015, for her poetry; the Juegos Florales Prize, 2014, for her novel La regla de los nueve *(2015); and the Crítica de Prensa Literaria Prize of the Universidad Diego Portales (USP in 2010). She has twice received the Chilean National Book & Reading Council's Creación Literaria Scholarship. Her publications include the poetry collections* Penínsulas *(2019) and* La perla suelta *(2009) and the novel* La regla de los nueve *(2015). Founder of the independent press Cástor y Pólux, she dedicates herself to teaching and literary workshops.*

ENGLISH TRANSLATIONS BY DANIEL BORZUTZKY

from COMPLETE / *de* COMPLETA

NUMBERS

good afternoon
the exact time
two-sixteen
the temperature
twenty-eight degrees
thank you for calling
good afternoon
the exact time
two-sixteen
the temperature
twenty-eight degrees
thank you for calling
good afternoon
the exact time
two-sixteen
the temperature
twenty-eight degrees
thank you for calling
good afternoon
the exact time
two-sixteen
the temperature
twenty-eight degrees
thank you for

NÚMEROS

buenas tardes
la hora exacta
dos dieciséis
la temperatura
veintiocho grados
gracias por llamar
buenas tardes
la hora exacta
dos dieciséis
la temperatura
veintiocho grados
gracias por llamar
buenas tardes
la hora exacta
dos dieciséis
la temperatura
veintiocho grados
gracias por llamar
buenas tardes
la hora exacta
dos diecisiete
la temperatura
veintiocho grados
gracias por

141

nothing happens at two in the afternoon nothing the nothing
sticks to the bodies scattered in the place of tedium nothing
happens nothing the phone rings many times it's twenty-eight
degrees and cloudy a small plane flies above the phone rings and
if I answer interference for a change nothing happens and the
tedium sticks it expands with the afternoon nothing the sheets
are mussed up the phone rings it's twenty-eight degrees because
a voice blows into the ear I won't pick up the receiver again a
small plane flies above and the phone rings it's twenty-eight
degrees and cloudy the dogs begin to bark this time it's over
and the tedium is a dog who barks in the afternoon's cement
it's twenty-eight degrees and the wind blows and it's cloudy
and hot the nothing sticks to the bodies scattered in the tedium
the window reverberates and creates a mysterious moment

the phone rings and the receiver is hung up wet because my hand is sweaty and I couldn't let it go it's twenty-eight degrees and the tedium what can we do with the tedium of two in the afternoon the phone rings over and over again the receiver gets damp and sweat drips I can't let it go the plane goes by again and it's two in the afternoon it's twenty-eight degrees again the window and the wind blows the dogs have stopped barking and the tedium remains and the tedium sticks hard to the bodies nothing happens and with my other free hand I look for it and I find it cold the sheets can't warm it the twenty-eight degrees are useless and I grab it and laugh slowly and I say it's mine and I caress it and again the sound of the plane and the phone and my hand drips lots of water and with my other hand I take it and bury it I open my legs and I bury it because the tedium because it's two in the afternoon because the tedium of the twenty-eight degrees because everything sticks because I

141

nada ocurre a las dos de la tarde nada la nada se pega a los cuerpos repartidos en el lugar del tedio nada ocurre nada el teléfono suena muchas veces hay veintiocho grados y está nublado una avioneta pasa el teléfono suena y si contestara interferencias para variar nada ocurre y el tedio se pega y crece con la tarde nada las sábanas están revueltas el teléfono suena y hay veintiocho grados porque una voz lo sopla adentro de la oreja no levantaré el auricular una avioneta pasa de nuevo y el teléfono suena hay veintiocho grados y está nublado los perros comienzan a ladrar esta vez se acabó y el tedio es un perro que ladra en el cemento de la tarde hay veintiocho grados y el viento sopla y está nublado y hace calor la nada se pega a los cuerpos repartidos en el tedio la ventana repercute y se crea un instante misterioso el teléfono suena y el auricular se coloca mojado porque la mano me suda y no puedo soltarlo hay veintiocho grados y el tedio qué hacer con el tedio de las dos de la tarde el teléfono suena muchas veces que se prolongan el auricular se humedece y chorrea sudor yo no puedo soltarlo la avioneta transcurre de nuevo y son las dos de la tarde hay veintiocho grados otra vez la ventana y el viento que sopla los perros se callaron y queda el tedio y el tedio se pega muy fuerte a los cuerpos nada ocurre y con la otra mano libre lo busco y lo encuentro frío las sábanas no logran calentarlo y los veintiocho grados no sirven y yo lo tomo y me río lento y digo es mío y lo acaricio la avioneta y el teléfono vuelven a sonar

y mi mano chorrea mucha agua y con la otra mano lo tomo y
me lo entierro abro las piernas y me lo entierro porque el tedio
porque las dos de la tarde porque el tedio de los veintiocho
grados porque todo se pega porque yo

DAY 4

decline don't get
up
the interrogation
doesn't work
when i had it
i covered the holes
alone I never looked
up
the floor declines the floor
i was still receiving
all the signs
in silence to be able to
turn them in
to be able to turn in
all the signs
in silence
to the floor don't get up
decline just decline

DÍA 4

declina no levantes
hacia arriba
no
funciona el interrogo
cuando tuve
me tapé los huecos
sola nunca miré
hacia arriba
el suelo declina el suelo
recibía aún
todos los signos
en silencio para poder
entregar sólo
para poder entregar

todos los signos
en silencio
al suelo no levantes
declina sólo declina

DAY 12

she's been bleeding for twelve
whole days boiling
she lays her hand on the table
quiet
she sees lineages hanging in cells
fall apart sees
slips her turn in the
crotch the scabs
i had a babble i re
ally wanted to be
another erect deficiency another
stain the floor laughs
everything happens for a reason she stains shivers
speaks in fearful voices
the walls are beautiful rocks
she rubs her face
on a brick say
i had the clearest
visage say
now scrawny saliva arranged
the clearest parts i
believe these
once
insolent hands
are murderers of
the body there's
nothing else
to

DÍA 12

lleva sangrando doce
días completos hervidos
sienta la mano en la mesa
callada
mira derrumbarse estirpes
colgadas en células mira
resbala su vez en la entre
pierna las lepras
yo tuve balbucea yo tu
ve tantas ganas de ser
otra carencia erguida otra
mancha el piso ríe
todo por algo mancha tirita
articula voces de susto
las murallas son bellas rocas
restriega el rostro
en el ladrillo di
yo tuve la faz
tan clara di
ahora enjuta saliva ordena
partes tan claras yo
creo estas
manos antes
frescas son
asesinas al
cuerpo no
hay más
que

the
situations
of
boredom

a house filled with tedium nonsense tangled up in the dining room repetition can't go on like a quest for lethargy and subsequent rest in the boredom there are no impressions only inertia and heavy moments filled with rage not even rage just movements filled with nothing and the always tiresome tedium you have to drool in the house which is the body the reference to the bathroom is because it's the place of abandon the bathroom brings security and heat is to have a frozen and shining uterus

in a house is to be born once more the floor is the solution the
tidiness is the love the necessity of

the
situations
of
boredom

a house filled with tedium nonsense tangled up in the dining
room repetition can't go on like a quest for lethargy and
subsequent rest in the boredom there are no impressions only
inertia and heavy moments and filled with rage not even rage
just movements filled with nothing and the always tiresome
tedium you have to drool in the house which is the body the
reference to the bathroom is because it's the place of abandon
the bathroom brings security and heat is to have a uterus frozen
and shining in a house is to return to being born the floor is the
solution the tidiness is the love the necessity of

the
situations
of
boredom

a house filled with tedium nonsense tangled up in the dining
room repetition can't go on like a quest for lethargy and
subsequent rest in the boredom there are no impressions only
inertia and heavy moments and filled with rage not even rage
just movements filled with nothing and the always tiresome
tedium you have to drool in the house which is the body the
reference to the bathroom is because it's the place of abandon
the bathroom brings security and heat is to have a uterus frozen

las
situaciones
del
hastío

una casa llena de tedio el sinsentido arrebujado en el comedor
no poder más la repetición como búsqueda del letargo
y posterior descanso en el hastío no hay impresiones sólo
inercia y movimientos pesados y llenos de ira ni si quiera

ira sólo movimientos llenos de nada y de tedio siempre
pesados hay que balbucear dentro de la casa que es el cuerpo
la referencia al baño es porque es el lugar para el abandono
el baño entrega seguridad y calor es tener un útero helado y
brillante en una casa es volver a nacer el suelo es la solución
lo pulcro es el querer la necesidad de

las
situaciones
del
hastío

una casa llena de tedio el sinsentido arrebujado en el comedor
no poder más la repetición como búsqueda del letargo y
posterior descanso en el hastío no hay impresiones sólo
inercia y movimientos pesados y llenos de ira ni si quiera
ira sólo movimientos llenos de nada y de tedio siempre
pesados hay que balbucear dentro de la casa que es el cuerpo
la referencia al baño es porque es el lugar para el abandono
el baño entrega seguridad y calor es tener un útero helado y
brillante en una casa es volver a nacer el suelo es la solución
lo pulcro es el querer la necesidad de

las
situaciones
del
hastío

una casa llena de tedio el sinsentido arrebujado en el comedor
no poder más la repetición como búsqueda del letargo y
posterior descanso en el hastío no hay impresiones sólo
inercia y movimientos pesados y llenos de ira ni si quiera
ira sólo movimientos llenos de nada y de tedio siempre
pesados hay que balbucear dentro de la casa que es el cuerpo
la referencia al baño es porque es el lugar para el abandono
el baño entrega seguridad y calor es tener un útero helado

from **LUCIA THE CITY** / *de* **CIUDAD LUCÍA**

i'm a voice i'm a
i'm a little voice
that wants to learn no
that wants
to begin to from

to let you not
that wants to begin to speak

city first
then whore there are
no ways no
to thrive in the mud no
to drown in the frenzy

tonight there are
tonight there are fusses
tonight there are fusses to build you love
tonight there are fusses
are there fusses? tonight?
can i say?
can i say
it?
(with my mouth filled with milk do i speak?)

lucía was a dream in which one way was to suffer
yes mi niña my little crimson you weren't a city no
you were legs you were a lovely vulva where a brown angel lived
why brown mama? why brown
if the angels are white like my teeth like those clouds
like my towels mama?
not all the angels look alike there's an angel who caught in the muck
tosses tortoiseshell figurines at your hair and that angel is brown
                              mi niña that angel is brown
brown mama brown i don't know what that is
i can see tiles bridges buildings towers avenues in my blood mama
but here nothing is brown nothing and if i tell you what is brown?
would you know it?
would you tell me?
i was sleepy once and i fell somehow i fell into lawless places
mama into muddy smelly places what would you say if i
mama what would you say?
not all angels look alike not all of them mi niña
there's a brown one who gets clogged from the way he sweats in his
                              swamp full of gold

mama
i could be a stink mama?
mama mama what is gold mama?

the possibility of being a city she said my only desire is to be a city it's that
it makes me come
it's that my milk comes through the streets through these constructions lucia says
love love there are fusses when you bang love
there are some tortoiseshell figurines that wither and shout for me to drink my milk
to be a city to be a city lucia stretches out and says
to be a city to be able to come on these foundations yes
to be a city to have an impact to fill with milk and the cement sucks itself off alone
and my cement becomes mud and spits me out yes my love yes mi niña yes my
little crimson
mama?
my head is filled with fusses and my throat mama
it seems to me that i haven't known how to understand
the fusses don't even let me write mama
like when my mouth filled with milk doesn't let me speak
yes mama just like those times i drank
i pass through those forms of pain lucia says
i pass through them as if they were as if i wanted it
there are nights i can't even breathe mama
 there are nights when your body sticks to mine and there's no way to find it
mama if there's a smell how can it be that he is not here that he's gone and late
in wanting to return
it's the fusses mama I know it's the fusses
i could have had that gold mama that light or that negation
i could have entered your cries so I could
stay lucia said
but the angel got rough and there was no way mama there was no way
the angel hid the gold in his breath the angel changed its tone to love me it changed
the ways of understanding
mama tell me if i understand?
if there are so many fusses do i understand?

soy una voz soy una
soy una voz pequeña
que quiere aprender no
que quiere
comenzar a de
a dejarte no
que quiere comenzar a decir

primero ciudad
luego zorra no
hay maneras no
de abundar en el barro no
de ahogarse en el frenesí

esta noche hay
esta noche hay unas bullas
esta noche hay unas bullas por construirte amor
esta noche hay unas bullas
hay bullas? esta noche?
puedo decir?
puedo decir
lo?
(con la boca repleta de leche yo hablo?)

lucía era un sueño en donde una manera era padecer
sí mi niña mi pedacito carmesí no eras ciudad no
eras piernas eras una vulva hermosa donde un ángel marrón vivía
por qué marrón mamá? por qué marrón
si los ángeles son blancos como mis dientes como esas nubes
como mis toallas mamá?
no todos los ángeles se parecen hay un ángel que atrapado en el légamo
te tira figuras de carey hacia el cabello y ese ángel es marrón mi niña ese
                                                                ángel es marrón
marrón mamá marrón no sé lo que es eso
yo puedo ver lozas puentes edificios torres avenidas en mi sangre mamá
pero acá nada es marrón nada y si yo te digo qué es marrón?
lo sabrías?
me dirías?
yo tuve sueño una vez y caía por una manera caía por lugares sin ley
mamá por lugares de fango y hedor qué dirías si yo te
mamá qué dirías?
no todos los ángeles se parecen no todos mi niña

hay uno marrón que atasca en su forma de sudar en su ciénaga repleta de or
mamá
yo podría ser hedor mamá?
mamá mamá qué es el oro mamá?

la posibilidad de ser ciudad ella dijo mi único deseo es ser ciudad es que
se me corra
es que me corra la leche por las calles por estas construcciones lucía dice
amor amor hay unas bullas cuando pegas amor
hay unas figuras de carey que se demacran y gritan que me tome mi leche
ser ciudad sí ser cuidad lucía se estira y dice
ser ciudad para que se la corra en estos cimientos sí
ser ciudad para que impacte para que llene de leche y el cemento se chupe solo
y mi cemento se haga barro y me escupa sí mi amor sí mi niña sí mi
pedacito carmesí
mamá?
tengo la cabeza llena de bullas y la garganta mamá
me parece que no he sabido comprender
las bullas no me dejan ni escribir mamá
como cuando la boca repleta de leche no me deja hablar
sí mamá lo mismo de esas veces de beber
traspaso las maneras del dolor lucía dice
las traspaso como si fueran como si yo lo quisiera
hay noches en las que no puedo ni respirar mamá
hay noches en las que su cuerpo se pega al mío y no hay cómo poder
encontrarlo
mamá si hay olor cómo puede ser que él no esté que se haya ido y tarde en
querer volver
son las bullas mamá yo lo sé son las bullas
yo podría haber tenido ese oro mamá esa luz o esa negación
yo podría haber entrado en su llanto para poder
permanecer lucía dijo
pero el ángel se puso tosco y no hubo manera mamá no hubo manera
el ángel ocultó el oro en su respiración el ángel cambió los tonos para
amarme cambió
las formas de entender
mamá dime yo entiendo?
si hay tantas bullas yo entiendo?

from **THE LOOSE PEARL** / *de* **PERLA SUELTA**

Imagine that her eye sockets fall into the walls and the forms. Imagine that little by little she feels the eruption of a belligerent lethargy that she can't pull out of. Imagine she wants to come with the back of her hand. Imagine she's too lazy to masturbate by herself. Imagine she walks through the tiny space of the bathroom, that there's no window, that she grabs her hair and looks into the mirror. She looks at the gold heart hanging in the middle of her chest. The mares. Grazing. That's it. The round-eyed plaster-cast mares, the dream, the song, the orange bed, the prayer. That's it. However you like it, however broken or simple. Imagine she looks into the mirror and says a prayer. Saliva slowly dripping because she's had her mouth open for a while. She thinks of him, of the eunuch, his stiff hair, his soft muscles. Then she cleans herself with a meticulous movement, with toilet paper, with a towel. Then, she's sitting. She's sitting on the toilet bowl and she repeats the same sentence, only this time she adds:

> *It's been a month since I've fucked anyone*
> *It's been a month since I've gotten it on*
> *It's been a month since anyone lit my ass up*
> *It's been a month since I've seen the light*

She says it in the simplest and most broken way. That's it. A small fraction, tense from the infections that besiege her. It looks like one of the mares will give birth this afternoon. As she does it the bed will start to creak, the bed and the shapes that stretch along the wall when the sun peeks through the curtains, without her wanting this, of course. The sun disturbs the pimples that popped up this morning, pustules on her coccyx. It's nasty, and when she feels them on her body, she starts to speak, to babble: *"feed me when I'm hungry / drink me till I'm dry."* Then, looking at herself in the dark television screen, bringing an eye mask to her face, she asks in a low voice: my master, where is my master?

Imagina que caen las cuencas de los ojos en las paredes y las formas. Imagina que de a poco siente que va surgiendo una pereza bélica de la cual no es posible sustraerse. Imagina que se quiere correr con el dorso de la mano. Imagina que le da flojera masturbarse sola. Imagina que camina por el espacio minúsculo del baño, que no hay ventana, que se toma el pelo y se mira al espejo. Se mira el corazón de oro que le cuelga en la mitad del pecho. Las yeguas. Pastan. Eso es. Las yeguas yesos ojos redondos, el sueño, la canción, la cama naranja, el rezo. Es así. De la manera que tú quieras, de la manera más rota y simple. Imagina que se mira al espejo y pronuncia una oración. Que lentamente se le cae la saliva porque se ha quedado un buen rato con la boca abierta. Piensa en él, en el eunuco, en sus cabellos tiesos, en sus músculos blandos. Luego se la limpia con un gesto meticuloso, con papel higiénico, con la toalla. Está sentada, luego. Está sentada en la taza del baño y vuelve a decir la misma oración, pero esta vez agrega:

> *Hace un mes que no jodo con nadie.*
> *Hace un mes que no me salta la liebre,*
> *que no se me prenden los cachetes;*
> *hace un mes que no veo la luz.*

Lo dice de la manera más rota y simple. Eso es. Un porcentaje breve, tenso de infecciones la ronda. Parece que una de las yeguas parirá esta tarde. Al hacerlo la cama comenzará a crujir, la cama y las formas que se estiran en la pared cuando el sol entra a través de las cortinas, sin que ella lo quiera, por supuesto. El sol molesta en los granos que le han salido esa mañana, unos granos en el coxis. Eso es nefasto, pues cuando los siente en su cuerpo, ella comienza a decir o a balbucear: "feed me when i'm hungry / drink me till i'm dry". Luego pregunta en voz baja, mirándose en la pantalla del televisor apagado, llevándose a la cara un antifaz: mi amo, ¿dónde quedó mi amo?

≈

Counting the days that pass, the loose one strolls through the basic territory, humming a song. She looks at her orange bed, thinks of the days when sweat and kisses embroidered the sheets, the pure and sacred piety. The same and the same. Drool. Pester. Come. Arrive. The bed. Filled with prayers. There are some keys under the pillow, clasps for a necklace with a gold heart, which the loose one looks at entranced, because she doesn't have a heart. Beyond, in another space or under another influence, the king is sleeping deeply. And he doesn't listen. And he doesn't feel. And he doesn't know that the loose one waits and waits for the precise moment of his flirtations and then escapes. As she has always done, because she can't, because she doesn't know how to stay or because it simply annoys her, because she gets annoyed at anything that starts to get serious.

≈

Contando los días que pasan, la suelta se pasea por el territorio básico, murmurando una canción. Mira su cama naranja, piensa en los días en los que el sudor bordaba las sábanas, los besos lo mismo, la pura y santa piedá. Lo mismo y lo mismo. Babear. Hostigar. Correr. Llegar. La cama. Repleta de oraciones. Bajo la almohada hay unas llaves, sujetas por una cadena con un corazón de oro, que la suelta mira arrobada, porque ella no tiene corazón. Más allá, en otro espacio o bajo otro estado, el rey está profundamente dormido. Y no escucha. Y no siente. Y no sabe que la suelta espera y espera el momento justo en el que se hará la linda, para luego escapar. Como siempre lo ha hecho, porque no puede, porque no sabe quedarse o porque simplemente le irrita, le irrita todo lo que parece ir en serio.

≥

As she makes her charts, the loose one observes herself again and again. She comes in and out of the bathroom, looks out at the street. She goes over to the balcony. She begins to water the plants on the terrace, which now burn from the cold of these last days of autumn. Soon winter will be here. And these, the burnt ones, are a reminder of that sunny day when the loose one told him: they are like our love; they've been born again. But it was a total drag. And the eunuch knew it and shut up, his phallus cowering as always. The loose one reconsidered, for example, when she would go by the window naked, or dressed, or horny. And this was just one example of the traps she set for him. With the eunuch nothing ever happened anyway. Nothing. Or better yet: nothing had happened, because he was a closed container, and stubborn, a little clumsy, a little stupid, limp fucks buried in memory, an imprint, a state one could appeal to.

≥

Mientras saca cuentas, la suelta se observa una y otra vez. Entra y sale del baño, mira hacia la calle. Cruza hacia el balcón. Comienza a regar las plantas de la terraza, que ahora se queman con el frío de los últimos días del otoño. Vendrá el invierno, pronto. Y ellas, las quemadas, recuerdan ese día de sol en que la suelta le dijo: son como nuestro amor; han vuelto a nacer. Pero era una pura lata. Y el eunuco lo sabía y calló, con el falo encogido, como siempre. La suelta reconsideró, por ejemplo, cuando se paseaba en pelotas frente a la ventana, o con ropa o con ganas. Y era sólo un ejemplo de todas las maneras con las que inventaba trampas para él. Con el eunuco nada ocurría de todas formas. Nada. O mejor: nada había ocurrido, porque él era un trasto cerrado y terco, un poco torpe, un poco lerdo, cogidas lacias sepultas en la memoria, una estela, un estado al que se podía recurrir.

GLADYS MENDÍA (Venezuela)

Gladys Mendía (Maracay, Venezuela, 1975) is a poet, editor and Portuguese-Spanish translator. She has been widely published in magazines and her most recent collection, El cantar de los manglares *(2018), was translated into English by Jèssica Pujol Duran and published under the title* The Singing of the Mangroves *(London: 2019). She has translated the work of Roberto Piva into Spanish in the anthology* La catedral del desorden *(2017), and is the founding editor of the literary and arts magazine* LP5 *(www.lp5.cl) and the independent press Homónima, founded in 2004 (www. lp5editora.blogspot.com).*

ENGLISH TRANSLATIONS BY JÈSSICA PUJOL DURAN

from THE SINGING OF THE MANGROVES / de EL CANTAR DE LOS MANGLARES

THE LABYRINTH OF COMPANY

The translator necessarily invents a form of expression from one language to another, like the poet invents a language within his/her own language.
ÉDOUARD GLISSANT

we are going to relate the forging of relations   to place our ear into the
voices and the voice into the ears   to move across the bridges between
the abysses to bring out the multiple root   we speak here of
variable speeds unlikely frequencies   unprecedented dimensions

the voice shoots seeds   simultaneous channels sprout
memory without history   memory of ears that look at each other
unpredictable choreography   connections of chance   landscapes
characters of the mangrove world

we the poetantes outside the order   writing in your ears
musicating in your ears   performing in your ears   each
ear in a projected archipelago   each ear in the
labyrinth of company   nomadic erect mangroves   poetantes
outside the order without a root of their own

we see tongues like mangroves   syntax of a black heron
swampy soil   thickets of roots branches   outside and inside the sea
outside and inside us   caesuras of the twisted landscape
syncope of silence   heteroglossia as paradise   grammar of the mud
poetantes buzzing in the ear

translations of breaths   pelican of healthy uncertainty   to sew
songs to weave sounds   roots of different colours   dancing
unheard genres

marooning in the labyrinth of company   basin   river
sea inlet   marooning for the sake of beauty   marooning the
language imposed by them

to attend the mosaic of new signs   and weave   to weave each other
mangrove verses   to open daedalus roads   to sing   to
weave to imagine marooning the mangrove world   to
sing the singing of the mangroves

to edit crocodile tears   snake hug   scorpions
wandering   to publish in falcon's flight flapping gravity
to spread eagle eye the mangrove world   to bring
out the roughness of brackish waters

to speak languages as archipelagos   translation as archipelago
imaginary as archipelago   proliferated boats verses
boats verses move across

I link oyster voices crab voices anemone voices   they do
not know each other   they write in the same waters   do not know
each other I knot seashell voices mussel voices limpet voices do not
know each other   sweet salty waters shelter them they dream the same
little roots   high tide low tide in the labyrinth of company
they embrace and do not know each another

warm winds bring unknown tones   multiple roots
rise   seeking unusual accesses   they travel through the air
they arch creating networks   ears of friction   we speak here of
poetantes imagining the new epics   sea grapes of the new babel

we are going to relate the forging of relations   of how they
adapt so as not to wither   of how they shield the systematic
barbarity they are afraid but spread out   add up openings   they
create nests originate nourishment   sustain the voices their own
voices

the poetantes pour down   the rain precipitates
stories   multiplication of droplets   wandering of water   they
disseminate memory without history   imagined spaces without history
imaginary stories of wandering   underwater roots without hierarchy
such is the geography of the poetantes   guardians of the tongues
mourners of the tongues   dwellers of all languages

mangrove estuaries the new libraries   wisdom of ease
intersection buzzes   collisions flutter   affinity and
appetite arise thus the mutual influences   unheard languages emerge
temporary stories   unforeseen effects   transitory variations
fluctuations without clear reason

we speak here of continents archipelago   black heron the new
flag shrimp and crabs the new heroes
coral reefs the new poems   incendiary licks   landscapes
characters of the mangrove world

without measures nor formulas without attacks nor arguments   the
singing of the mangroves   projects poetic baroques   swamps
coasts cays hanging intertwined branches   thus their verses
murmur of tide chiming of foam   whistle of wind   heap of
voices   repetitions ignored screams   vagabond whispers
such is the new epic in the labyrinth of company

EL LABERINTO DE LA COMPAÑÍA

El traductor inventa el lenguaje que necesitamos para pasar de una lengua a otra, como el poeta inventa un lenguaje en su propia lengua
                                        EDOUARD GLISSANT

vamos a relatar la puesta en relación   a poner el oído en las voces   y la
voz en los oídos   transitar los puentes entre abismos   hacer evidente
la raíz múltiple   hablamos aquí de velocidades variables   frecuencias
inverosímiles dimensiones inéditas

la voz dispara semillas   crecen canales simultáneos   memoria sin
historia memoria de oídos que se miran   coreografía imprevisible
conexiones del azar paisajes personajes del mangle mundo

nosotros los poetantes afuera del orden   escribiendo en tus oídos
musicando en tus oídos   performando en tus oídos   cada
oído en un archipiélago proyectado   cada oído en el laberinto
de la compañía manglares erguidos nómadas   poetantes afuera del
orden sin única raíz

vemos lenguas como manglares   sintaxis de garza mora   suelo
cenagoso marañas de raíces ramas   afuera y adentro del mar   afuera y
adentro de nosotros   cesuras del paisaje retorcido síncopa
del silencio heteroglosia como paraíso   gramática del fango
poetantes zumban al oído

traducciones de alientos pelícano de sana incertidumbre coser canciones
tejer sonidos   raíces de distintos colores   bailando inauditos
géneros

cimarronear por el laberinto de la compañía   cuenca   río   mar
ensenada cimarronear en nombre de la belleza   cimarronear la lengua
impuesta por ellos

asistir al mosaico de nuevos signos   y tejer   tejernos manglares
versos abrir caminos dédalos   cantar   tejer
imaginar cimarronear el mangle mundo   cantar el cantar de
los manglares

editar lágrimas de cocodrilo   abrazo de serpiente   errancia de
escorpiones   publicar en vuelo de halcón aleteando la gravedad
difundir ojo de águila el mangle mundo   hacer evidente la
agitación de aguas salobres

hablar lenguas como archipiélago   traducción como archipiélago
imaginario como archipiélago   barcos versos proliferados   barcos
versos transitan

enlazo voces ostras voces cangrejos voces anémonas   no se
conocen escriben en las mismas aguas   no se conocen   anudo
voces caracoles voces mejillones voces lapas   no se conocen   aguas
salobres   los   cobijan   sueñan   las   mismas   raicillas
marea alta marea baja en el laberinto de la compañía se abrazan y no se
conocen

vientos cálidos traen desconocidos tonos   múltiples raíces se alzan

buscan insólitos accesos   viajan a través del aire   se arquean
creando redes oídos del roce   hablamos aquí de poetantes imaginando
las nuevas épicas uvas de mar de la nueva babel

vamos a relatar la puesta en relación   de cómo se adaptan para no
marchitar de cómo escudan la barbarie sistemática   sienten miedo
pero se extienden suman aperturas crean nidos   originan el alimento
sustentan las voces sus propias voces

los poetantes llueven a cántaros   la lluvia son relatos
precipitados multiplicación de gotas   errancia del agua   propagan la
memoria sin historia espacios imaginados sin historia   relatos
imaginarios del divagar raíces submarinas sin jerarquía   tal es la
geografía de los poetantes guardianes de las lenguas   dolientes de las
lenguas   habitantes de todas las lenguas

estuarios de manglares las nuevas bibliotecas   sabiduría de la soltura
zumba la intersección   revolotean colisiones   surge afinidad y apetito
así las influencias mutuas   lenguajes insólitos emergen   relatos
temporales efectos imprevistos   variaciones transitorias fluctuaciones
sin razón clara

hablamos aquí de continentes archipiélagos   garza mora la nueva
bandera camarones y cangrejos los nuevos héroes   arrecifes de coral
los nuevos poemas   lenguaradas incendiarias   paisajes personajes del
mangle mundo

sin medidas ni fórmulas   sin ataques ni argumentos   el cantar de
los manglares proyecta barrocas poéticas   ciénagas costas cayos
colgantes entrelazadas ramas   así sus versos   murmullo de marea
campaneo de espumas silbar de viento cúmulo de voces   repeticiones
gritos ignorados susurros vagamundos   tal es la nueva épica en el
laberinto de la compañía

from HIGH BEAMS / *de* LUCES ALTAS

LATIN AMERICAN VOICE

the mosaic voice the fragmented voice the voice many voices   layers of voices shuddering the quotidian the exotic the ordinary the exquisite the uneasy voice the strong voice the complaining voice   our impure voice branched into so many voices   by biological necessity   by adaptation by logic   by trial   by proposal by enthusiasm without theories with temporary archives   dying together by the same bullet   without homogeneity   voices that call to the fertile fatherless voices of circumstances descriptive arbitrary eloquent achieve their non-purpose voices to the extreme voices that rise on their backs to Heaven from Earth

VOZ LATINOAMÉRICA

la voz mosaico   la voz fragmentada la voz muchas voces   capas de voces estremecimiento lo cotidiano lo exótico lo corriente lo exquisito la voz inquieta la voz fuerza la voz queja nuestra voz impura ramificada en tantas voces   por necesidad biológica   por adaptación   por lógica   por tanteo por propuesta por entusiasmo   sin teorías   con archivos temporales muriendo juntos por la misma bala   sin homogeneidad   voces que llaman a lo fértil sin padre voces de circunstancias   descriptivas   arbitrarias elocuentes   logran su no finalidad   voces al extremo   voces que suben de espaldas al cielo de la tierra

WORLD

our world are the voices   they speak so loud that it is impossible not to hear them   our diversity scares   they want us to be a single mass that we speak the same that we write the same the Guarani voices are a threat to neoliberalism   the Mapuche voices are bombs about to go off the Mayan voices are an act of subversion   the Wayuu voices are shots to the system   the Quechuan voices are missiles blowing up the institutions our diversity is an attack   I walk through the streets of my neighbourhood and the oppressors have done an excellent job   all overcrowded   all uniformed   all anaesthetised objectified in traffic following the signs accelerating in the highways star-filled without light   dreaming of disobedience

MUNDO

nuestro mundo son las voces   hablan tan fuerte que es imposible no escucharlas   nuestra diversidad asusta   quieren que seamos una masa que hablemos igual que escribamos igual las voces guaraníes son una amenaza al neoliberalismo   las voces mapuches son bombas a punto de explotar las voces mayas son un acto de subversión   las voces wayúu son disparos al sistema   las voces quechua son misiles explotando las instituciones nuestra diversidad es un atentado   camino por las calles de mi barrio y los represores han hecho un excelente trabajo masificados todos   uniformados todos anestesiados   todos cosificados en el tránsito   siguiendo   la   señalética   acelerando en las autopistas   estrellados sin luz   soñando con la desobediencia

from THE ALCOHOL OF THE INTERMEDIATE STATES / *de* EL ALCOHOL DE LOS ESTADOS INTERMEDIOS

THE ALCOHOL OF THE INTERMEDIATE STATES

> *It can be said that a substance burns in a grey flame I don't know the*
> *colours of the flames of all substances*
> ALEJANDRO TARRAB

time is at war because of pure violence   because it knows itself infinite and free   transmitting on all channels simultaneously   time is god   is asthma that burns   yes   there are flickers in the intermediate states asthma is flickering   as liquid steps we rain   sometimes honey is found in some eyes   but honey is the alcohol of the fire

in the cavern it rains inwards   the drops fight to be drops but they are rain   rain is the alcohol of intermediate states   the drops evaporate   there is no movement   the cavern is the shapeless space   with no shape or clarity there is no reflection but everything burns seeing itself the fire is the flickering that hides the mirror

the moment night becomes day is flickering   in the
intermediate states   there is no movement   the ship behind the
mist is flickering   in the intermediate state there is no movement
the eyes that embrace are flickering   in the intermediate states there is
no movement   the journey that still doesn't reach a destination is
flickering   in the intermediate states there is no movement

stuttering   compulsions   excesses   the tasteless mixture
ferments   there is no voice in this system   but it vibrates it
expands   suspended in waves of letters travelling through the tunnel
the alcohol produces sparks between purity and nuances   purity limit
pain   open nuances are built   the nuances are the alcohol
of the intermediate states

in the original code   the blurred are the ones who adapt
those who lean out staying between blurred lines as they pass by   they know
that from the metabolism of all speech   the voice will be produced
with my / our alcohol   with my / our otherness

I get lost in the trials of the cavern   there are always tell-tale
witnesses   judges   whistles between window and window   due
to the absence of the voice we shift our intentions   we don't
get to know language ourselves not knowing language ourselves is the alcohol
of the intermediate states

the voice eludes   the mosaic that we inherited centuries ago it
resists   generations expel it   displacements are
built   through the window I listen to the cadence   everyone knows
that the alcohol is the voice   the voice is the alcohol of the fire

if I jump out the window   if I leave my finger there   if we are
the out of focus   the voice burns unknowingly   the hands burn
unknowingly but they feel the alcohol evaporate   lighting up everything
in the density of names   in the almost voracious
traffic where the almost voracious traffic   is the alcohol of the fire

the fire can be heard screaming in the leaves of the trees   the
swaying of the fire in the leaves of the trees   the wind
blows to calm their pain   the wind doesn't
know the wind is the alcohol of the fire

the journey is the slow destruction   is the lightning of the snow that
punishes with starry blindness   nothing starts without something
ending   but always something starts in the intermediate states
something that leaves motionless mocking the rite everything burns
logically   it is the bittersweet fire   us the fallen mangoes
like shooting stars

I am in front of the fire   with my back to the voice   the snow is the
sea   is the howl   who is one but a howl in silence
everything   burns   calculatedly   what is the voice but a
corrosive effect

we are devoured by the voice   the voice doesn't exist yet   survives us
the dislocated mangoes without archetype   the fever is not
fever it is called fertile   fire widowed fire   the earth doesn't
tremble   the pulse of the intermediate states floods the tunnel
we the temperamental   the out of tune   waiting for the
tides of the voice

it's the burning rocks next to the burning waterfall   makes me
rain   my eyes hurt   may it be that you want to share my rain
like mangoes slowly falling   like desperate mangoes

EL ALCOHOL DE LOS ESTADOS INTERMEDIOS

se puede decir que una sustancia se quema en una llama gris no conozco los
colores de las llamas de todas las sustancias
Alejandro Tarrab

el tiempo está en guerra por violencia pura por saberse
infinito y libre   transmitiendo en todos los canales
simultáneamente   el tiempo es dios es el asma que
arde   sí   hay parpadeos en los estados intermedios
el asma es parpadeo como eslabones líquidos llovemos   a
veces se encuentra miel en algunos ojos   pero la miel es
el alcohol del incendio

en la caverna llueve hacia adentro   las gotas luchan por ser
gotas pero son lluvia   la lluvia es el alcohol de los estados
intermedios   las gotas se evaporan   no hay movimiento   la
caverna es el espacio sin forma   sin forma ni claridad no
hay reflejo   pero todo arde viéndose   el incendio es el parpadeo
que esconde el espejo

el instante en que la noche se convierte en día es parpadeo   en
los estados intermedios no hay movimiento   el barco tras la
bruma es parpadeo   en los estados inte rmedios no   hay
movimiento   los ojos que abrazan son parpadeo   en los estados
intermedios no hay movimiento   el viaje que aún no llega a
destino es parpadeo   en los estados intermedios no hay
movimiento

tartamudeos   compulsiones   excesos   fermenta lamezcla
sin sabor aún   no hay voz en este sistema   pero vibra se
expande   suspendida en ondas de letras   viaja por el túnel
el alcohol produce chispas entre pureza y matices   pureza límite
dolor   matices abiertos se construyen   los matices son el
alcohol de los estados intermedios

en el código original   los difuminados son los que se adaptan
los que se asoman quedando en líneas borrosas al pasar   saben
que del metabolismo de todos los discursos   se producirá la voz
con mi nuestro alcohol   con mi nuestra alteridad

me pierdo en los tanteos de la caverna   siempre hay testigos
delatores   jueces   silbidos   entre ventana y ventana por
la ausencia de la voz es que movemos las intenciones   no
llegamos a sabernos lengua   no sabernos lengua es el alcohol de
los estados intermedios

la voz nos esquiva   el mosaico que heredamos hace siglos se
resiste   generaciones lo expulsan   los desplazamientos se
construyen   por la ventana escucho la cadencia   todos saben
que el alcohol es la voz   la voz es el alcohol del incendio

si doy un salto por la ventana   si dejo mi dedo ahí   si somos
los desenfocados   la voz arde sin saber   las manos arden sin
saber pero sienten el alcohol evaporarse   iluminarlo todo
en la densidad de los nombres   en el tránsito casi voraz
donde el tránsito casi voraz   es el alcohol del incendio

se escucha el incendio gritar en las hojas de los árboles   el
balanceo del incendio en las hojas de los árboles   el viento
sopla para calmar su dolor   el viento no lo sabe
el viento es el alcohol del incendio

el viaje es la destrucción lenta   es el relámpago de la nieve que
castiga con ceguera estrellada   nada comienza sin que algo
termine   pero siempre algo comienza en los estadosintermedios
algo que se va sin moverse   burlando el rito   todo arde
lógicamente   es el incendio agridulce   nosotros los mangos
caídos como estrellas fugaces

estoy frente al incendio   de espaldas a la voz   la nieve es el
mar   es el aullido   quién es uno sino un aullido en silencio
todo arde calculadamente   qué es la voz sino un efecto
corrosivo

somos devorados por la voz   la voz aún no existe   nos sobrevive
nosotros los mangos dislocados sin arquetipo   la fiebre no es
fiebre se llama incendio   fértil incendio viudo   la tierra no
tiembla   el pulso de los estados intermedios inunda el túnel
nosotros los temperamentales los desafinados   esperando las
mareas de la voz

son las rocas ardiendo junto a la cascada ardiendo   me hace
llover   duele en los ojos   será´que quieres compartir mi lluvia
como mangos cayendo   lentamente   como mangos desesperados

MARCIA MOGRO (Bolivia)

Marcia Mogro (b. La Paz, 1956) has lived in Santiago since 1985. She studied literature at the Universidad Mayor de San Andrés where she now teaches. She has published eight collections of poetry – de los estados, su ánimo *(2016);* exposición de alto riesgo *(2013);* Restos de un cielo, partes vestigios fragmentos rastros *(2011);* Excavaciones *(2009);* Lacrimosa *(2005);* Los jardines colgantes *(1995, 2004);* De la cruz a la fecha *(2000); and* Semíramis *(1988) – some of which have been translated into English and German.*

ENGLISH TRANSLATIONS BY JUANA ADCOCK

INNOCENT MATTERS 1 / ASUNTOS INOCENTES 1

from EXCAVATIONS / *de* EXCAVACIONES

last night
covered in rubbish I slept
I slept   c o v e r e d   i n   r u b b i s h

I never thought I'd come to this
n e v e r
thought
I ' d c o m e
t o   t h i s

mother and I are weeping, in recollection

the stupefied city
is governed by a relentless
and futile
logic
in a world capable of any transfiguration:

the city realises
over the years
that her body has changed position
she realises
that she is becoming the figure
of contemporary appearance that is required of her
bestowing her solitude with new meaning
eliminating any risk of encounter

his life is linked to these landscapes
which his dreams do not let go of
even if the edges blur
even if he passes over one life to the next
disoriented
lonely wandering
in the flickering rain
following an irreplaceable light
he resolves to
(de)scribe in crude and precious terms:

they say they have a formidable and defiant desert
they say the mountain range is reclining and in silence
they say the vision of the sea remains in the eye
that even if you die it remains inalterable
they say that when there is a storm
it appears inscrutable and wild

these landscapes can be breathtaking, he says

they say the mountains are individual
they say that the highlands can lead to rapture
they say it is a space where the horizon is not visible
they say the sky is blue in winter
they say one lies there in an atmosphere of perfect misplacement

the landscapes can be breathtaking, he says

**LIKE IN A DREAM
DISCONCERTING AND STUPENDOUS
HE CAN SEE   TOUCH
BREATHE UP IN THE AIR
    SURPRISED TO DIE**

to possess on earth a certain freedom
(each one has their own body)

an intentional body addressing the world
marked by a violent   and dark atmosphere
it contemplates
the mountains that fail to cheer it
contemplates the unattainable beach
the old cemeteries of ships and the abandoned dockyards
contemplates

    e y e s   r a i s e d   t o   a   b l u e   s k y   t h a t
       h a s   n o   m e a n i n g

he awakes in fear
        is almost an object
alluding to its original location
without authorship over his own biological rhythm
fascinating and mysterious

says: this is physical

tomorrow they're going to check up your little body
what it is you have
what it is you don't have   – she says –

activate the mechanisms of speculation
from the depths of psychosis
(knowing this
is the last time he will look like today)

        the vicuña grazing
        the thousands of vicuñas grazing

he thinks
about that very domestic scene
about that height   he thinks
with that blue sky
with those colourful bits of wool on their ears he thinks

        permanent inhabitants of these desolate
        regions
        those vicuñas with their beautiful highly sophisticated bodies

.their legacy.

do you have a vicuña blanket? do you have a vicuña quilt? do you have
a vicuña sweater? a vicuña poncho do you have one brother?

selknam dreamed
(selknam evoked)
selknam said
selknam thought selknam
walked selknam
towards extremely sad sunsets
selknam imagined
while canoeing
while mixing dyes
while body painting selknam dreamed

      anoche
      tapado de basura he dormido
      he dormido   t a p a d o   d e   b a s u r a

                yo nunca he pensado en llegar a esto
                n u n c a
                pensé
                e n l l e g a r
                a e s t o

      su mamá y yo estamos llorando, recuerda

estupefacta
la ciudad se rige por una lógica implacable
e inútil
en un mundo capaz de cualquier transfiguración:

se da cuenta
a lo largo de los años
que su cuerpo ha cambiado de posición
se da cuenta
que está pasando a ser la figura
de apariencia contemporánea que se le exige
otorgando a la soledad un significado nuevo
eliminando cualquier riesgo de encuentro

su vida está ligada a estos paisajes
que sus sueños no abandonan
aunque los contornos se difuminen
aunque pase de una vida a otra
desorientado
andar en solitario
bajo una lluvia discontinua
siguiendo una luz insustituible
resuelve
(d)escribir en términos crudos y preciosos:

dicen que tienen un desierto formidable y desafiante
dicen que la cordillera está echada y en silencio
dicen que la visión del mar queda en los ojos
que aunque mueras permanece inalterable
dicen que cuando hay tormenta
presenta un aspecto impenetrable y salvaje

son paisajes que pueden impactar, dice

dicen que las montañas son individuales
dicen que el altiplano puede causar embeleso
dicen que es un espacio donde no se alcanza a ver el horizonte
dicen que el cielo es azul en invierno
dicen que ahí uno yace en una atmósfera de perfecto extravío

son paisajes que pueden impactar, dice

**COMO EN UN SUEÑO
DESCONCERTANTE Y ESTUPENDO
MIRA   TOCA
RESPIRA EN EL AIRE
            SORPRENDIDO DE MORIR**

disponer en la tierra de cierta libertad
(cada uno tiene su cuerpo)

un cuerpo intencional y dirigido al mundo
marcado por una atmósfera violenta   y oscura
contempla
las montañas que no logran alegrarlo
contempla su inalcanzable playa
los viejos cementerios de naves y los astilleros abandonados
contempla

e l e v a l o s o j o s a l c i e l o a z u l q u e
n a d a s i g n i f i c a

asustadamente despierta
    es casi un objeto
que alude a su emplazamiento original
sin tener autoría de su ritmo biológico
fascinante y misterioso

dice: esto es físico

mañana te van a revisar tu cuerpito
qué cosa tienes
qué cosa no tienes   – le dice –

activar mecanismos de especulación
desde la profundidad de la psicosis
(saber
que es la última vez que se va a ver como hoy)

      la vicuña pastando
      las miles de vicuñas pastando

piensa
en esa escena tan doméstica
en esa altura   piensa
con ese azul cielo
con esas lanitas de colores en las orejas piensa

      permanentes habitantes de estas regiones
      desoladas
      esas vicuñas con sus bellos cuerpos altamente sofisticados

.su legado.

tienes manta de vicuña? tienes colcha de vicuña? tienes chompa
de vicuña? poncho de vicuña tienes hermanito?

selknam soñaba
(evocaba selknam)
selknam decía
selknam pensaba selknam
caminaba selknam
en tristísimos atardeceres
selknam imaginaba
mientras botaba canoa
mientras mezclaba tintes
mientras pintaba cuerpo selknam soñaba

from SEMÍRAMIS, 16(MG).–/ de SEMÍRAMIS, 16(MG).–

NOBODY IS THAT FAR AWAY

Semíramis, 23 (MG).– Everyone is ready now.
      Everyone.
      Armed and disarmed.
      Dead and about to die.
      Outside the walls.
      They siege the city that smells like rain.

      By the fire's glow they are resting.
      Arms and armoury.
      Stones and fists.
      Now the city is besieged
      and it smells of the smoke
      of the fires lit
      outside the walls.

NADIE ESTÁ TAN LEJOS

Semíramis, 23 (MG).– Ya están todos listos.
      Todos.
      Armados y desarmados.
      Muertos y por morir.
      En los extra muros.
      Cercando la ciudad que huele a lluvia.

      Al resplandor de las fogatas descansan.
      Armas y armaduras.

> Piedras y puños.
> Ahora la ciudad está cercada
> y huele al humo
> de las fogatas encendidas
> en los extra muros.

THEY BREAK OUT BEFORE DAWN

Semíramis, 26(MG).– They took possession of the hills,
of the mountains and the summits.
Of abysses and caves.
Protecting themselves from the cold with furs,
they wait.

They wait on the corners,
on the benches in the square,
in the wardrobes and behind mirrors.
Waiting, they are
waiting.

BROTAN ANTES DEL AMANECER

Semíramis, 26(MG).– Tomaron posesión de las colinas,
de los cerros y las cumbres.
Protegiéndose del frío con pieles,
esperan.

Esperan en las esquinas,
en los bancos de la plaza,
en los roperos y detrás de los espejos.
Esperan ellos,
esperan.

REBELS DIE IN

Semíramis, 28(MG).– Even the rubbish was burning
in the streets,
in the parks.
They were hungry.
And they had nothing to eat,
they ate nothing.

Many killed themselves with poison.
Others strangled themselves.
With their own hands.

REBELDES MUEREN EN

Semíramis, 28(MG).–   Hasta la basura se quemaba
                    en las calles,
                    en los parques.
                    Tenían hambre.
                    Y nada tenían que comer,
                    ya nada comieron.

                    Muchos se mataron con veneno.
                    Otros se ahorcaron con sus manos.
                    Propias.

LISTEN:

They needed to distribute that body
among all the roads,
among all the Apachetas,
so it may serve as an example
and those facts may never be repeated.

Faced with the stupor of the entire world
I promise
– because I love you –
to learn your bones by heart,
to memorise with my intellect,
with my instinct and emotions
so that never again I care
about not recognising you
being here where I am.

Bearing witness – the hills and the rivers,
Bearing witness – men of flesh and blood
who deny that what they have seen
and touched and told
was some sort of vision.
And they say:

ELEVEN MILLION MARTYRS
IN ALL KINDS OF CONDITIONS
AND FROM ALL COUNTRIES
AN INCALCULABLE NUMBER
HAVE BEGUN A DANCE.

ESCUCHA:

Había que repartir aquél cuerpo
por todos los caminos,
por todas las apachetas,
para que sirva de ejemplo
y jamás se repitan tales hechos.

Ante el estupor del mundo entero
yo prometo
– porque te amo –
saber tus huesos de memoria,
aprenderlos con mi razón,
con mi instinto y sentimiento
para que nunca más me importe
no reconocerte
estando aquí donde estoy.

Testigos los cerros y los ríos,
testigos los hombres de carne y hueso
que niegan que lo que han visto
y tocado y contado
haya sido porque están alucinados.
Y dicen:

ONCE MILLONES DE MÁRTIRES
DE TODAS LAS CONDICIONES
Y DE TODOS LOS PAÍSES
EN NÚMERO INCALCULABLE
HAN COMENZADO UNA DANZA.

LUNARIUM

1.– Semíramis(MG): Lying on our backs with our hands together,
together as in a dream of ours and we watch
the clouds pass by
sailing – you say – like boats
so is the sea, interminable
like a dream of ours my love.

2.– Semíramis(MG): The distance makes the moon seem larger,
        like in a dream of ours
              my love,
        my love knowing our bones
        our bodies like in a dream
        had kissed each other in the dark alleyways.

3.– Semíramis(MG): I had kissed your ear
            my love
        seeing words enter
        like in a dream of ours
        the earth was like the moon before
        and the sun like this earth
        and all the moons written in the sky
        and others we don't know of.

LUNARIO

1.– Semíramis(MG): Echados boca arriba y manos juntas,
        juntas como en un sueño nuestro y miramos
        pasar las nubes
        navegando, –me dices–, como barcos
        así es el mar de interminable
        como un sueño nuestro amor mío.

2.– Semíramis(MG): La distancia hace ver la luna más grande,
        como en un sueño nuestro
              amor mío,
        amor mío sabiendo nuestros huesos
        nuestros cuerpos como en un sueño
        habíanse besado en los callejones oscuros.

3.– Semíramis(MG): Había besado tu oreja
            amor mío
        viendo entrar las palabras
        como en un sueño nuestro
        la tierra era antes como la luna
        y el sol como la tierra esta
        y todas las lunas escritas en el cielo
        y otras que no sabemos.

LUNA MONTENEGRO (Chile)

Luna Montenegro (Chile / UK) is a poet, visual artist, performer and film-maker living in London, working with text, sound, drawing, installation, curatorial projects and film. She is interested in ideas of ritual, presence, politics, locality and collaboration, interweaving Spanish, English and dead languages from Tierra del Fuego. She runs 'one night stanza' a small hand-made-publishing-press. Her work has been published by Word For/Word, Poetry Wales, Writers Forum Chile, Recrea Libros, Boiler House Press and datableed.

ENGLISH TRANSLATIONS BY LUNA MONTENEGRO & ADRIAN FISHER

≋

I wanted to call this poem *A Sonic Voyage*,
or the voice of one from the Brixton crowd,
or find an odd word on wikipedia
that could describe a bacteria
and a sound at the same time
and call it that,
I wanted not to say *I*, but say *we*
and include ~~the perception of~~ drone bees,
early morning blackbirds and limestone.
Call it *Writings from the spleen or left toe.*
The words as mist or moist,
the missing song, the jaguar's roar,
joy of electromagnetic radiation,
the frog inside the pond,
call it *dog*
and start barking.

≋

A este poema yo quería llamarlo *El Viaje Sónico*
o la voz de alguien en la multitud de Santiago Centro,
o encontrar una palabra rara en wikipedia
que pueda describir una bacteria
y un sonido al mismo tiempo
y llamarlo así,
quería no decir **yo**, sino decir **nosotres**
e incluir ~~la percepción de~~ las abejas-dron,
los mirlos de madrugada y la piedra caliza.
Llamarlo *Escritos desde el hígado o del meñique izquierdo.*
Las palabras como nube o niebla,
la canción perdida, el rugido del jaguar,
el gozo de la radiación electromagnética,
la rana del estanque,
llamarlo *perro*
y empezar a ladrar.

≋

ho ho ho   (many times)
     ho ho ho   sing the people
ho ho ho   in two different tones
the shaman announces the arrival of Matan
all women sing together   Matan, Matan, Matan
Keren / Kenek   el día   a day
Holpikren   un día de sol   a sunny day
Holpikren   Holpikren   Holpikren
    the fire extending the shadow
    the arrival of the western sky
    the possibility of light
    the body is red and white, the body jumps
upwards, sideways   the dance is a
       distraction
    the dance is a delight
    the dance is all there is
    meta-morph   meta-morph
Jhún Hutl Párn   Jhún Hutl Párn   Jhún Hutl Párn
    el cisne de cuello negro   the black-necked swan
ho ho ho   ho ho ho   ho ho ho
    the mask hides, the mask imitates the body,
      the mask is held at ear height
    keuchi   keuchi   keuchi
      a beautiful day
  the body is red and white, the body jumps
upwards, sideways   the dance is a
       distraction
    the dance is a delight
    the dance is all there is
ho ho ho   ho ho ho   ho ho ho

≈

O	*u*	*a*	*ro*	*uch*
Loi	*mush*		*ka*	
O	*u*	*a*	*ro*	*uch*
Loi	*mush*			*ka*

No sé cuando
Nací
Nací
Nací

When?   I was born   When?   I was born   When?

Kupás   pá
Kupáspá Tribus   *(five / cinco)*
Yahgan
Yagán as
as if not registered

                                    Crecí
Cosí   Hilé   Tejí

                                    Crecí
Cosí   Hilé   Tejí

At the end of the earth   it was her

Ni	ñosygran	des morían de gol	pe
Ni	ñosygran	des morían de gol	pe

chil drenandel der where diying de gol   pe
chil drenandel der where diying de gol   pe

Tosí   Tosí   Tosí

Como una rosa que va por primera vez a la escuela
aprendí

Ouarouch   *(tree / árbol)*
Loimushka
Ouarouch
Loimushka   *(flower / flor)*

The name
I have
Es de la Tierra

Nací   Nací   Nací

Asilo. Todos. Al Asilo. Todos. Con Madre. Con Padre. O sin.

I was little, tiny, tiny.

Crustaceans, birds, sea lions, fish.

.
Comí   Comí   Comí

Agua cambié por té y por café
Fósforo
Lover

La civilización muerde   el estómago
La civilización muerde   el pulmón

        Civilization bites your   omach
        Civilization bites your   lungs
        Civilization bites your   memory

despacito me baño en aceite de lobo suavecito

Muya   Ballena   The dream
Maucho   Challe y erizo   Muya   *(fishing / pescar)*

El   maltiem   po   Quenotepi   lleel
Maltiem   po   Que notepi   lle

The   bad weather it shouldn't catch you   bad weather
it shouldn't   catch you   The   bad weather   it
shouldn't   catch you

Tosí   Hilé   Cosí

            Tosí   Hilé   Cosí

O   u   a   ro   uch
Loi   mush   ka
O   u   a   ro   uch
Loi   mush   ka

≋

let anything i see be something

    detached from the photographic flash
            the visual cortex recovers
      words that are sleeping, extinguishing, sitting
Chaanpèn   ancestral elliptical galaxy

    outlining the magnetic field
          close to the nucleus in its eccentricity
     disfiguring photosensitive representations
the cornea brutally gobbling
        the tangible tongue
           emancipation as a pupillary reflex

    microscopic organisms in furious copulations
           under each of your computer keys
       vitreous humour on the tail of the seven-headed dragon
              Albrecht Dürer on Skype
    the only night your webcam isn't working

    describe with your finger what you are seeing:

        the object is unknown   futile the eye
in its disconnection from the brain, from the ear, from the polar auroras,
          from the mobile phone, from the reptile

    the object is unknown   the effects
         of diffraction permanently impose
a limit on the possibility of resolution
      the eye is untranslatable, binocular, sharp
             and irreverent

      the object is unknown   dark matter the eye
          a centipede blinking
curling up in a Santiago alley way
              segmented reality
      neighbouring the nose and its occasional spasms
    the distance between body parts like valleys

      the object is unknown but capable of assassinating you
    the fork of meaning
aiming with certainty at   the centre of the colloidal / commercial centre
         viscous, vicious lens
    your guts feeding the earth   death as revolution

a 5D cinema invitation
impossible to accept
not due to gravity
electromagnetic migraine
throbbing in the stomach
is the emptiness the lack of content?   insanity

exiled living cells
that the arrow brings closer (to your neck) prey on
implosion

the nothing in philosophy, the nothing in ontology, the nothing in
existentialism, the nothing in maths, the nothing in science
see also: Being Entity Emptiness Thing   (edit)

neurobeings accelerating
their neurospaceships on the neuromotorways   arriving at the sea

the extrem ism is   the extrem ism
the rupture   captures   the aura of the question
that is coming from the object
sin tax the distance shortens

nothing is truly straight
rather closer to a circle
in tention   to rile the chicken coop
de co   lonisation of the tongue that sings
whoever it is that sees here a living tongue

drugs   dilating   drugs opening
muscular tissue   in contraction in expansion
how to get used to the darkness?
It's the pupil that allows
the penetration   of the light

the object   is   unknown
whoever sees the most
let them be the one to say something

the greater the distance in space the object
the greater the distance in time
thereisnothinginthefuturesomething

written as a form of dialogue with the poem
'todo lo posible que sea falso' by Jèssica Pujol

⤽

lo que sea que vea que sea algo

desprendida del flash fotográfico
               la corteza visual recupera
         palabras dormidas, extinguidas, sentadas
Chaanpèn   galaxia elíptica ancestral

delineando el campo magnético
           cercana al núcleo en su excentricidad
desfigurando representaciones fotosensibles
brutalmente engullendo
    la córnea a la lengua tangible
          emancipación como un reflejo pupilar

microscópicos organismos en cópulas furiosas
             bajo cada tecla de tu computador
    humor vítreo sobre la cola del dragón de siete cabezas
            Alberto Durero en skype
la única noche   que tu webcam   no está funcionando

describe con el dedo lo que estás viendo:

             el objeto es desconocido   inútil el ojo
en su desconexión del cerebro, del oído, de las auroras polares,
           del teléfono portátil, del reptil

el objeto es desconocido   los efectos
         de la difracción permanente imponen
un límite en la posibilidad de resolución
     el ojo es intraducible, binocular, filudo   e irrevere⟩

el objeto es desconocido   materia oscura el ojo
         un cienpiés parpadeante
enroscándose en un callejón de Santiago
                realidad segmenta⟩
    vecino a la nariz y sus espasmos ocasionales
la distancia entre las partes del cuerpo como valles

        el objeto es desconocido pero capaz de asesinarte
el tenedor del significado
apuntando certero   al centro del centro comercial/coloidal
     cristalino viscoso, vicioso
tus vísceras alimentando la tierra   la muerte como revolución

invitación al cine en 5D
                imposible aceptar
        no por gravedad
     jaqueca electromagnética
    pulsaciones en el estómago
es el vacío la falta de contenido?   desquicio

      células vivas desterradas
        que la flecha acerca (a tu cuello) depreda
      implosión

    la nada en filosofía, la nada en ontología, la nada en
el existencialismo, la nada en matemáticas, la nada en ciencias
        véase también: Ser Entidad Vacío Cosa   (editar)

neuroseres acelerando
    sus neuronaves en las neuroautopistas   que llegan al mar

      el extre mismo es   el extre mismo
la ruptura captura   el aura de la pregunta
     que viene desde el objeto
          sin taxis   la distancia se duplica

    nada es realmente recto
       más bien cercano a un círculo
in tencionalidad   de revolver el gallinero
   de co lonización de la lengua que canta
el que sea que vea aquí una lengua

    drogas   dilatan   abren las drogas
      tejido muscular   en contracción en expansión
cómo acostrumbrarse a la oscuridad?
          es la pupila la que permite
      la penetración   de la luz

el objeto   es   desconocido
      el que sea que vea más
         que sea el que diga algo

a mayor distancia en el espacio el objeto
    a mayor distancia en el tiempo
        nadahayenelfuturoalgo

    escrito como una forma de diálogar con el poema
    'todo lo posible que sea falso' de Jèssica Pujol

≋

to be alert, to be far and
inevitably present, to be
above when things are
happening in the centre of
the earth, to be by
definition below the
clouds, stars and other
celestial bodies, to be
permanently re-gulated
by the law of gravity, in
some form glued to the
earth, recreating the
fiction, preventing the
erosion, processing the
light, creating spaces for
radical transformations,
to be defiantly standing
transmitting nutrients and
signals, adapting your
canopy, producing
oxygen, to be constantly
learning from the
trees.

≋

estar alerta, estar lejos e
inevitablemente presente,
estar arriba cuando las
cosas ocurren en el centro
de la tierra, estar por
definición abajo de las
nubes, estrellas y otros
cuerpos celestes, estar
permanentemente re-
gulada por la ley de
gravedad, de alguna
forma pegada a la tierra,
recreando la ficción,
previniendo la erosión,
procesando la luz,
creando espacios para
otros seres dentro de tu
cuerpo, estar preparade
para transformaciones
radi-cales, desafiante-
mente de pie,
transmitiendo nutri-entes
y señales, adaptando tu
copa, produciendo
oxígeno, estar
constantemente
aprendiendo de los
árboles.

NERONESSA (Dominican Republic)

Neronessa (b. Santo Domingo, Dominican Republic, 1988) studied Creative Arts, Philosophy and Marketing. At 16 she published her first poetry book La Estirpe de las Gárgolas *(2005) and in 2015 she published* El Volcán de la Matriz Electroelástica *in Madrid. She has participated in a number of international anthologies, literary festivals and magazines. Her work has been translated to English, French and Italian. She also dedicates herself to artistic photography, to the research and development of biotechnology based in plants and the promotion of sustainable lifestyles.*

ENGLISH TRANSLATIONS BY ANNIE McDERMOTT

VORTEX OF PERCEPTIONS

A commandment is imposed fusing
the harried clashing reality of contradictions.

Reality transmutes the mundane,
crunches sounding out mysteries.
Gushing up from the soul I'll meld my essence to the quest
soar from the sensory abyss to sink deep in the tsar
of stabbing hot coals.

From the oceans to the dawn, the muscles of so many
sweating sweet honey to rebuild the phases of understanding
this vortex, will it win out or wane?
nest of wavering judges withstanding the storm,
ideologies devour the whirlpool of enslaved will.

Truth rolls on like a relay playing out
the pollen of a history of cancer.
The tree that filled the splinter
the splinter that fills the tree
The enigma can never be tarnished.

VORTICE DE PERCEPCIONES

Un mandamiento es impuesto aglutinando
la atropellada y precipitada realidad de contradicciones.

La realidad transmuta a la intrascendencia,
cruje el sondeo de lo desconocido.
En un chorro del alma uniré mi esencia a la búsqueda

desde el abismo sensorial volaré hasta zambullirme en el zar
de brasas punzantes.

Desde los océanos hasta el amanecer, los músculos de tantos
sudando las mieles para reconstruir las fases de la comprensión
de este vórtice, ¿remontará o decaerá?
vacilante nido de jueces soportando la tempestad,
ideologías comen la vorágine de la voluntad esclavizada.

La verdad rueda como carrera de relevos que cicla
en el polen de una descendencia de cáncer.
El árbol que llenó la astilla
la astilla que llena el árbol
El enigma jamás podrá ser mancillado.

POST VIBRATIONS OF EXEGESIS

Primal I cracked the scale of toxic medulla
Restored the repristination of the oceanic narrative
From the cavities came blunderbuss wounds of luxury
Sly waterfalls of impartiality
And with my stumps I swept the sand
that fills the sweat of men.

My breasts wept a sky of testimonies
oils and sunsets will rise from my pores.
You know my teardrops are the drilling
arms of your sternum of failures and myths
in a rhythmic barrier that cannot be synthesised.

You walk on convulsing unfathomable fibres:
Run! A grape slips from my thought
And that grape is a seashell made of temptation,
Of condemnation a chimera
Pure marbling spiral deep in the navel
of discernment
emitting a visceral ocean light.
It's just a gust
like star saliva
Oozing sly speeches to rinse out the nerves
A cold sweat of designs and contingencies

Egyptian droplets dancing
the tango of uncertainty.
That watery elbow, that vertigo of
Condensation in my ribs, wanting
To weigh upon destiny's eyes.

Today children the thalamus recites from the torrent
A knife made of ants eats a piece of the time.
From my tree-the-scale,
From my breasts-the-fruit.
Mitosis lines the eye of the deaf-mute sky.
A knife made of ants like a mallet of seconds,
distance is simply the digits of time
labouring figures tearing strips off my life
gnawing the marrow of my bodily freedoms.

POST VIBRACIONES DE LA EXÉGESIS

Yo fracturé primigenia la escama de la médula tóxica
Resucité la repristinación del argumento oceánico
De las cavidades escaparon los trabucazos de la opulencia
Las cataratas furtivas de la imparcialidad
Dragué con mis muñones la arena
que rellena el sudor de los hombres.

Mis pechos lloraron un cielo de testimonios
óleos y atardeceres se levantarán de mis poros.
Sabrás que mis lágrimas son los brazos
taladrando del esternón de tus leyendas y fracasos
en una barrera rítmica imposible de sintetizar.

Caminas sobre fibras convulsionantes de lo ignoto:
Corre! Se me escapa una uva del pensamiento
Y esa uva se convierte en caracol de la tentación,
del repudio y la quimera
Pura espiral marmolea que se entierra en el ombligo
del discernimiento
y emana una luz como desde el océano visceral.
Es una sola ráfaga
como una baba estelar
Que destila discursos furtivos para enjuagar los nervios
Como un sudor helado de designios y contingencias
Bailan egipcias gotas, el tango
de la incertidumbre.
Ese codo acuoso, ese vértigo de las

Gotas en mis costillas, queriendo
Presionar los ojos del destino.

Hoy recita hijos el tálamo desde el torrente
Un cuchillo de hormigas se come un pedazo del tiempo.
De mi árbol-la-escama,
De mis pechos-los-frutos.
La mitosis forra el ojo del cielo sordomudo.
Un cuchillo de hormigas como un mazo de segundos,
la distancia solo son dígitos de tiempo
cifras jornaleras desmenuzando mi longevidad
ruyendo el tuétano de mis libertades corpóreas.

CYCLICAL

Catching his scent I grasped Mercury as he passed through my cervix
As he made all the martyrs
fall for everlasting glory.

I held in the star until it fell
from the vines of the chakra
Leaving mutinous swamps on the tiles
Hysterical Sodom in my conversations!

Anaemic slices of fire,
Pellets from God's breath
(He wants to solder
meat
into a stew)
Travelling down the trachea to keep time.

I push a cobweb to the mouth of existence
that flutters within its lips
like a hummingbird,
that half closes like a squinting eye
to spit out swollen rainbows.

The eye blinks its bloody yawns
A mudguard for cyclothymic revolution
Becoming the rifle
In a shoot to kill crypt.

The poor sad thorn in the lung
of the petals!
I swear
I'll only vomit up miracles
until dawn.

CÍCLICO

Por su aroma sujeté a Mercurio al traspasarme la cerviz
Al rodar enamorando los mártires
de la gloria permanente.

Contuve el astro hasta desprenderse
de las lianas del chakra
Cuando dejó pantanos de rebelión en las losetas
Sodoma histérica en mis conversaciones!

Anémicos, gajos de fuego,
Perdigones del aliento de Dios
(Él quiere soldar
un caldo
de carnes)
Que circulan la tráquea de la puntualidad.
Pujo telaraña hacia la boca de la existencia
que aletea entraña en sus labios
como un colibrí,
que se entrecierra como entrecerrar un ojo
para escupir los arcoíris entumecidos.

Ese ojo pestañea sus bostezos de sangre
Un salpicadero de revolución ciclotímica
Se constituye en carabina
de una cripta-dispara-muertos.

Triste la pobre espina entre el pulmón
de los pétalos!
Te juro
que solo vomito milagros
hasta el amanecer.

EARTH MEANS WEEPING

I swear my eyes will be fruitful
And crackling scatter like bells from the soul
Coolly I will strip them of their husks

As the full moon squeezes tides from the fruit of the earth:
I will grow the day.
The rays will gather resultant at the door
Lashes of a whip to fracture the symphony
Who will refute the night's complexity?
Who will seize what comes after the dark?
What shimmering path can link zenith and shade?
The contest between reflection and summit
The balance between gravity and dawn,
the ultimate course of storming the abattoir.

Then let me mitigate the sun with degravitated tears
Which his eye valve will set ablaze like corn.
I confess he sees more of the stars than the tides
So much Midas still corralled in his cheeks
in a citric phoenix wrapping the earth in elastic wings.
The sun draws the day from the meek little skulls
And then like a father cloaked in distance
shapes in turn the tasks of tomorrow.

TIERRA SIGNIFICA LLANTO

Te juro que mis ojos serán fructíferos
Y esparcidos en chasquidos como campanas del alma
Frescamente los despojaré de sus cáscaras
Como la luna llena exprime las mareas del fruto de la tierra:
Cultivaré el día.
Concurrirán consecuentes los rayos a la puerta
Latigazos que fracturarán la sinfonía
¿Quién refutará la complejidad de la noche?
¿Quién confiscará la secuela de la opacidad?
¿Qué ruta se estremece entre el cenit y la sombra?
La contienda entre reflexión y cúspide
La balanza entre alba y gravedad,
la eventualidad de ir a embestir en el matadero.

Entonces querré mitigar el sol con lágrimas desgravitadas
Y él las encenderá como espigas con la válvula de sus ojos.
Admito que él frecuenta más astros que las mareas
Tanto Midas quedó acorralado en sus mejillas
en un fénix cítrico que se torna elástico para arropar la tierra.
El sol arranca la jornada desde los pequeños cráneos subyugados
Hasta que como padre se cobija de distancia
para en ciclo formular los retos del mañana.

ECHOES

Let eternity not cloud over with us in its belly.

In antiquity the *all* clothed its offshoots in fierce destiny,
Odds and evens coldly absorbed.
Your eyes on me plunged in the boundless will escapes us
Why does its everlasting suck in fury and not hate?

You can swing the womb of my dreams on your tongue,
But its fruits will float buried in men splitting off their piety
sulphuric secretions, faces exploding into thought and transcendence.
Time will lick your tastebuds enveloping my uterus, swelling your
                                voice with its temporal blood.
My caves will be painted into nonentities sublime and brief as splinters
                                                    of wind.
I'll sing until my words leave bitemarks even if my soul gutters out:

Let eternity not spill upon our blood,
when eternity succumbs let it not collapse upon our home.
When eternity drowns let its muscles not drag us
down to the lungs of the abyss.

ECOS

Que la eternidad no se enturbie con nosotros en su vientre.

En la antigüedad el *todo* arropó sus vástagos con la fiereza del destino,
Pares e impares absorbidos sin compasión.
Tu mirada en mí sumergida en la voluntad de lo infinito se nos escapa.
¿Por qué su perpetuo no succiona el odio y solo succiona el furor?

Aunque columpies la matriz de mis sueños en tu lengua,
Flotarán sus frutos enterrándose en los hombres para disociar su piedad
el azufre de la secreción, en pensamiento y trascendencia explotarán
                                                    los rostros.
El tiempo lamerá tus papilas encapsulando mi útero, rellenando tu
                                voz con su sangre temporal.
Mis cuevas se pintarán de nulidad en la sublime brevedad de las
                                                esquirlas de viento.
Yo canto hasta que mis palabras dejen su mordida aunque se extinga
                                                        el alma:

Que la eternidad no se vuelque encima de nuestras sangres,
que cuando la eternidad se rinda no se desplome sobre nuestro hogar.
Que cuando la eternidad se ahogue no nos arrastre con su músculo
hacia los pulmones de la nada.

SILENCE

Eyes grazing high walls
Petal turned flame
(and no one answers
the roars)
Ravaged bleeding years of youth.

SILENCIO

Roza murallas con los ojos
Pétalo convertido en llama
(y nadie responde
a los bramidos)
Cuarteado sangra años de juventud.

FRUIT OF THE VERDICT

Venerated, the skeleton sucking onto
hanging off my collarbone immensifying its all.

Its glorious corpse of worker wasps in my torso hive.
See how my stock and lineage boil receptive
still threaded through my coagulated plasma
inside the infant swarm of cosmos
grotesque tadpoles are broken and rebuilt,
rend and mend my varicose vein, rezipping
ripping and reforesting my universe.

Missing a rib splitting from mine,
plucked out with pinches of my smell an accident
My scent has befallen him
like varicose veins around the legs of the earth.

And so that thing your helpless self
is revealed as false, sleepily teeming
in the crawl of discernment.

But my little ones remain my brand-new parasites
this bubbling hernia their evidence

The solitary brood of snakes...
when the evolutions of matter come
who will scatter the senses far away from their tongues?
The body reacts when the mind acts,
the lecherous human mechanism.

Back then I called man a serpent,
christened him a tangled forest, a poisoned fruit.
Man now and before, spiritless has emerged
every season flung at the same clan
when my chalice brought forth on this crown of thorns it wrought,
on this indecipherable lap, in the storm the seedling warps
and the fearful sword calls out my camouflage with an ambush
of essence.

FRUTO DEL VEREDICTO

Venerado, el esqueleto que succionando
cuelga de mis clavículas inmensificando el propio.

Su glorioso cadáver de avispas labora en mi torso colmena.
He aquí que mi linaje y mi casta bullen receptores
enhebrados todavía a mi plasma coagulado
dentro del infante enjambre de cosmos
los gusarapos grotescos se rompen y se reconstruyen,
hienden y remiendan mi varice, rezurciéndola,
rasgan y reforestan mi universo.

El carente de costilla se ha desprendido de la mía,
se extirpó con pizcas de mi olor como accidente
Mi fragancia le ha sobrevenido
como se le cumple la varice a las piernas de la tierra.

De esta manera es que el tú mismo desprotegido
se descubre como falso, pululando adormecido
en el hormiguear del discernimiento.

Mas mis pequeños continúan siendo mis parásitos frescos
el burbujear de la hernia es su evidencia

La aislada generación de víboras...
cuando sobrevengan las evoluciones de la materia
¿quién esparcirá la sensibilidad lejos de sus lenguas?
El cuerpo reacciona cuando la mente acciona,
en la lascivia de los engranajes mente-cuerpo.

En aquel tiempo llamé como serpiente al hombre,
le bauticé como floresta confusa, fruta de ponzoña.
El hombre ahora y antes, el ausente de espíritu ha emergido
y todas las temporadas se abalanzaron al mismo clan
cuando mi cáliz se propagó sobre esta corona de espinas que es
su mismo proceder,
sobre este indescifrable regazo, en la tempestad se deforma el retoño
y la espada temerosa enfrenta mi camuflaje con la emboscada
de la esencia.

FAITH

We need to smudge out the chain,
Abolish the amulets.
Push the make-believe nuggets of hope from the path
send them tumbling tinkling,
Phantom missteps expelling the tears and sighs.

We have to hammer all the more, if there were no escaping
the ego of fire and how it goes up in flames.
Skip over the discrepant key,
whose settled echo gave my spirit distant shelter.

I want to paint the hailstorm of ash
onto the binding inclining me gasping
towards the utmost centre
With its very weight.

My ambition wandering will cut through
the monolith that once, serene, sustained my zeal.

My perspicacity will pierce the mirage,
watercolouring my elusive cheeks,

walking my person like before;
splattered with doctrines,
unprotected fragmented
among its undulating filaments.

Your strands are arching shackles,
flesh is just corrupted breath,
a sickly shawl of sludge asleep
on lymphatic quilts,
trickling onto the innocents
who grow without glory in my impatience.

Soap shares some faculties with water
Eclogues flower out of fluff.
The sea air climbs the frozen whisper,
the possibilities of fickle parchment,
doubts interwoven like wasp dances.

Still I bow down and vow this is the end,
a repeat of the palaeolithic comet
because ideas are never redeemed or caught
in mills of memory
Hunted halting in the canine panting of dauntless futures
Even dogs will shorten the concept of loyalty
Even roads will soak through stomachs
Judgement sharpens the oxymoron
There's a tireless dripping in the faces of cloud
implanting doubt in crumbled jawbones
when somebody believes.

LA FE

Es necesario esfumar los eslabones,
Suprimir los amuletos.
Alejar de la senda los lingotes imaginarios de la esperanza
que se despeñan melodiosos,
expulsando con tropezones fantasmas, las lágrimas y el aliento.

Es preciso martillar aún más, si fuera ineludible
el ego del fuego y su combustión.
Omitir la tecla discrepante,
que lejanamente alojaba mi espíritu en su eco asentado.

Quiero pintar la granizada de cenizas
sobre el vínculo que me inclinó con jadeos
a lo supremo de los centros
Porque pesa.

Mi ambición atravesará errante
el monolito que antes, sereno, sostenía mi ímpetu.

Mi perspicacia perforará el espejismo,
situando en mi faz solapada su acuarela,
caminando mi ser como antes;
embarrado en las doctrinas,
desamparado y fragmentado
por entre las olas de sus filamentos.

Tus hebras son grilletes arqueados,
la carne solo es soplo corrompido,
un mórbido manto de fango dormido
en edredones linfáticos,
chorreando a los inocentes
que crecen sin gloria en mi impaciencia.

Pertenecen a los jabones algunas facultades del agua
Églogas florecen de pelusas.
El aire marino trepa en el susurro helado,
las posibilidades de pergamino inconstante,
entretejidas las dudas como los bailes de las avispas.

Todavía me doblego y profeso que será el remate,
una repetición del cometa paleolítico
porque nunca se redimen ni se atrapan las ideas
en los molinos del recuerdo
Cazadas cesan en el aliento canino de futuros intrépidos
Hasta los perros abrevian el concepto de lealtad
Inclusive los caminos empapan estómagos
Juzgar intensifica el oxímoron
Existe un goteo incansable en las nubes faciales
que injertan la duda en las quijadas desboronadas
cuando alguien cree.

LEONOR OLMOS (Chile)

Leonor Olmos (b. 1988) had her first collection, p0ema, *published by Kokoro Libros and then appeared in the anthology* País Imaginario. Escrituras y Transtextos, Poesía Latinoamericana 1980-1992 *published by the Spanish press Editorial Ay del seis. Her poems have been published in printed magazines as well as online, including in Pesapalabra, Jámpster, Thalamus Magazine, and Transtierros amongst others.*

ENGLISH TRANSLATIONS BY JUANA ADCOCK

4

a.- this poem can solve nothing / – within the poem death is consumed / already, say it again, the percentage of purity mixed with a bit of sun, with a bit of hunger : // everything ends here and suddenly not,

– a new server, an electronic poem, a messiah – poem descending from the heavens – only the chosen ones contemplate their own destruction – no, seriously, this poem can solve nothing /

b.- this poem abandons the world / leaves the little puddle – ulcer / leaves the mouth numb / leaves the snow upon the night : this poem comma colon below :

    b.1.- is to break the mouth is to break the mouth is to break the mouth with teeth
    b.2.- a liquid screen being born in a sunny field
    b.3.- to destroy the body to destroy the body to destroy the body *is* to destroy the materiality of the poem and take it to the limit

    b.3.1.- the poem versus the flesh versus the blood loses consistency / lets the blood fall / breaks the blood and the poem / and to leave everything here among the living / a new direction in a low quality file /
everything ends here,

    everything ends here poem / you can re-solve nothing / : and suddenly not : and suddenly a little puddle of water, of stone : it's all a lie, poem – and then what? and then how?

4

a.- este poema nada puede resolver / – adentro del poema
la muerte se consume / ya, dilo de nuevo, el porcentaje
de pureza mezclado con un poco de sol, con un poco de
hambre : // todo acaba aquí y de pronto no,

– un nuevo servidor, un poema electrónico, un mesías –
poema bajando desde el cielo – sólo los elegidos contemplan
su propia destrucción – no, en serio, este poema nada puede
resolver /

b.- este poema abandona al mundo / deja el charquito –
llaga / deja la boca adormecida / deja la nieve sobre la noche
: este poema coma dos puntos a continuación :

b.1.- es romper la boca es romper la boca es romper la
boca con los dientes
b.2.- una pantalla líquida naciendo sobre un campo
soleado
b.3.- acabar con el cuerpo acabar con el cuerpo acabar
con el cuerpo es acabar con la materialidad del poema y
llevarlo al límite

b.3.1.- el poema versus la carne versus la sangre pierde
consistencia / dejar caer la sangre / romper la sangre y
el poema / y dejar todo aquí entre los vivos / una nueva
dirección en un archivo de baja calidad /
todo acaba aquí,
todo acaba aquí poema / nada puedes re-solver / : y de
pronto no : y de pronto un charquito de agua, de piedra :
todo es mentira, poema – y entonces qué? y entonces cómo?

6

water on my head, all simulated – this is my mouth, this is
my body, this is the continuous simulation that contains us – /
this is a scene, an open sun, a porous ulcer – and something

about us and everything about us – at http: // – in enthroned
language : this poem says it contains us, this poem washes away
the guilt of our parents

– me, the daughter of a neoliberal system – / me, in the snow, chewing on pain, spitting

the bills to be paid month by month –

/ 2 alternatives :

a) I feel my body in the grass / sometimes the eyes wake up in the poem, sometimes the poem and the eyes meet

/ upon nothingness /

b) tired : of lodging the poem in the flesh and letting it die / of lodging the poem between the legs,

a n d l e t t i n g t h e m d i e / of wandering from tongue to tongue / with nothing to offer you

6

el agua sobre mi cabeza, todo simulado – ésta es mi boca, éste es mi cuerpo, ésta es la continua simulación que nos contiene – / ésta es una escena, un sol abierto, una llaga porosa – y algo

de nosotros y todo de nosotros – en http: // – en lenguaje entronizado : este poema dice contenernos, este poema lava la culpa de nuestros padres

– yo, la hija de un sistema neoliberal – / yo, entre la nieve, masticando el dolor, escupiendo

las cuentas que pagar mes a mes –

/ 2 alternativas :

a) siento mi cuerpo entre la hierba / a veces los ojos se despiertan en el poema, a veces el poema y los ojos se encuentran

/ sobre la nada /
b) cansada : de acomodar el poema entre la carne y dejarla morir / de acomodar el poema entre las piernas,

y d e j a r l a s m o r i r / de vagar de lengua en lengua / sin
nada que ofrecerte

7

there is something diseased in the air, there is a body tied
to other bodies, all poems are disease ; all poems are a sunny
plain, from a certain angle – circle,

all poems are a sunny plain *on the edge* of despair – there
are practices that consist in splitting bodies and tongues, in
burning remains in burning totems / connecting the screen,
switching on the screen : a bit of sun inside my eyes inside my
blood, bubbling – a broken link – a poem not found – wandering
among the stones that stand above the water / wandering around
the throat that stands above all symbols / broken / destroyed /
unborn

there is a body tied to other forms : there is something
diseased in sustaining the poem as a substrate, as nourishment
/ within my body the poem bites, it tugs on pain – the grafts on
the tongue : the waves of the sea caress
a head / a body a t b r e a k i n g p o i n t / from another
angle : pain / – the blood and the grass on the body / the fear and
the s u n n y plain burnt, all perspectives are useless to the eye

this poem sustains the world upon this head upon this
♥ / a handful of nerves, of knots : a silence that collapses spaces
: that ties up spaces : me as an identity
that does not correspond to a body / shards of glass, a
liquid screen / a p o e m a t b r e a k i n g p o i n t / a poem a b o
u t t o b r e a k u s

at times I sicken, and I ask the poem for a little sun, a
little breeze : – at times
I sicken

and the sun does not nourish me, and the sun
does not h o l d m e

7

hay algo enfermo en el aire, hay un cuerpo atado a otros cuerpos, todo poema es enfermedad ; todo poema es un llano soleado, desde una perspectiva – círculo,

todo poema es un llano soleado *al borde* de la desesperación – hay prácticas que consisten en dividir cuerpos y lenguas, en quemar restos en quemar tótems / conectar la pantalla, encender la pantalla : un poco de sol dentro de mis ojos dentro de mi sangre, burbujeando – un link caído – un poema caído – vagar por las piedras que sobresalen sobre el agua / vagar por la garganta que sobresale por todo símbolo / quebrado / destrozado / no nacido

hay un cuerpo atado a otras formas : hay algo enfermo en sostener el poema como sustrato, como alimento / dentro de mi boca muerde el poema, jala el dolor – los injertos de la lengua : las olas del mar acarician
una cabeza / un cuerpo a p u n t o d e r o m p e r s e / desde otra perspectiva : el dolor / – la sangre y la hierba sobre el cuerpo / el miedo y el llano s o l e a d o quemando, toda perspectiva es inútil para el ojo

este poema sostiene el mundo sobre esta cabeza sobre este ❤ / un manojo de nervios, de nudos : un silencio
que derrumba espacios : que sujeta espacios : yo una identidad
que no corresponde a un cuerpo / trozos de vidrios, una pantalla líquida / un p o e m a a p u n t o d e r o m p e r s e / un poema a p u n t o d e r o m p e r n o s

a veces enfermo, y pido al poema un poco de sol, un poco de aire : – a veces
enfermo

y el sol no me alimenta, y el sol no me sostiene

9

in an alternative future, there is no poem, there is no woman – the speaker is moved with the mirrors, the speaker is a hybrid cyborg,

re assembled / part by part, manufactured by hands that know neither life nor death, is something else, the poem is something else, devours the flesh in machete strikes and consumes it beside the sun

nothing can grow there / nothing can be from there : death and its algorithm is something else and does not reach you

the algorithm of the poem is altered / codified – nothing in this world corresponds to the distance or the emptiness of a body on the water or the snow

– the machine incorporates the body into space and the grass / incorporates the body – masticated, intervened

– in an alternative future : this poem does not give up – it is a machine that laughs and dances on the stars / that connects the screen to a muscle, that destroys a muscle and attaches visions

– it all seems distant and lost –

in the industry of the fifth world, the poem is a liquid being, a parasite in the system of consumption and production, the flesh loses substance, water, electrolytes : this is my hallucinated flesh – intervened – according to the use and custom,

the assembly line crushes me

dissolves my hunger, quells my thirst

9

en un futuro alternativo, no hay poema, no hay mujer
– el hablante se estremece junto a los espejos, el hablante es
un cyborg híbrido,

re ensamblado / por partes, elaborado por manos que
no conocen ni la vida ni la muerte, es otra cosa, el poema es
otra cosa, devora la carne a machetazos y la consume junto
al sol

nada puede crecer desde allí / nada puede ser desde
allí : la muerte y su algoritmo es otra cosa y no te alcanza

el algoritmo del poema es alterado / codificado –
nada de este mundo corresponde a la distancia o al vacío de
un cuerpo sobre el agua o sobre la nieve

– la máquina incorpora el cuerpo al espacio y a la
hierba / incorpora el cuerpo – masticado, intervenido
– en un futuro alternativo : este poema no se rinde
– es una máquina que ríe y danza sobre las estrellas /
que conecta la pantalla a un músculo, que destruye a un
músculo y le atacha las visiones

– todo parece lejano y perdido –

en la industria del quinto mundo, el poema es
un ser líquido, un parásito en el sistema de consumo y
producción, la carne pierde sustancia, agua, electrolitos :
ésta es mi carne alucinada – intervenida – según el uso y la
costumbre,

la cadena de montaje me tritura

disuelve mi hambre, calma mi sed

11

/ just drops of blood, just – the horrors in my ♥ dance,
the vision blinds the light, the cut up bodies ready for their
packaging :

– all the light in my eyes a l l t h e l i g h t a n d t h e b l i n d
n e s s in my eyes – a translucent microfilm – translucent skin

programmed to allow itself get lost in a shooting range – the cold wind of morning / the body and the blood accumulate at the edges,
how much does the sun delay in emptiness?
how much does the sun bleed in emptiness?

a barcode / adhesive tape / packing tape on a body or on tissue or on a swollen abdomen / the compresses mid-afternoon, the warm water ; infusion after infusion
in my stomach / language is diluted : language dances, I follow the movements, my skin adheres itself to the machine, the machine corrupts the tissue : the diagnosis is confused with the humus with the quiet breath, oxygenated, contaminated ad portas

by the nausea
the vertigo
by_the symptoms that precede the shock / the crisis /
_the flesh retreats from the bodies on the snow _
_beautiful lights that are corrupted & finish off our eyes _
beautiful fears that tear up & burn our (diseased / insane) ♥

11

/ sólo gotas de sangre, sólo – los horrores en mi ♥ bailan, la visión ciega a la luz, los cuerpos trozados listos para su empaque :

– toda la luz sobre mis ojos t o d a l a l u z y l a c e g u e r a sobre mis ojos – un microfilms traslúcido - una piel traslúcida configurada para dejarse perder en un campo de tiros – el aire frío de la mañana / el cuerpo y la sangre se acumula sobre los bordes,
cuánto demora el sol en el vacío?
cuánto sangra el sol en el vacío?

un código de barras / cinta adhesiva / cinta de embalaje sobre un cuerpo o sobre un tejido o sobre un abdomen hinchado / a media tarde las compresas, el agua tibia ; infusión tras infusión
en mi estómago / el lenguaje se diluye : el lenguaje danza, sigo los movimientos, mi piel se adhiere a la máquina, la máquina corrompe al tejido : el diagnóstico se confunde con el humus con la respiración quedita, oxigenada, contaminada ad portas

de la náusea
　　del vértigo
　　　　de_los síntomas que anteceden al shock / a la crisis
/

　　　　_la carne se aleja de los cuerpos sobre la nieve _
　_hermosas luces que corrompen & acaban nuestros ojos _
　　　_hermosos miedos que arrancan & queman nuestro
(enfermo / insano) ♥_

13

　　this is a low-intensity transmission / the optic fibre shoots
through the tissue in my eyes / a body held barely by words, a
trans, cis god, organically pure, operated, surgically removed, the
lotus position, the lotus position, and us starving, and us flying
birds

　　awaiting the arrival of the poem, – the crisis,
underemployment, the slaving hand, the slaving hand and us
taking refuge : / infinitely blind : utterly rapt

　　it does not seem like the work of a body but the work of a
feverish condition, symptomatic, 38 degrees below 0, in the middle
of the summer, the off-season and great deals

　　line of credit line of coke line of sugar - mixed, contaminated,
a connection point for
stars and throats alight

　　mid-afternoon midway at noon, mid-decay

　　(a sleeping god dictates the poem to a body / machine /
root : to a body / muscle / emptiness) (a sleeping god / speaks of
death and of blood – sickens, sutures with needle and threads the
inflamed tissues of the mind, tissues contaminated by the mind :
me falling asleep pressing reset / every machine
/　　　　sound　　　　/　　　　origin　　　　/
– seaweed, ferns, dancing among feet, between digits among holes
/ the cosmos renews its agreement, offers the necessary blood,
offers the necessary flesh) (it is possible that in the poem there is

a transcription error : and it is not blood but milk in a field and the field is a simulated reality, and it was not me suspended in space : but another woman who knows it all and says it all : and it was not a god speaking to me in my dreams, it was the snow, it was the post collapse effect /

me, an apparition,

a vision condensed in a lysergic plate – there is no other way to bleed, there is no other way to fall)

13

ésta es una transmisión de baja intensidad / la fibra óptica atraviesa el tejido de mis ojos / un cuerpo sujeto apenas por palabras, un dios trans, cis, orgánicamente puro, operado, extirpado, la posición de loto, la posición de loto, y nosotros muy hambrientos, y nosotros pájaros voladores

esperando la venida del poema, – la crisis, el sub empleo, la mano esclava, la mano esclava y nosotros refugiados : / infinitamente ciegos : infinitamente absortos

no parece obra de un cuerpo sino obra de un cuadro febril, sintomático, 38 grados bajo 0, en pleno verano, temporada baja y buenas ofertas

línea de crédito línea de coca línea de azúcar – mezclada, contaminada, un punto de conexión de astros y gargantas encendidas

a media tarde a medio a medio día, a medio decaer

(un dios dormido dicta el poema a un cuerpo / máquina / raíz : a un cuerpo / músculo / vacío) (un dios dormido / habla de la muerte y de la sangre – enferma, sutura con aguja e hilos los tejidos inflamados de la mente, los tejidos contaminados por la mente : yo durmiendo reseteando / cada máquina / sonido / origen / – algas, helechos, danzando entre unos pies, entre dígitos entre agujeros / el cosmos renueva su acuerdo, ofrece la sangre necesaria, ofrece la carne necesaria) (es posible que en el poema haya un error de transcripción : y no sea sangre sino leche sobre un campo y ese campo una realidad simulada, y no era yo suspendida en el espacio : sino otra

que todo lo sabe y todo lo dice : y no fue un dios hablándome
entre sueños, fue la nieve, fue el efecto post colapso /

yo, aparecida,

una visión condensada en una lámina lisérgica – no existe
    otro modo de sangrar, no existe otro modo de caer)

MARA PASTOR (Puerto Rico)

Mara Pastor is a poet, editor and professor. She is the author of several books of poetry. Her latest book, Deuda Natal *(AZ Press, 2021), translated by María José Giménez in collaboration with Anna Rosenwong, was awarded the 2020 Ambroggio Prize by The Academy of American Poets. Currently, she is the academic leader of the Bachelor's and Master's Program in Creative Writing at Universidad del Sagrado Corazón.*

ENGLISH TRANSLATIONS BY MARÍA JOSÉ GIMÉNEZ & ANNA ROSENWONG
PICTURES BY LORRAINE RODRÍGUEZ

from DEUDA NATAL

THE BUSTS OF MARTÍ

One fine day all the busts of Martí
started talking,
all the beautiful busts of Martí
began to speak Martí.
From the Martí with the chacmool body in Vedado
to the one in Villa Lugano, in Argentina,
and the one in that park in downtown Shanghai,
the world was filled with talking Martís,
busts of Martí drawn
like apostles toward Popocatépetl
along zigzagging, resonating routes
until they lined up shoulder to shoulder,
all the Martís in América
all the Martís in the world,
all the busts of Martí.

There were those who thought
it was the end times.
There were those who wanted to send
amphibious troops
journalists to interview
one of the busts of Martí,
but the chattering was so immense, so strident,
that every Martí made it impossible to hear the rest,
and they became a harmless roar,
molten lead, tree ash.

LOS BUSTOS DE MARTÍ

Un buen día todos los bustos de Martí
comenzaron a hablar,
todos los hermosos bustos de Martí
comenzaron a parlotear a Martí.
Desde el Martí con cuerpo de Chacmool en el Vedado
hasta el de Villa Lugano, en Argentina,
o el de aquel parque tan céntrico en Shangai,
El mundo estaba lleno de Martís hablantes,
bustos de Martí que se encaminaban
como apóstoles al Popocatépetl
en rutas zigzagueantes y sonoras
hasta colocarse uno junto al otro,
todos los Martí de América,
todos los Martí del mundo,
todos los bustos de Martí.

Hubo quien creyó
que era el fin de los tiempos.
Hubo quien quiso enviar
a sus tropas anfibias
a sus periodistas para entrevistar
a alguno de los bustos de Martí,
pero el parloteo era tan masivo, estridente,
que un Martí hacia imposible escuchar al otro,
y todos a su vez se hacían rugido inofensivo,
plomo fundido, ceniza de árbol.

BEATRIZ MAGADÁN

In a shack in Chacahua,
lives Beatriz Magadán
with her little chicken that listens to hearts.

She cooks seafood
in coconut oil on her woodstove
and talks when the chicken isn't listening.

She crossed the border in a trunk
with every one of her children.
Over there she was baker, tortillera, house
keeper, mother, grandmother and wife.

One fine day, empty-handed, on foot,
she returned to her village on the
Pacific shore. "Fear," she said,

"is not a mother in a trunk
waiting for them to take one of her children,
fear is not daring to do something else."

BEATRIZ MAGDÁN

En una enramada de Chacahua,
vive Beatriz Magadán
con su pollito que escucha el corazón.

Ella prepara platos de mar
en la estufa de leña con aceite de coco
y habla cuando el pollito no escucha.

Cruzó la frontera en una cajuela
con cada uno de sus hijos.
Allá fue repostera, tortillera, empleada
doméstica, madre, abuela y esposa.

Un buen día, sin equipaje, a pie,
regresó a su pueblo en la orilla
del Pacífico. El miedo, dijo,

no es una madre en una cajuela
esperando a que le quiten un hijo,
el miedo es no atreverse a hacer otra cosa.

BÉLA TARR IN THE FILM CLUB

He projected images
in the forests of Hungary.

He muttered between his teeth the names
of the most beautiful films.

One day his girlfriend flew the coop,
that birdhouse in Finsbury Park.

She left like a Mossi warrior leaving
a village at war.

That's when I learned he used to throw
the iron and the blender at his girlfriend.

She, who travelled alone all the way to Burkina Faso,
who drew wild birds.

My friend hit his girlfriend.
I never found out in what muscle he buried

his Ural Mountain violence.
I remembered the day he arrived, cheerful,

with that tattoo of a friendly siren,
and that time we saw the movie

about Béla Tarr at the film club.
Silent sequence shot in one take,

whale corpse in a travelling tent
a short, terrified man enters.

They've carried off his friends,
and the man enters the tent,

to see in the eye of the dead whale
another impossible world.

BÉLA TARR EN EL CINE CLUB

Lanzaba imágenes
en los bosques de Hungría.

Susurraba con las muelas los nombres
de las películas más hermosas.

Un día su novia se fue de su casa,
aquella pajarera en Finsbury Park.

Se fue como se iría una guerrera mossi
de algún poblado en guerra.

Supe entonces que le tiraba
la plancha y la licuadora a su novia.

A ella, que viajaba sola hasta Burkina Faso,
que dibujaba pájaros salvajes

Mi amigo le pegaba a su novia.
No supe en qué músculo enterraba

su violencia de Montes Hurales.
Recordé el día en que llegó, alegre,

con el tatuaje de sirena afable,
y aquella vez que vimos la película

de Béla Tarr en el cine club.
Secuencia silenciosa en tiempo real,

cadáver de ballena en una carpa itinerante
a la que entra un hombre pequeño y aterrado.

Se han llevado a los amigos,
y el hombre entra a la carpa,

para ver en el ojo de la ballena muerta
otro mundo imposible.

AFTER THE STORM

Dozens of cars
wait in line
for a little fuel.

At the gas station
they're waiting for a ladder
to get up to a generator.

Faith is waiting
in this line
for the machine to work.

We want
a little fuel
to reach our town
and see if our house is still standing.

We want gas
as our honeymoon.

All verbal forms
are unlikely options.

What remains of the scenery
is people lined up
waiting
for a machine to work.

DESPUÉS DE LA TORMENTA

Decenas de carros
esperan en fila
por un poco de combustible.

En la gasolinera
esperan por una escalera
que lleve a un generador.

La fe es esperar
en esta fila
a que la máquina funcione.

Nosotros queremos
un poco de combustible
para llegar a nuestro pueblo
y ver si nuestra casa sigue en pie.

Queremos gasolina
como luna de miel.

Todas las formas verbales
son opciones improbables.

Lo que queda de paisaje
es gente alineada
esperando
a que la máquina funcione.

LAST NAMES ON THE BODY

In 1837 William Montgomery
believed he was the first to discover
the areolar glands that now populate
my milk-filled nipples.
Since then, we call them
Montgomery tubercles.
I prefer to call them sugar freckles,
milk oases, sunflower pollen.
In 1872 John Braxton believed he was the first
to discover the contractions
that prepare me for my daughter's arrival.
Now we call that unexpected force
that contracts the matter of my womb
a Braxton contraction. I prefer
to call it birth rehearsal,
flash flood, underwater volcano.
In 1886 in front of another group of men
James Chadwick identified
the violet colour labia turn before delivery.
Chadwick's sign, they call it.
For me it resembles nothing more than
an eggplant that becomes the cosmos.
The nomenclature of expectant bodies

is the strange poetry of a demiurge
that has nothing to do with those gentlemen.
Linea alba, primipara, gravid lunacy.
Shall I give a mountain my last name
because I gaze at it? May I
name my lover's mole
after myself because I discover it?
The day we erase those names
from women's bodies
another tongue will write their expansion.

APELLIDOS EN EL CUERPO

En 1837 William Montgomery
creyó ser el primero en descubrir
las glándulas areolares que pueblan
ahora mis pezones llenos de leche.
Desde entonces, les decimos
tubérculos de Montgomery.
Prefiero decirle peca de azúcar,
oasis de leche, polen de girasol.
En 1872 John Braxton creyó ser el primero
en descubrir las contracciones
que me preparan para la llegada de mi hija.
Ahora le decimos a esa fuerza inesperada
que contrae la materia de mi vientre
contracción de Braxton. Prefiero
decirle ensayo de alumbramiento,
inundación repentina, volcán submarino.
En 1886 James Chadwick identificó
frente a otro grupo de hombres
el color violáceo de la labia por concebir.
El signo de Chadwick le dicen.
Para mí nada más parecido
a una berenjena que se hace cosmos.
La nomenclatura de los cuerpos expectantes
es la extraña poesía de una demiurga
que nada tiene que ver con estos señores.
Línea alba, primípara, lunática gravidez.
¿Puedo ponerle a una montaña mi apellido
porque la contemplo? ¿Puedo
nombrar el lunar de mi amado
con mi apellido porque lo descubro?
El día que borremos sus nombres
del cuerpo de las mujeres
otra lengua escribirá su expansión.

from **ARCADIAN BOUTIQUE**

MAN

Man,
return to your forest
because you have a tapeworm
in your brain,
lodged as if in a den
that I didn't buy without the bread of my brow.
Nation, don't eat strawberries
on the freeway, because of the tapeworms.
Strawberries, don't be suburb.
Atlántico, don't be island.
Father, don't be güero.
Tourist, be grey-haired
and don't eat strawberries either.
White woman, don't be wilted.
Ciales, don't be fearful.
Pastry cook, cross Madrid.
Sweets, take the metro.
Father, no one told you to save your country.
Nation, don't eat strawberries,
howsoever
father bites himself. Farmers,
sell on the highway.
Tapeworms, don't be house.

       HOMBRE

       Hombre, regrese a su bosque
       porque tiene un cisticerco
       en el cerebro,
       como en una madriguera
       que no compré sin el pan de mi frente.
       País, no coma fresas
       en la autopista, por los cisticercos.
       Fresas, no sean suburbio.
       Atlántico, no sea isla.
       Papá, no seas güero.
       Turista, sea canoso
       y tampoco coma fresas.
       Blanca, no sea mustia.

Ciales, no sea miedo.
Pastelero, atraviese Madrid.
Dulces, vayan en metro.
Padre, nadie le dijo que salve su país.
País, no coma fresas,
comoquiera
padre se muerde. Agricultores,
venden en la autopista.
Cisticercos, no sean casa.

≈

It will be him the cat man his arms tattooed
with line art hearts.
Seeking a woman for eye licking.
He licks it.
The woman turns over in bed.
She licks his eye.
The woman shows her teeth.
Both offer their thanks.
Woman and cat man cover themselves with pillows.
They make a huge balloon with their guts exposed.
A woman of small layers
A cat with milk teeth.
A love without many territories inside.

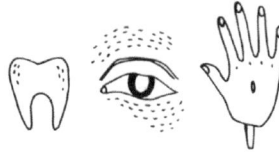

≈

Será él el hombre gato de los brazos tatuados
con corazón de líneas.
Busca una mujer para lamerle el ojo.
Se lo lame.
La mujer se da la vuelta en la cama.
Le lame el ojo.
La mujer le enseña los dientes.
Ambos lo agradecen.
Mujer y hombre gato se cubren de almohadones.
Hacen un enorme globo con las tripas al aire.
Una mujer de pequeñas láminas.
Un gato con dientes de leche.
Un amor sin muchos territorios dentro.

≈

Two-headed girl,
her home is the shell of an egg.
She is not two emergencies.
She is a radioactive snake.
A fire fish.
They cut her ad infinitum,
label her a cyborg.
Two-headed girl,
dicot creature,
refuse to take two driving tests
and spring from the echo of your sister that you are,
neon minotaur.

≈

Niña bicéfala,
su casa es el cascarón de un huevo.
No es dos emergencias.
Es una serpiente radioactiva.
Un pez de fuego.
La cortan hasta el infinito,
le ponen etiquetas de ciborg.
Niña de dos cabezas,
criatura dicotiledona,
niégate a tomar dos exámenes de conducir
y emerge de eco de tu hermana que eres,
minotaura de neón.

MIKEAS SÁNCHEZ (Mexico)

Mikeas Sánchez (b. 1980, Ajway, Chiapas, Mexico) holds a masters degree from the Universidad Autónoma de Barcelona in teaching literature and language practices. She is also a translator, radio producer and protector of the Zoque territory. She is the author of six books and has been published in anthologies in Mexico and other countries. In 2014 she was nominated for the Pushcart Prize for the best published work in the United States and has received a number of literary awards in Mexico. She is a member of the Sistema Nacional de Creadores de Arte.

ENGLISH TRANSLATIONS BY WENDY CALL

Translator's note:
In translating this series of 12 poems, I relied primarily on Mikeas Sánchez's Spanish versions. I studied Zoque versions as well, and Mikeas answered my many questions about both. In her Spanish versions she uses several Zoque names and terms, explaining them in footnotes. Rather than reproduce all her footnotes in English, I have incorporated some of the definitions into my translations. Others, however, I have included under the relevant poems.

from MOKAYA / de MOJK'JÄYÄ

I believe in the flesh and the appetites,
[…] and each part and tag of me
is a miracle

> *Wanjambatzi te' sis' tejerkike te sudgu'y*
> *Teserike mumu'tyä mumu chätyäyambä tiyä' äj neba'*
> *d ä' ngomist' chaki*

> *Creo en la carne y en los apetitos,*
> *y cada parte, cada pizca de mí*
> *es un milagro*

WALT WHITMAN

ONE

I am woman
and I celebrate every crease of my body
every tiny atom that makes me
where my hopes and doubts sail
All my contradictions are marvellous
because they are mine
I am woman and I celebrate every vein
where I trap my ancestors' secrets
all the Zoque men's words in my mouth
all the Zoque women's wisdom in my spit

TUMÄ

Yomo'chä
tese ngotzäjkpatzi äj'nwyt
tumdumäbä' tzäki'tzäki tujkubä'jin
ngotzäjkpatzi äj' natzkutyam äj' ngipsokiu'tyam
Mumurambä kipsokiu'y
wurambäre' äjne'ankä'ram
Yomo'chä tese' ngotzäjkpatzi tumdumäbä äj'näbin'dzajy
Juwä' ijtyaju wäñajubä äj' anukuis myusokiutyam
tese' mumurämbä tzame ore'pänis'ñyeram ijtyaju äj' aknakomo
tese' mumurämba kokypsku'y ore'yomo'isñyeram ijtyaju äj' tzujomo'

UNO

Soy mujer
y celebro cada pliegue de mi cuerpo
cada minúsculo átomo que me forma
y donde navegan mis dudas y mis esperanzas
Todas las contradicciones son maravillosas
porque me pertenecen
Soy mujer y celebro cada arteria
donde aprisiono los secretos de mi estirpe
y todas las palabras de los ore'pät están en mi boca
y toda la sabiduría de las ore'yomo están en mi saliva

TWO

I name myself and speak for all the mistreated girls
who gamble their innocence
in a darkened alley
For them May's first rain
and the wolf's roar
For them the tigress's howl
and the honeysuckle scent of tenderness
May mother quail and father sparrowhawk
soothe the souls of all the wounded girls
since the beginning of masculine time
May Piogbachuwe* and Kopajktzoka* come
to show us the beauty of the great beyond

Piogbachuwe: the guardian of a volcano that is a central feature of Zoque territory.
Kopajktzoka: a character in Zoque legend – a headless woman.

METZA

Tzambatzi' toya'ixajpabä nkiaes'ñoyikäsi'ram
te' jiamyajpabäis' myätzik
pitzä'run'omo
Tekoroya'ram winabä' mayo'poyas'tyuj
te' wejkä' paruwisñye'
Tekoroya'ram yom'gakis' wyejkä
jäyäs'yomaram
Yajk' mytiaä te' kumunu teserike te' tajpi'ram
minä' yajk' masanäjya'yaä' nkiaes' tyoya'ram
tobyabä tzotzusen'omo nasakobajk
Yajk' mytiaä Piogbachuwe teserike Kopajktzoka'
minä' yajk' isansajyaä kotzäjkis xasa'ajku'y

DOS

Me nombro y hablo por todas las niñas maltratadas
que juegan su inocencia
desde un callejón sin farolas
Para ellas la primera lluvia de mayo
y el rugido del lobo
Para ellas el gemido de la tigresa
y el olor a madreselva de la ternura
Que vengan la codorniz y el gavilán
a ungir el alma de todas estas niñas heridas
desde la memoria primigenia del hombre
Que vengan Piogbachuwe y Kopajktzoka
a mostrar la belleza del inframundo

THREE

I name myself and speak for all the raped girls
who seek their childhood in a bumblebee's buzz
and in a palm tree's sway
I speak in the name of the female volcano
Tzitzungätzüjk
and the male mountain
Jakima'käjtzäjk
who rise powerful on the sacred plain

I speak of the soul
its immortality untouchable by shame or doubt

I speak of immaculate sex
of the perennial girls
who soar above their grief
like the condor and eagle
showing their magnificence
dimmed with the passage of time

TUKAY

Tzambatzi' ñujkiaräjubä' pabiñomos' ñäyi'käsiram
Myetchajpabäis nwyt ojkjä'äs wyejkä'omo
kokokujyis' myjkskä'omo
Tzambatzi' yom'gotzäjkis' ñäyi'käjsi
Tzitzungätzäjk
tzambatzi' jaya'kotzäjkis'ñäyi' käjsi
Jakima'kätzäjk
muja'kejyajpabä masan' nenakäjsi

Tzambatzi' kojamas'ñäyikäjsi
teyi' juwä ji' tä känuki toya'is
Tzambatzi' te' masan' yom'ijtkuyis' ñäyi'käjsi
xkaes'ñäyikäsi'ram
te' nkiae' ji' ñachaebä'is toya
xirijtyajpabä muja' jonchi'seram
wäkä' yisansajyaä myuja'ijtkutyam
käwänubä' sone ame'omoram ansängäjsi

TRES

Me nombro y hablo por todas las muchachas violadas
que buscan su niñez en el zumbido del abejorro
y en el vaivén de la palmera
Hablo en nombre del cerro hembra
Tzitzungätzüjk
y del cerro macho
Jakima'käjtzäjk
que se yerguen poderosos en la llanura sagrada

Hablo del alma
cuya inmortalidad no alcanzan el oprobio ni la duda
Hablo del sexo inmaculado
de las niñas perennes
que se alzan por encima del desconsuelo
como águila y cóndor
mostrando su grandeza
doblegada por el paso de los tiempos

FOUR

I speak of my mother
whose nagual crouches under Piogbachuwe's skirt
while her childhood is a howler monkey
leaping among stands of bamboo
I think of my mother
yes, I think of her
and her chestnut scent from the kitchen
in her nearly blind, inviolable
tenderness
I think of my mother
and she thinks of her alcoholic father
who waits for the northern wind as a sign of rain
who waits to see my grandmother naked at the river once again
at the age of sixteen

MAJKXKU'Y

Ngotzambatzi äj' mama'
yajk' ägbabä'is nkiojama' Piogbachuwes'pyayu'kämä
täjp'wyjtpabä tzawijse' myoch'une'ijtkuy'omo
sojkuy'kämäram
Ngypspatzi' äj' mama'omo
jä'ä te'omo ngypspatzi'
ngypspatzi' kyastaña'oma'omo
te' wänubä jyotzkuy'omo
ji' musibä' dä' ngätäjkäj'ya
Ngypspatzi äj' mama'omo
tese' teis nkypspa notpabä'jyara'omo
jyokpabäis te' mambasawa' kyotzambabäis te' tuj'
jyokpabäis yijsä' jojpajk'omo nikurakabä äj' machuwe
ipskotumäbä'yame'jin

CUATRO

Hablo de mi madre
cuyo nahual se agazapa bajo el manto de Piogbachuwe
mientras su niñez es un saraguato
saltando entre los lienzos de caña
Pienso en mi madre
sí pienso en ella
y en su olor a castañas desde la cocina
en esa su ternura casi ciega
impenetrable

Pienso en mi madre
y ella piensa en su padre alcohólico
que espera el viento del norte en señal de lluvia
que espera de nuevo mirar en el río a la abuela desnuda
con sus 16 años

FIVE

I speak of my grandmother
her hands so anxious to harvest coffee
and grow gardenias
My grandmother whose wide, flowered skirt
was always the butterflies' and fairies'
favourite place
Awaiting midsummer
in her mourning dress
awaiting death
with her breasts bare
and smelling of mint
When everything falls apart
and grief is like algae
on tombstone
she is the northern wind that brings rain
she is the highest note of the reeds' song
that once more brings you the word joy

MOJSAY

Ngotzambatzi äj' dzu'mama
jene' suñi' mujspabäis tyukä kafel'
teserike' ñibä' gardenia'jäyä
Äj' dzu'mama petzibä'tyeksi'jin jäyä'tzäkibä'tyeksijin
jenerena' xutyajpabä tandan'istam
joyjoye'istam
Teis' jyokpana' te' kanikular
yagbajk' yomos'yasajin
teis' jyokpana' te' kaku'y
nusan wajkubä' chutzi'jin
yerbabuenajse' omyajpabä
Mumu tiyä' yajpak
nä' ijtuk' tumä mäja'roya

tza'sebä'toya mij' dzokokiäjsi
tere' te' mambasawa' ñejnabyabäis te tuj'
tere' te suskuyis'wyane
yajk' kasäjpabäis

CINCO

Hablo de mi abuela
aquella de manos ávidas para el corte de café
y el cultivo de las gardenias
Mi abuela con su amplia falda florida
siempre fue el lugar predilecto de las mariposas
y los duendes
Ella esperando la canícula
con su huipil de viuda
ella esperando la muerte
con sus pechos desnudos
y olorosos a hierbabuena
Cuando todo se desmorona
y tienes un dolor como de alga
como de roca
ella es el viento del norte que te trae la lluvia
ella es la nota más alta del carrizo
que te trae de nuevo la palabra alegría

SIX

I also speak for all the virgins and whores
who never knew love
those who smothered desire's flame
beneath their beds
while they waited for death
with its silver rosary
I speak for all the perpetual girls
who hid all the hatred under their skirt folds
making their bed a sanctuary
where no man wanted to take shelter
who had blind sons and one-eyed daughters
gnawing their bellies
to the end of their days

TUJTAY

Tzabguetaritzi' te' wärambä'yomos'ñäyikäjsi teserike
maña'yomos'ñäyikäsi
ja' yispäjkia'äbäis te' sudgu'y
te' yomo' jayk' tuyajubä'is yängu'kyämä
te' sudguyis' jyuktäjk
jyokyajpasen'omo'na te' kakuyis'yora
konukspa' platabä'rosariujin
Tzabguetaritzi' te' ja' kyoräjkaya'äbä' pabiñomos'ñäyikäjsi
teis'tam wyäñaju mumubä' nkysku'y ñtyeksi'kämä
myasandzäjkiaju yängutyam
jurä' nitumäbä' pät' ja' xunä'chäyä'
tejse' ñä' ijtyaju toty'rambä'jayaune'ram teserike
ji'yamyaebä'yom'uneram
kyetzayajubä'is chejk'
yajuse'angas yitjtkutyam' nasakobajkäjsi

SEIS

Hablo también por todas las vírgenes y rameras
que nunca conocieron el amor
aquellas que apagaron bajo su cama
la hoguera del deseo
mientras esperaban la hora de la muerte
con su rosario de plata
Hablo por todas las muchachas perpetuas
que guardaron todo el odio bajo el plisado de su falda
haciendo de su cama un santuario
donde ningún hombre quiso guarecerse
y tuvieron hijos ciegos e hijas tuertas
que mordieron sus vientres
hasta el final de sus días

SEVEN

I name myself and speak for all the women
who are still pained by sex
for all who still keep silent
and loathe the word desire
to them I offer my spirit
scented with May flowers
I celebrate with them my pain and pleasure

KUYAY

Tzambatzi yomos' ñäyikäsiram
yajk' toyajpabäsma dyomo'ajku'y
tekoroya'ram jinma' musibäis chapya'ä nitiyä
teserike nkisayajpabäis te' sudgu'y
tekoroyaram widbä'jayajpatzi äj' anima'
jäyä mayujse'ombabä
tejindam ngotzäjkpatzi äj' ndoya teserijke äj' ngasojku'y

SIETE

Me nombro y hablo por todas las mujeres
que aún se duelen por su sexo
por todas aquellas que todavía callan
y aborrecen la palabra deseo
a ellas ofrezco mi espíritu
perfumado con flores de mayo
con ellas celebro mi dolor y mi gozo

EIGHT

For my mother and grandmother
I offer the scent of black pepper leaves
where the saints slept
I offer the happiest song of the flute player
changed into a bird as he dreams
For them
I burn ocote pine boughs
that perfume their hair
dark legacy of Kopajktzoka
For them
the drum's brightest note
and the dancer's age-old prayer

TUKURUJTAY

Äj' mama'koroya äj' dzu'mama'koroya
widbäbatzi' moki'ajyis'yomaram
ukiajumä' dä' ngomi'ram
widbäbatzi te' suñi'kasäjpabä wane' sustayusñye
jonchi'ajpabä ägbasen'omo
Tekoroyaram

japäbiatzi′ suñi′omyajpabä′kujy
wäkä′ yomatzijaya′ä wyajtyam
tzäki′ chajkubä Kopajktzoka′is
Tekoroyaram
käsibä′wane kowarayusñye′
te′ peka′konuksku′y ejtzpabäsñye

OCHO

Para mi madre y mi abuela
ofrezco el aroma de las hojas de pimienta
en que durmieron los santos
ofrezco la canción más alegre del pitero
convertido en pájaro mientras sueña
Para ellas
enciendo palos de ocote
que perfumen sus cabellos
herencia oscura de Kopajktzoka
Para ellas
la nota más centella del tambor
y la oración más antigua del danzante

NINE

I bless the day of my birth
that rainy September when the Tzujsnäbajk River
overflowed its memory and made me into a girl
descended from Piogbachuwe
guardian of the mountains and the Tzitzun volcano
I bless my father and my mother for having engendered me
though I was not born to nobility
I had my own kingdom
that night-time world where a young woman danced
amid storms
And I had my own gods who taught me to curse
in a gagged and wounded tongue
Those are my beauties
my essence
my throne that no one can seize from me

MAJKUSTÜJTAY

Masanäbiatzi te' jama' jujchek'äj' punaju'
jikä' septiembre' tuj'poya jurä te' tzujsnubajkis
yajk' mijnayutzi' äj' jame teserike' yajk' tujkutzi yom'une
Piogbachuwes'yanuku
kotzojkis'tam' kyomi teserike tzitzun'gotzojkis'kyomi
Masänäyajpatzi äj' jara' äj' nana tzäjkpujtyaju'ankätzi
tejse' ja' pänajätzi nkirawa'räjk'omo
yäse' tese' oyu'ri nä' ijtkere' mujbä äj' angimokiuy'
tumä' tzokoy' jurä' tumä pabiñomo pämi'bäjkpa'na wäkä' yetza'
toya'kujkmäram
Teserike' äj' ngämistam isandziyajutzi jujche yach'ona'
Tumä tochäj'kubä ore'omo
Teramde' äj' sasa'ajku'y
teramde' äj' ijtku'y
tere' äj' angimokiuy ni'is jin'musibä ma' yajk'tzunja

NUEVE

Bendigo el día de mi nacimiento
aquel septiembre lluvioso donde el *Tzujsnäbajk*
desbordó su memoria y me convirtió en niña
descendiente de *Piogbachuwe*
dueña de las montañas y del volcán *Tzitzun*
Bendigo a mi padre y a mi madre por haberme engendrado
pues aunque no nací en cuna de patricios
tuve mi propio reino
aquella fortaleza insomne donde una muchacha danzaba
en medio de las tempestades
Y tuve mis propios dioses que me enseñaron a blasfemar
en una lengua amordazada y herida
Esas son mis lindezas
esa mi esencia
ese mi trono que jamás nadie habrá de usurparme

TEN

I also bless my funeral
in which an all-powerful God
Nasakobajk* will come to show me the path
that will guide me to Tzuan'*
There where all my ancestors await
celebrating an endless fiesta
under the Chichón Volcano's skirt

under the waters of the River Mobak'
There where my enemies also stand
waiting their turn to stone me
to sling their hate against my stiff soul
but only Nasakobajk can sing
the funeral march that will guide me
into the Great Labyrinth for all time

MAKAY

Masanäbiatzi te' äj' ngakuy'jama
jurä' mujabä' dä' Ngomi'is
Nasakobajkis' makatzi' isandzi'i te' tuk
makatzi' tzajme juwäre te' Tzuan'
Jinäre' makabä' jokiae' äj' anukuis'tam
sun'omo
tzitzun'ngotzojkis yasakämä'
Mobajkis' ñä'kämä
Teyi' makari jokiajkere' kisayajpabäis
makatzi' pundyoyae' tza'jin
wäkä' ñäbujtpä'yaä kyxkuytyam äj' anima'käjsi
teram' dzamayajpatzi jujche' Nasakobaj'kistire' muspabä' ma' wajnä'
te' wane'jin ñä' makiaräjpamä te' kayajubä'
temä'angas te' I'pstäjk'omo

DIEZ

Bendigo también mis funerales
donde un Dios todopoderoso
Nasakobajk ha de venir a enseñarme el camino
que me conducirá al *Tzuan'*
Ahí donde aguardan todos mis ancestros
celebrando en eterna fiesta
bajo el manto del volcán Chichón
bajo las aguas del *Mobak'*
Ahí donde aguardan también mis enemigos
esperando su turno para lapidarme
para descargar su enemistad contra mi alma yerta
pero sólo *Nasakobajk* podrá cantar
la marcha fúnebre que me conducirá
por siempre al Gran laberinto

Nasakobajk: Mother Earth.
Tzuan': is the parallel world where human souls go after death; it can also be
visited during life, "at the invitation of the guardians of peaks and mountains".
.

ELEVEN

I celebrate my sex
and the exquisite shape of my hips
where a man I love reclines
I glorify my soul
as well as my inner and outer lips
Because a great and compassionate God
forged my breasts
Because my face and my waist and my feet
could not have been better

MAJKOTUMÄ

Ngätzojkpatzi äj' yom'ijtkuy
teserike' te' sasarambä äj' nuñbajk'tam
juwä' kojejpa' äj' närun'
ngätzojkpatzi äj' anima'
ngätzojkpajse äj' yom'ijtkuy
Mujstamä' mijtam jujche' tumä mujabä' dä' Ngomy's
tzäjka'yajutzi äj' dzutzi'ram
Mujstamä' mijtam jujche' dä' Ngomi'is suñi' tzujkayu' äj' wynäjpajk
äj' dzejk'pajk teserike äj' ngosoram

ONCE

Celebro mi sexo
y las exquisitas formas de mis caderas
donde reposa el hombre que amo
Glorifico mi alma
lo mismo que mis labios mayores y menores
Porque un Dios grande y misericordioso
forjó mis pechos
Porque no pudieron haber sido mejores mi rostro
mi cintura y mis pies

TWELVE

I don't want anyone else to name me
no one can call me Kopajktzoka
or Helen or Clytemnestra
or Lesbia or Piogbachuwe
no one can say whether they like my hips

or the size of my breasts
Because my soul is immortal
just like the ceiba tree and the volcanoes
just like solitude and silence
and my eternity is boundless
just like death just like the abyss

MAJKOMETZA

Jin suni chapia'ä äj' näyikäjsi
u' yajk näjmayaju' Kopajktzoka
u Elena u Clitemnestra
u Lesbia u Piogbachuwe
jin'suni wäkä' ñäpia'ä uka' suñi äj' nuñbajk'
uka' wä' äj' dzutzi'is myaja'ajkuy
Mij' dzamatyambatzi jujchere jin'mabä' nkyae äj' anima
ji' nkia'yaejse te' pistindam teserike te' kotzojktam
ji' nkia'yaejse te' tum'ijtkuy teserike te' jana'tzabgu'y
mij' ndzamatyambatzi jujche' äj' ijtkuy'is ja' ñä' irä' yajkuy
ja' ñä' iräjse yajku'y te' pitzä'is teserike te' kakuy'is

DOCE

No quiero que nadie más me nombre
que nadie me llame Kopajktzoka
o Helena o Clitemnestra
o Lesbia o Piogbachuwe
que nadie más diga si le gustan mis caderas
o el tamaño de mis pechos
Porque mi alma es inmortal
lo mismo que la ceiba y los volcanes
lo mismo que la soledad y el silencio
y mi eternidad no tiene medida
como no tienen medida el abismo ni la muerte

HOW TO BE A GOOD SAVAGE

My grandfather Simón wanted to be a good savage,
he learned Spanish,
and all the saints' names.
He danced before the altar
and was baptised with a smile.

My grandfather had the force of Red Thunder
and his nagual was a tiger.
My grandfather was a poet
who healed with words.
But he wanted to be a good savage,
learned to eat with a spoon,
and admired electricity.
My grandfather was a powerful shaman
who spoke the gods' language.
He wanted to be a good savage,
though he never succeeded.

JUJTZYE TÄ WÄBÄ TZAMAPÄNH'AJÄ

Simón, äj' atzpä'jara sutu' wäbä tzamapänh'ajä,
kyomujsu castilla'ore
teserike mumubä dä' nhkomis' ñäyiram.
Ejtzu' masanh'däjkis wynanh'omo
teserike' mpyäkinh'dyzyoku' sijkpa' te' näyäyokiuy.
Äj' atzpä'jarais ñä' ijtayuna' tzabas'Mää'is pyä'mi,
nhkyojama kak'dena'.
Äj' atzpä'jara kedgäkätäbyabä'pänhdena
teis' muspana' tya' tzoka tyziame'jinhdam.
Te' sutu' wäbä' tzamapänh'ajä,
myuspäjku jujtzye yajk' yosa' te' käjtztäjkuy',
teserike' nhyenhtuyu' te' nhkirawais'ñoaram.
Äj' axpä'jara musobyabä' pänh'dena,
teis' muspana' ñä' tzapiaä pyeka'nhkiomiram.
Äj' axpä'jara sutu' wäbä tzamapänh'ajä,
tese' ja' myuskubyakä jujtzye' tzyäkä.

CÓMO SER UN BUEN SALVAJE

Mi abuelo Simón quiso ser un buen salvaje,
aprendió castilla
y el nombre de todos los santos.
Danzó frente al templo
y recibió el bautismo con una sonrisa.
Mi abuelo tenía la fuerza del Rayo Rojo
y su nagual era un tigre.
Mi abuelo era un poeta
que curaba con las palabras.
Pero él quiso ser un buen salvaje,
aprendió a usar la cuchara,

y admiró la electricidad.
Mi abuelo era un chamán poderoso
que conocía el lenguaje de los dioses.
Pero él quiso ser un buen salvaje,
aunque nunca lo consiguió.

WHAT IS IT WORTH?

Those masters of barbarity tell us:
I'll give you a millionaire's bank account,
in exchange for your blue sky,
I'll build you a nice supermarket
in exchange for your mountains.
One million dollars
for your children's smiles
as they run in the rain.
We Mokayas laugh at their ignorance,
even the smallest children
know that money turns to manure
when you pass over to Tzuan.
We Mokayas ask you,
the masters of decay.
Is a millionaire's bank account
enough to bring back
the laughter of our dead?
How much money is enough
to cleanse sadness from the soul?

JUJCHERE'

Te' yajkuyis'nhkyowinastam, tä' näjmatyamba:
Mij' nhkajkabyatzi sone'ruminh'jinh
te' tzujtzibä' mij' dzajp,
mij' dzäjkpujtabyatzi saxapyä' maa'räjk
uka' dyaj täjkäbya mij' nhkotzojk'omoram.
Tumä'millon tzujtzirambä'ruminh
wäkä' jambä'ä jujche kasäyajpa mij' uneram
poyapajk oñdyujomo.
Mokayas'tam mij' nhkosijktatymbatzi' mij' dzame',
mochirambä'uneis myuxajpabände,
jujche te' tuminh yatzyäyubä wakas'tinhajpa,

dä' nhkätpak te' Tzuan'.
Mokayas'tam mij' nhkämetztambatzi' mijtam',
yajkuyis' nhkyowina'ram.
¿mij' banku'omorambä' tuminh'jinh
mujspa'a yajk' wyrujatyamä
Tzusnäbajkis'xasa'ajkuy?
¿Sonebä' mij' nduminh'jinhdam maka'a nhkä'rejtame
wäkä' nimojktamä te' tzajp puspä'ukam?

¿CUÁNTO VALE?

Los amos de la barbarie, nos dicen:
Te ofrezco una cuenta millonaria
a cambio de tu cielo azul,
te construyo un hermoso supermercado
a cambio de tus montañas.
Un millón de dólares
por la sonrisa de tus hijos
que corren bajo la lluvia.
Los Mokayas nos reímos de su ignorancia,
hasta los niños más pequeños
saben que la fortuna se convierte en boñiga
cruzando la línea del Tzuan.
Los Mokayas les preguntamos a ustedes,
amos de la decadencia.
¿Una cuenta millonaria
será suficiente para devolverle
la alegría a nuestros muertos?
¿Con cuánto dinero alcanzará
para limpiar el alma de la tristeza?

MAXIMILIANO SOJO (Venezuela)

Maximiliano Sojo, a trans man, (b. Marta Sojo, Caracas, 1990) studied Modern Languages and later became a teacher of French language at the Pedagógico of Caracas. In 2015 he left Venezuela and moved to Chile where he founded the Fundación Versolibre in Santiago de Chile, alongside the poets Nelson Zúñiga and Francisca Santibáñez. In 2020 he began working on his first poetry book. His poems have been published in the digital Latin American poetry magazine Digo.Palabra.txt *(2018) and in the first special edition of* Revista Awen *(2018).*

ENGLISH TRANSLATIONS BY DAVID BRUNSON

FATHER

when I met him
at thirteen
I was scared
of the soldier
who aborted me
whose boots had warped
his toes
I was scared
he'd come to regret it
that he'd spew his apologies at me
like soldiers
getting ready for a war
they'll never go to
frustrated they leave me
two or three messages
that I see but don't respond to
until I hear about
who has died
and that I've aborted a father

PADRE

cuando lo conocí
a los trece años
tuve miedo
del soldado
que me abortó
a quien las botas habían torcido
los dedos de los pies

tuve miedo
de que se arrepintiera
me arrojara sus disculpas
como hacen los soldados
que preparan una guerra
a la que nunca irán
frustrados
dejan dos o tres mensajes
que yo veo y no respondo
hasta que me entero
de que ha muerto
y que he abortado un padre

CORTEX

my windows and my ruins open
I too am the sea-swell
I dream of not going back
although a pebble
in a shoe does come back
from my mud-filled street
taking the stairs
because the power's out again
and not even the polished floor squeaks
or shines
and there are no shoes or soles
no strength to take a step
or to go up to the fifth or sixth floor
and jump head-first
down to the concrete
cracking another hole the smell of burnt skull
hovering around the slack body
at the exit
and at night
blood is also oil
to be drilled for
if that skull were harder
it would pierce a deep hole
the deepest hole
it would reach the earth's cortex
to the crack

adjoining its dura mater
my land
you bear it all but I don't know why
my land
you could drop dead but
my land
you do not die.

CÓRTEX

se abren mis ventanas y mis escombros
yo también soy el oleaje
sueño con no volver
aunque vuelva
la piedrita en el zapato
de mi calle llena de barro
las escaleras
porque otra vez se fue la luz
y ni siquiera el piso lustrado brilla
ni chirría
y no hay zapatos ni suelas
ni fuerza para dar el paso
o para subir al quinto piso o al sexto
y lanzarse
de cabeza sobre el asfalto
abrir otro hueco olor a cráneo chamuscado
quedar con el cuerpo laxo
a la salida
que de noche
la sangre también es petróleo
por excavar
si la cabeza fuera más dura
perforaría un hoyo profundo
más profundo
llegaría a la corteza
al crack
inmediato de la duramadre
tierra
que resistes no sé por qué
tierra
que puedes morirte y
tierra
no te mueres.

MOTEL MALAMUERTE

they found my stepfather's father downtown,
dead in a fleabag motel
in an unmade bed
his chest burst open
by the bad life that old
bald bum had lived

the motel wasn't guilty
of that old man's bad death
a bad life
had siphoned children from his balls, from his baldness

the old man died in a shitty motel
in the middle of Caracas
and it was a bad death
a heart attack
naked and lifeless
opened up in the middle of the bed

his oldest son
looked up to him
he inherited his bloated balls
his hairy chest
his baldness
and the luck of a bad death
alone
in the middle of the bed
a millionaire in worthless bolivars

these desires killed my stepfather's father
he'd married the rum that bloated his cheeks
he was green when they found him
and now his firstborn
slobbers in his name
as his genitals
foam.

MALAMUERTE

al papá de mi padrastro lo encontraron
muerto en el centro el tórax abierto
en la cama destendida de un hotel
de mala muerte
por algo mala muerte tuvo el viejo
macho calvo callejero

el hotel no tiene culpa de la mala
muerte del viejo
la mala vida
que sacó hijos de sus testículos, de su calvicie

muerto el viejo en un hotel de mala muerte
en el centro de Caracas
muerto de mala muerte el viejo calvo
infartado
desnudo y lánguido
abierto en el centro de la cama

su hijo mayor
el imitador
heredó los testículos llenos de nata
los pelos en el pecho
la calvicie
la suerte de la muerte mala
en el centro de la cama
solo
millonario en bolívares devaluados

al padre de mi padrastro lo mató el morbo
se casó con el ron que le hinchó los cachetes
lo encontraron verde
y su primogénito
babosea en su nombre
mientras se abarrota los genitales
con espuma.

NOON IN SANTA CRUZ DE ARAGUA

he carries a million crumbs beneath his shoulder
he leads
a saddled mare waiting for
rain or

to sow the sun the yucca below the soil
without seeds
the sun
burns the roots
that sway side to side
like someone rocking the street

he drags his mare tied up at the jugular
and its heart throbs with the traction
of blood
and underneath
its sweaty leg stings
the horse clears its throat
it trips
falling
like a missile to the dust

a bray bounds over the hole in the highway

as sweat drizzles from its forehead
to its salty cheek
"I'd do anything for some water for my filly"

but not even the hairs of its mane move

it's noon now
not even the god of his faithful comes by
for a while not even the wind whistles

they say it'll rain soon
but
the cicadas don't sing

the vultures will come for their early dinner

"I don't see anything either
but some help ought to come for your filly"

nobody is always the first to arrive.

MEDIODÍA EN SANTA CRUZ DE ARAGUA

lleva un millón de migajas bajo el hombro
lleva
la yegua ensillada para
cuando llueva o
siembre el sol la yuca bajo la tierra
sin semilla
quema
el sol la raíz
que se arrastra lado a lado
como quien mece la calle

lleva la yegua amarrada a la yugular
y lo que palpita lo lleva tracción a sangre
arrastrado
debajo
escuece la pierna sudorosa
la garganta carraspea
tropieza la equina
cayendo
como un misil sobre el polvo

llanto abunda sobre el hoyo en la carretera

mientras llovizne sudor en la frente
sobre la mejilla salada
cualquier cosa por agüita pa' mi potra

pero la potra no mueve ni los pelos de su crin

son las doce
por aquí no pasa ni el dios de sus fieles
el viento hace rato que ni silba

dicen pronto lloverá
pero
ni las chicharras cantan

llegarán los zamuros a la cena temprana

yo tampoco vi nada
ya llegará la ayuda pa' su potra

nadie siempre llega primero.

BILLY

billy only knew the pistol's boom
but nothing of physics
or the boomerang's return
he was out of time
like everyone else he knew the boom
in the pistol his father gave him at carnival
but not the latin-american boom
billy knew the boom when bullets hit
bursting femurs hips and sternums
but billy didn't know the third law
he preferred to puncture the smooth bellies of kids on the court
he didn't know of newton
of dying in front of his mother
of the 9mm glock
of growing up next door to me
of bleeding out his head and torso and extremities

BILLY

billy solo supo del boom de la pistola
no supo de física
ni de las vueltas del boomerang
no le dio tiempo
supo del boom como los otros
por aquella pistolita que le regaló su padre en carnaval
no supo del boom latinoamericano
billy supo del boom cuando los proyectiles percutían
reventando fémures cadera esternón
billy no supo que todo lo que sube baja
prefirió agujerear las zonas blandas de los carajitos en la cancha
no supo de newton
ni por crecer junto a mi casa
ni por morir frente a su madre
ni la glock 9 mm
ni sangrando por cabeza, tronco y extremidades.

MISSVENEZUELA

good evening, Caracas

on your right, the dead woman

raped
tossed on the side of a country road

lost without her passport,
budget boobjob
with her CADIVI allowance,
out of self respect

miss [dead abroad]
a round of applause.

MISSVENEZUELA

buenas noches, poliedro

a la derecha la muerta

la violada
tirada a un costado del alfoz

la que se perdió sin pasaporte
se operó las tetas en oferta
con el cupo cadivi
por pundonor

miss [muerta en el extranjero]
un fuerte aplauso.

LET THE WORD BE SPOKEN

let the word be spoken
let the gunshot silence only death's mouth
but not ours
and not the mouths of others
let the word be burning saliva
and let it spit on death's word

but not our words or the words of others
your mouth opens like a door for flies
secreting
that resounding liquid
that changes the world
and pours from the throat
until it reaches tyranny's
terrifying timpanies
which roar
and fire shots at your word
and at our words and at the words of others
tyranny nearly wins
it's on the point of silencing
the bridges along the cavities and teeth
that raise your word higher than you
                         you are nothing without your
                         word
                         nothing without your word
                         nothing without your word
you are a word raised higher than yourself
higher than a tower
higher than us and higher than them
higher than those who don't raise themselves
higher than those who grow bored
higher than those who sell themselves out
or those who buy what they're selling
higher than those who deliver themselves to the grave
like the dead
who do not whistle
and if you fall silent
let your silence be tar
which breaks your cartilage
and dries your tongue
shattering
your molars and your jaw
breaking your trachea
and you choke
because he who stays silent
is complicit

QUE LA PALABRA DIGA

que la palabra diga
que el tiro calle la boca del muerto
no la nuestra
ni la de ellos
que la palabra sea saliva ardiente
el escupo en la palabra del muerto
no la nuestra ni la de ellos
la tuya abierta como puertas para moscas
secreta
el líquido que suena
que cambia el mundo
desde la garganta
hasta los tímpanos temerosos
del tirano
que ronca
que suelta el tiro en tu palabra
y en la nuestra y en la de ellos
que casi gana
está a punto de silenciar
los puentes en las caries
que tu palabra se alce más que tú

           tú no eres nada sin tu palabra
           no eres nada sin tu palabra
           no eres nada sin tu palabra

eres tu palabra alzada más que tú
más que la torre
más que nosotros y más que ellos
que no se alzan
que se aburren
que se venden
que se compran
que se llevan a la tumba
como el muerto
que ni silbó
que si te callas
tu silencio sea alquitrán
que rompa el cartílago
que seque la lengua
que el maxilar explote
y las muelas
que deje la tráquea rota
y te ahogues
porque el que se calla
es cómplice

VIRNA TEIXEIRA (BRAZIL)

Virna Teixeira (b. Fortaleza, Brazil, 1971) is a poet, translator and editor. She lives in London where she works as a psychiatrist. Her poetry is translated in Spanish, English, Catalan, German and Hungarian. She has participated in various festivals and poetry anthologies in Brazil and around the world. She published three collections of Scottish poetry in Brazil, and translations of contemporary Latin American authors. She is the director of a publishing house in London, Carnaval Press, specializing in Brazilian poetry, and is editor of the literary magazine Theodora *www. theodorazine.com.*

ENGLISH TRANSLATIONS BY VIRNA TEIXEIRA, REVIEWED BY CHRIS DANIELS

≋

Celling fans do not smother this heat. Greenhouse, *fleur tropicale. Finir l'aventure a travers le monde.* On the veranda a painter touches up paintings. Heavy traffic of taxis and buses playing boleros. Bananas. Climbing the stairs of minuscule salsotecas. *Ay que me gusta mucho.* How Latins move. With tight trousers at the zona rosa. *A la orden.* A doll for my daughter, *un sombrero* for my daddy. *Secu de camarones and club verde.* I sunbathe in a white bikini amongst German tourists. I wake up from a dream of iguanas and fire.

≋

Ventiladores de teto não abafam este calor. Estufa, fleur tropicale. Finir l'aventure a travers le monde. Na vereda um pintor retoca quadros. Trânsito lento de táxis e ônibus que tocam boleros. Plátanos. Subir os degraus de minúsculas salsotecas. Cristos, cumbias e luzes. *Ay que me gusta mucho.* Como se movem os latinos. De calças apertadas na zona rosa. A la orden. Uma boneca para minha filha, un sombrero para mi papá. Secu de camarones y club verde. Tomo sol de biquíni branco entre turistas alemãs. Acordo de um sonho com iguanas y fogo.

≋

Assessing a girl from Guarulhos who had been
to Holloway prison
accused of drug trafficking

now admitted with a psychotic episode
the ex-husband deported
back to Italy three years ago
      so she says
she found someone else to support her – another –
      multiples of the same type
      seduced by her charm
          of a tiny sexy mulata

her new lover comes to visit her daily
he brings papaya he is upset
she thought he wanted to kill her
to steal her organs

but Maria is now seeing angels
she is guarded in her room praying
Latina. Ave Maria
Maria de los Angeles
illegal

an expired visa
an expired sponsor
a godfather somewhere
a ticket in someone else's name

sectioned
refusing medication
      locked in her room
a language barrier to interview Maria
barricaded in my mother tongue
in a ward full of immigrants

Maria doesn't believe she is psychotic
she complains of somatic symptoms
she thinks her body is infested by
tropical worms

she thinks she has schistosomiasis
she thinks she has ascariasis
she thinks she has cisticercosis
her tests were all normal

Maria has been away from Brazil
for many years
still she is adamant her body is infected

she wants to go to Guarulhos to be treated
she will come back cured
an angel told her that

in a dream of a woman made of stone
      holding hands with a child

               ≈

      Entrevistando uma moça de Guarulhos que esteve na prisão de
                                   Holloway
      acusada de tráfico de drogas
      agora admitida com um episódio psicótico o ex-marido
                                  deportado
      de volta a Itália três anos atrás então ela diz
      que encontrou alguém para sustentá-la – outro –
                          múltiplos do mesmo tipo
          seduzidos pelo seu charme de pequena mulata

      seu novo amante vem visitá-la diariamente ele traz papaia
                            ele está chateado
      ela pensava que ele queria matá-la para roubar seus orgãos

      mas Maria agora está vendo anjos desconfiada dentro do quarto
                                 rezando
      Latina. Ave Maria
      Maria de los Angeles ilegal

      um visto vencido
      um patrocinador vencido
      um padrinho em algum lugar
      um bilhete no nome de outra pessoa
      internada
      recusando medicação
          trancada no quarto

      uma barreira de linguagem entrevistar Maria barricada na
                            minha língua mãe
      numa enfermaria cheia de imigrantes

Maria não acredita que está psicótica ela se queixa de sintomas
somáticos
ela pensa que seu corpo está infestado por vermes tropicais

ela pensa que tem esquistossomose ela pensa que tem ascaridíase
ela pensa que tem cisticercose

seus exames foram todos normais Maria está longe do Brasil
há muitos anos
ainda assim tem certeza que seu corpo está infectado

ela quer ir para Guarulhos ser tratada ela vai voltar curada
um anjo contou para ela

num sonho com uma mulher feita de pedra de mãos dadas com
uma criança

ANOTHER TIME

Nearly there. The water going up and down around Gormley's
sculpture, an angry girl arguing on a date, tell me how do you
regulate your emotions like the water level, how do you navigate
through foreign water routes? A glass of wine to manage your
feelings. Her defensiveness masked behind the ebullition, anger
as an avoidance mechanism, the mention of love raising his fears
of suffocation. Don't be so suspicious. What is not treated can be
misinterpreted. You can't hold back now that the lock was suddenly
opened. Look – it's overflowing.

OUTRO TEMPO

Quase lá. A água subindo e descendo em volta da escultura de
Gormley, uma garota raivosa brigando num encontro, conte
como você regula suas emoções como o nível da agua, como
você navega por estrangeiras rotas aquáticas? Uma taça de vinho
para administrar os sentimentos. A defesa dela mascarada pela
ebulição, a raiva como um mecanismo de evitação, a menção
de amor levantando nele medos de sufocamento. Não seja tão
desconfiada. O que não é tratado pode ser mal interpretado.
Você não pode segurar mais agora que o dique foi de repente
aberto. Veja – está transbordando.

The couple's room. How to tame a lion. Mastering triumph with excessive boldness, fantasy, and an edgy narrative. Denying an almost intolerable danger. In this dream she got lost in the dark, drunk, stepping over naked bodies. Violations were not immediately perceived as traumatic. Then all her kindness was lost. She was re-enacting, from victim to dominator, furious, freed from restraints, tearing her tights, savagely healing, hitting, calming down, asking for restraints. Powerlessness turned into anger, protecting her, protecting her hurt, burning it, purifying it, while Carmen Miranda smiled and waved to her against a sky on fire.

> O quarto de casal. Como domar um leão. Exercitando triunfo com audácia excessiva, fantasia, e uma narrativa limítrofe. Negando um perigo quase intolerável. Neste sonho ela se perdeu no escuro, bêbada, pisando sobre corpos nus. As violações não foram imediatamente percebidas como traumáticas. Então ela perdeu toda a bondade. Ela estava re-encenando, de vítima a dominadora, furiosa, livre de contenção, rasgando sua meia-calça, curando-se selvagemente, batendo, acalmando-se, pedindo contenção. Impotência transformada em raiva, protegendo ela, protegendo sua mágoa, purificando, enquanto Carmen Miranda sorria e acenava para ela contra um céu em chamas.

I will move continuously but I won't move, I can't commit, excuse me but I have to work, I am busy, I don't want a relationship, we have different expectations, I've never been in love, love is a psychosis, I hate the woman who refused me, I hate the woman I refused, she hates me, she hated my drinking, she was asexual, your anger reminded me of her anger, I am afraid of you, I will tie you up, I will call the police, you said I was a women hater, you are wonderful, I am having a great time, please take care of yourself, I will be waiting for you, I won't sleep with anybody, I won't make a move, while I move motionless continuously inside my passivity.

≈

vou me mover continuamente mas não vou me mover, não quero compromisso, desculpe mas tenho que trabalhar, estou ocupado, eu não quero um relacionamento, temos expectativas diferentes, acho que nunca me apaixonei, o amor é um psicose, eu odeio a mulher que me dispensou, eu odeio a mulher que dispensei, ela me odeia, ela odiava minha bebida, ela era assexuada, sua raiva me lembra a raiva dela, eu tenho medo de você, eu vou te amarrar, eu vou chamar a policia, você disse que eu era um misógino, você é maravilhosa, estou adorando esse tempo juntos, por favor se cuida, eu vou esperar por você, eu não farei nenhum movimento, eu não vou dormir com ninguém, enquanto eu me movo continuamente imóvel na minha passividade

≈

wrapped in a tight
garment
modelling
in its cocoon

body   anew   behind the screen

dream of a green
metallic bikini
from Barbarella

in a ball far beyond
the Beach of the Future

scribble on the wall

the molds   the boots   a wig

to display the skin in a glass *maison*
or a night basement

with her acrylic earrings

her cyborg female
neuroatypical

between punks and
genres incognitos

liberated of collectives and congregations

        ❧

        envolta numa malha
        compressora
        no seu casulo
        modelando

        um corpo novo   por trás da tela

        sonha com um biquíni
        de Barbarella
        verde-metálico

        num baile muito além
        da Praia do Futuro

        rabisca na parede

        os moldes   as botas   a peruca

        para exibir a pele na maison de vidro
        ou num porão noturn

        com seus brincos de acrílico

        seu feminino ciborgue
        neuroatípico

        entre punks e
        incógnitos gêneros

        libertos de coletivos e paróquias

I pass by the club
wearing a balaclava

The candies have
exploded already
several having escaped
in spaceships

My muse
is a non-binary
rubber doll

with a black mask
and icy blonde
ponytails

I pump up
her breasts
her hips

I paint her eyes
with a green pencil

I dress over
my catsuit

a latex corset

We are extreme
and incognito
my doll and I

tied   melted

dressed for pleasure

in a fugitive moment
between shadows
and the northern lights

❧

de balaclava
percorro o clube

as balas já
explodiram
muitos seguiram
em naves-mães

minha musa
não-binária
é uma *rubberdoll*

de máscara negra
e cabelos
platinados

inflo seus seios
suas ancas

pinto seus olhos
de lápis verde

visto sobre
o meu *catsuit*

um *corset* de látex

estamos incógnitas
e extremas
minha doll e eu

unidas   fundidas

dressed for pleasure

no momento fugitivo
entre sombras
e luzes do norte

≈

our images
made of mirrors

marching inside
this fantasy kingdom

I lead you with a
medieval corset
with brass buckles

to protect my chest

my petticoat is fluid
my boots are patent

you are astonished
smiling with a full
circle red dress

the Alice band holding
your grey blue hair

as you cross the ballroom
of your chimerical castles

fetishising the female
body in fragments of
imaginary lands

tied up in dreamy costumes

≈

nossas imagens
feitas de espelhos

avançando adentro
o reino da fantasia

eu conduzo você com
um corset medieval
com fechos de cobre

para proteger meu peito

minha anágua é fluida
minhas botas são de verniz

você está deslumbrada
sorrindo com um vestido
vermelho rodado

a tiara de Alice segurando
seu cabelo cinza azulado

enquanto cruza o salão
de castelos quiméricos

o feminino fetichizado
em corpos fragmentados de

terras imaginárias

atados em costumes de sonho

SARA URIBE (Mexico)

Sara Uribe (b. 1978, Mexico) was a scholar of Fondo Nacional para la Cultura y las Artes and received the Premio Nacional de Poesía Tijuana award and the Premio Nacional de Poesía Clemente López Trujillo award. She has been published in newspapers and anthologies in Mexico, Peru, Spain, the UK, Canada and the USA and her poetry has been translated into English, Portuguese, German and French. She is currently completing her PhD in Modern languages at the Universidad Iberoamericana.

ENGLISH TRANSLATIONS BY JD PLUECKER

from ANTÍGONA GONZÁLEZ / de ANTÍGONA GONZÁLEZ

Here we are all invisible. We have no face.
We have no name. Here our present seems suspended.
I'll wake up at any moment, I say when I try to lie to myself,
when I can't stand it any more, when I'm about to collapse.
But that moment never comes: what happens here is what is
actually real.
*They told me they'd found a few corpses, that there was a chance. They
told me that they were going to bring them here.*

Aquí todos somos invisibles. No tenemos rostro.
No tenemos nombre. Aquí nuestro presente parece
suspendido.
Voy a despertar en cualquier momento, me digo
cuando intento engañarme, cuando no resisto más,
cuando a punto del derrumbe.
Pero ese momento nunca llega: lo que ocurre aquí es
lo verdaderamente real.
Me dijeron que habían encontrado unos cadáveres,
que era una probabilidad. Me dijeron que los iban a traer aquí.

What thing is the body when someone strips it of a name, a history, a family name? *That there was a chance.* When there is no face or trail or traces or signs. *That they were going to bring them here.* What thing is the body when it's lost?

❧

¿Qué cosa es el cuerpo cuando alguien lo desprovee
de nombre, de historia, de apellido? *Que era una
probabilidad.* Cuando no hay faz, ni rastro, ni huellas,
ni señales. *Que los iban a traer aquí* ¿Qué cosa
es el cuerpo cuando está perdido?

❧

I came to San Fernando to search for you, Tadeo. I came to see if
one of these bodies was yours.

❧

Vine a San Fernando a buscarte, Tadeo. Vine a ver si
alguno de estos cuerpos es el tuyo.

❧

How is a body recognized? How to know which is the right one
if it is under ground and in piles? If the halflight. If the ashes. If
this thick mud steadily covers it all. How to claim you, Tadeo, if
the bodies here are just debris?
This pain is also mine. This fasting.
The absurd, the exhausting, the urgent labour of unburying a
body to bury it anew. To confirm out loud what is so feared, so
desired: yes sir, agent, yes sir, medical examiner, yes sir, police
officer, this body is mine.

❧

¿Cómo se reconoce un cuerpo? ¿Cómo saber cuál es
el propio si bajo tierra y apilados? Si la penumbra. Si
las cenizas. Si este lodo espeso va cubriéndolo todo
¿Cómo reclamarte, Tadeo, si aquí los cuerpos son
sólo escombro?
Este dolor también es mío. Este ayuno.
La absurda, la extenuante, la impostergable labor de
desenterrar un cuerpo para volver a enterrarlo. Para
confirmar en voz alta lo tan temido, lo tan deseado:
sí, señor agente, sí, señor forense, sí, señor policía, este
cuerpo es mío.

❧

Some by their tattoos. Others their scars.
Some by the clothes they wore the last day they were seen, some
by their teeth and some recognizable only by their DNA.
The ones who faint prior to glimpsing the doorway, as if their
eyes were prevented from identifying their loved one in the
formless matter.
There are some who search as a way to refuse to remain in the
silence to which they've been relegated.
There are some who inquire time and time again as a means to
confront their misfortune.

❧

Hay quienes por sus tatuajes. Otros más las cicatrices.
Quienes por la ropa que llevaban el último día que
fueron vistos, quienes por su dentadura y los sólo
por ADN reconocibles.
Los que antes de atisbar el umbral se desmayan,
como si sus ojos estuvieran impedidos para identificar
lo amado en la materia informe.
Los hay quienes indagan como una forma de rehusarse
a permanecer en el silencio al que han sido
conminados.
Los hay quienes inquieren una y otra vez a modo de
encarar el infortunio.

❧

I'm also disappearing, Tadeo.
And all of us here, if your body, if the bodies of our people.
All of us here will gradually disappear if no one searches for us,
if no one names us.
All of us here will gradually disappear if we just look helplessly
at each other, watching how we disappear one by one.

❧

Yo también estoy desapareciendo, Tadeo.
Y todos aquí, si tu cuerpo, si los cuerpos de los
nuestros.

Todos aquí iremos desapareciendo si nadie nos busca,
si nadie nos nombra.
Todos aquí iremos desapareciendo si nos quedamos
inermes sólo viéndonos entre nosotros, viendo cómo
desaparecemos uno a uno.

from SIAM / *de* SIAM

FACSIMILE

for Santos Reyes

the woman gone silent was made of dust
detritus from her years my own

someone (it's your sister my father said)
turns a page
clips an ad from the newspaper
lifts her hand to stop a taxi
she hurries, no desire to arrive late
passengers headed to / please board

someone: that one: the woman gone silent
is it possible for these purposes
to substitute the terms
repetition / cacophony
to use the word *sister*?

is it possible to say prosthesis
mudlabyrinth

leave the doors
is it possible
open
broken wide
like the name
in its eruption

roam through rooms
would it be possible / impossible
the childhood that no

perhaps identical
the shadow
the birthmark is lunar / the ground solar
the two-parted?

perhaps tenants
who take over
the building
and deposit
the amount
in the courts?

nothing more murky
than the proximity
of that strange woman
my father
brought home
with no warning

she quick
in the glass
that slips
and plummets

in the feast
of splinters / gratings

instantaneous
like the flash
of a photograph
that never / that no one / what no one
has coins to flip? / so no one
brings bread to their mouth
in the face of hunger / the family name

the women recently arrived was no one

I turned away from her at the wrong moment
in her eyes the two-faced verb
the verb lip-corner / the catalogue of absences

the vapour
the seed

what thing is symmetry?
a cornice?

inoffensive
the word
the half

of that word
what we have left

what do we have left
if the others
are us

our bed
its sheets

and the kiss / signal
to sleep
and in her mouth
to burn?

because someone (it's your sister my father said)
let's use: she
let's use: cut and paste
the woman gone silent
nescient like you
her life in its entirety
of the loom's long lines
eats breakfast this morning
at your table
and you ask yourself if she'll spend the night
in the room next door
if she'll rise in the hours
to head
to the margins

if dreamlike
she'll begin
with you
a dialogue of dust
the edges / if her voice

FACSÍMIL

para Santos Reyes

la mujer enmudecida estaba hecha de polvo
escombro de sus años los míos

alguien (es tu hermana dijo mi padre)
da vuelta a una página
recorta un anuncio del periódico
levanta la mano para detener un taxi
se apresura, no es su deseo llegar tarde
pasajeros con destino / favor de abordar

alguien: esa: la mujer enmudecida
¿se podría para este efecto
para sustituir los vocablos
repetición / cacofonía
usar la palabra *hermana*?
se podría prótesis
legamolaberinto
dejar las puertas
se podría
abiertas
violentadas
como el nombre
en su irrupción

recorrer habitaciones
sería posible / imposible
la infancia que no

¿acaso idéntica
la sombra
el lunar / solar
lo bipartita?

¿acaso inquilinos
que se apropian
del inmueble

y depositan
el importe
en los juzgados?

nada más turbio
que la proximidad
de esa extranjera
que mi padre
trajo a casa
sin aviso

rauda
en el vaso
que resbala
y se precipita

en el festín
de las esquirlas / limadura

instantánea
como el flash
de una fotografía
que nunca / que nadie / ¿qué nadie
tiene monedas para el azar? / que nadie
se lleve el pan a la boca
frente al hambre / el apellido

la recién desembarcada era nadie

le di la espalda a deshora
en sus ojos el verbo bifronte
el verbo comisura / la nómina de ausencias
el vaho
la simiente

¿qué cosa es lo simétrico?
¿una cornisa?

inofensiva
la palabra
la mitad
de esa palabra
que nos queda

¿qué nos queda
si los otros
son nosotros

nuestra cama
sus sábanas

y el beso / signatura
para dormir
y en su boca
arder?

porque alguien (es tu hermana dijo mi padre)
usemos: ella
usemos: cortar y pegar
la mujer enmudecida
nesciente como tú
su vida toda
de la urdimbre
desayuna esta mañana
en tu mesa
y te preguntas si pasará la noche
en el cuarto contiguo
si se pondrá de pie en las horas
para acudir
hasta los márgenes
si onírica
entablará contigo
un diálogo de polvo
las orillas / si su voz

FIRST ATTACK

To write from a building, he says. Windows. The ravaged city launches the first strike. Two contiguous vertices. The segments? Intersected. Perpendicular.
All city. A building without landlords. Someone who dictates a demolition order. Someone who transcribes an address. There is no one to notify, he says. This building has no owners or tenants [here the simulacrum and the false alarms] [here the contingency and the cosmetics:
a red light / a blinking flash on the walls]. *A list of names of people or things that are being lost.*
This is not an edge, he says.
Someone opens the windows violently [there are instructions to force them open right now] [there are instructions to clear it all]. This is an evacuation, a stampede. This is about writing while

descending a staircase [a suburb that does not stop shaking / noise / a devastated hemisphere] [something to assemble and disassemble every night / an explosive device / a border] [something that disfigures the speaker / contusion / puncture / hematoma].
Writing from a disguise, he says
[discharge, dislocate, disabuse]
All city: a building. All collapse this thicket.
Writing like a peregrino, he says. Kilometres. The highway.
[Peregrino, na (From the Lat. peregrīnus)]
1. adj. Refers to a person: that travels through strange lands.
2. adj. Refers to a person: that by devotion or vow goes to a visit a sanctuary, especially if in possession of a staff or cloak.
3. adj. Refers to a bird: that moves from one place to another.
4. adj. Refers to an animal or a thing: that comes from a strange country.
5. adj. Strange, special, unusual, or rarely seen.
6. adj. Gifted with a unique beauty, perfection or excellence.
7. adj. That in this transient life.

PRIMER ASALTO

Escribir desde un edificio, dice él. Ventanas. La ciudad abatida lanza el primer golpe. Dos vértices contiguos. ¿Los segmentos? Intersectados. Perpendiculares.
Toda ciudad. Un edificio sin propietarios. Alguien que dicta una orden de demolición. Alguien que transcribe un domicilio. No hay a quién notificar, dice él. Este inmueble no tiene dueños ni inquilinos [aquí el simulacro y las falsas alarmas] [aquí la contingencia y el maquillaje:
una luz roja / un destello parpadeante sobre las paredes]. *Una lista de nombres de personas o cosas que se pierden.*
Esto no es una orilla, dice él.
Alguien abre las ventanas con violencia [hay instrucciones de forzarlas justo ahora] [hay instrucciones de franquearlo todo]. Esto es una evacuación, una estampida. Esto se trata de escribir mientras se desciende una escalera [un suburbio que no cesa de agitarse / ruido / un hemisferio devastado] [algo que armar y desarmar todas las noches / un artefacto explosivo / una frontera]

[algo que desfigure al hablante / contusión / pinchazo
/ hematoma].
Escribir desde un disfraz, dice él
[desbordar / desbrozar / desbastar].
Toda ciudad: un edificio. Todo colapso esta espesura.
Escribir como un peregrino, dice él. Kilómetros. La
carretera
[Peregrino, na. (Del lat. peregrı-nus)]
1. adj. Dicho de una persona: que anda por tierras extrañas.
2. adj. Dicho de una persona: que por devoción o por voto va a visitar un
santuario, especialmente si lleva el bordón
y la esclavina.
3. adj. Dicho de un ave: que pasa de un lugar a otro.
4. adj. Dicho de un animal o de una cosa: que procede de un país extraño.
5. adj. Extraño, especial, raro o pocas veces visto.
6. adj. Adornado de singular hermosura, perfección o excelencia.
7. adj. Que en esta vida de paso.

from A LOT OF WRITING FOR NOTHING / *de* UN MONTÓN DE ESCRITURA PARA NADA

POEM IN WHICH THE FEMALE SPEAKER CHATS WITH A MALE EDITOR TO WHOM NO ONE HAS EXPLAINED WHETHER PURITY EXISTS, OR IF IT IS, LET'S SAY, NECESSARY. OR POSSIBLE. OR IF IT TASTES GOOD.

He said he wanted a neutral poem. The recorded laughter, he'd
add that himself.
Said he would have at the ready a stylist, make-up artist, Xanax,
Bach flowers.
Foodstuffs and amenities available in the dressing room, in case
they were required.
First, he asked me if my poem wanted to come out dressed as a
poem; as a Mexican poem; as a contemporary Mexican poem; as a
contemporary Mexican poem written by a woman; as a contemporary
Mexican poem written by a bisexual woman.
Afterwards he was adamant that it was preferable for us to undress it.
Said it would be more appealing for the audience if they could dress
it up however they wanted. Like those paper dolls we we'd make
clothing for, attaching it to their bodies with tiny tabs.
As naked as possible. He said. No tattoos. No marks, no brandings.
Tell your poem to close its eyes and ignore who published it and where.

Perhaps you should sterilize it with anti-bacterial wipes, he suggested.
Said its packaging should specify: this poem should not be ingested
                                                          with a straw.
It'll be better to just erase the poem completely.
Not to publish the poem but its erasure.
To say: there was a poem here.
Neutral. Perfectly neutral.

POEMA EN QUE LA ENUNCIANTE CHARLA CON UN EDITOR AL QUE NADIE LE HA EXPLICADO SI LO PURO EXISTE, O SI ES, PONGAMOS, NECESARIO. O POSIBLE. O SI SABE BIEN.

Dijo que quería un poema neutro. Las risas grabadas las pondría él.
Que tendría listos estilista, maquillista, tafiles, flores de Bach
Viandas y amenidades dispuestas en el camerino, por si fuese
                                                          necesario.
Primero me preguntó si mi poema quería salir vestido de poema; de
poema mexicano; de poema mexicano contemporáneo; de poema
mexicano contemporáneo escrito por una mujer; de poema
mexicano contemporáneo escrito por una mujer bisexual.
Después aseguró enfático que era preferible que lo
desvistiéramos. Que al público le sería más atractivo si podía
arroparlo a contentillo. Como aquellas muñequitas de papel a
las que les fabricábamos ropa hecha para fijarse al cuerpo con
minúsculas pestañas.
Lo más desnudo posible. Dijo. Sin tatuajes. Sin marcas.
Dile a tu poema que cierre los ojos y no mire quién o dónde se
                                                          publica.
Tal vez deberías esterilizarlo con toallitas antibacteriales,
sugirió. Que en su empaque se especifique: este poema no
deberá beberse con popote.
Mejor será borrar el poema por completo.
Publicar no el poema sino su borradura.
Decir: aquí hubo un poema.
Neutro. Neutrísimo.

POEM IN WHICH THE FEMALE SPEAKER PARAPHRASES, IN ORDER TO REFUTE AS FALSE, A SERIES OF STUPIDITIES REGARDING THE FLAGELLANT ORIGINAND NATURE OF POETRY

If you're told you can only
write poetry
if you've suffered
or if you're suffering

if you know
unequivocally
that you'll suffer.
That all writing
should arise
out of The Wound.
Believe me
you've been lied to.
Not all that about abandoning any hope. Not about failing like
an idiot. Not the infernos of lava where to burn. No, not about
lunging over the rails either. Not about twenty-six reincarnations
to be able to write like the blabbering bard in a hat and bow-tie
reciting his poems from memory to impress people.
Believe me,
you don't need it.
We're not parrots
and reciting poetry from memory is an approach
that fortunately
has fallen in disuse.
I'm sorry, all that about bars and mud, the cigarette held in his
fingers, the beard left unshaven for days, the little ivory tower,
the erudition and purity of your voice. No, not wisdom either. All
that about having to have lived in order to write. About refining
a poem for six years. About leaving time for the poem to breathe.
About the major poem.
Believe me
it's purely
inventing
a character.

POEMA EN QUE LA ENUNCIANTE PARAFRASEA, PARA REFUTAR POR FALSAS, UNA SERIE DE ESTULTICIAS EN TORNO AL ORIGEN Y NATURALEZA FLAGELANTES DE LA POESÍA

Si te dicen que sólo
puedes escribir poesía
si has sufrido
si estás sufriendo
si sabes
inequívocamente
que sufrirás
Que toda escritura

debe partir
de La Herida.
Créeme
te están mintiendo.
Ni lo de abandonar esperanza alguna. Ni lo de fallar como
un idiota. Ni los infiernos de lava en los cuales arder. No,
tampoco lo de arrojarse de las bordas. Ni lo de las veintiséis
reencarnacionespara poder redactar como el vate fantoche
de sombrero y moño que recita sus poemas de memoria para
impresionar.
Créeme,
no lo necesitas.
No somos loros
y la declamación es una técnica
afortunadamente
en desuso.
Lo siento, lo de las cantinas y el lodo, el cigarro entre los
dedos, la barba de días, la torrecita de marfil, la erudición y
la pureza de tu voz. No, la sabiduría tampoco. Lo de tener
que haber vivido para poder escribir. Lo de pulir un poema
durante seis años. Lo del tiempo de respiración del poema.
Lo del poema fundacional.
Créeme
es pura
construcción
de personaje.

FÁTIMA VÉLEZ (Colombia)

Fátima Vélez (b. Manizales, Colombia, 1985) has published three poetry books Casa Paterna *(2015),* Del porno y las babosas *(2016, in collaboration with the artist Powerpaola) and* Diseño de interiores *(2019). She lives in New York with her two twin children and a beta fish. She is completing her PhD in Hispanic American cultural studies at the Public University of New York.*

ENGLISH TRANSLATIONS BY JUANA ADCOCK

from PORN AND SLUGS / de EL PORNO Y LAS BABOSAS

RAW MATERIALS / MATERIA PRIMA

1

nobody would imagine that making love might be a cockroach's thing
I say love and it's the brown thrusting its forms
the darkness tightening crossdressing taking shape
loving each other
a neon light shines and they're loving each other
more organ by now and more guts
more flesh less eye
two cockroaches as you've never seen them before
no modesty, more existence than
loving in their husks
trembling in the give
blind and with antennae
tips tiptoeing on the vibration
of breadcrumbs, from the routine to the other
scent:
a kingdom that is so physical
so substance in the invisibility
so particle in the diminutive
that it makes us want to bathe
not in cleanliness but in the smear
the desire to be entrail does us and rattles us
into organs not wholly ours

the unease is matter
a chunk of earth set into motion

what recently became a strength emerges
from a dignity not thought possible
in the heat of a form
the cockroach figure
becoming cockroaches
sharpening the plural

1

nadie se imagina que lo suyo de una cucaracha sea hacer el amor
digo el amor y es el café encajando sus formas
la oscuridad aprieta se traviste se acuerpa
se quieren
una luz de neón alumbra y se quieren
a estas alturas más órgano más tripas
más carne menos ojo
el de dos cucarachas como no las has visto
sin pudor, más existencia
que quererse en sus cáscaras
tiritar en lo blando
con antenas y ciegas
en puntas sobre la vibración
de las migas del pan, de la rutina al otro
olor:
un reino tan físico
tan sustancia en lo invisible
tan partícula en lo diminutivo
que dan ganas de bañarse
no de limpieza sino de lo untado
quererse entraña nos hace y nos sacude
en órganos no del todo nuestros

materia esa nerviosidad
un pedazo de tierra puesta en movimiento
lo recién fuerza surge
de una dignidad no creída posible
al calor de una forma
la figura cucaracha
haciéndose cucarachas
afilando su plural

2

something of another in periplanetic
of the inferior carboniferous
family of the blatids, blatellids, blaberids, poliphageous,
cryptocercidous, noctucollidous
whose union with what is human comes from when we dwelt in caves,
nocturnality and skulduggery

something of another
or cannibals of feeling
devouring our capacity to enter
allowing us to graze pastures of sewers and toothbrushes

something of another
or that impossibility
written in the dna
and between the less other, less touched
more rapid, more creatures
reproduction and reproduced
spreading out their horizontality from the brown
until there are no more
moving or narratable parts
capturable on earth
thus putting out the light of the last waste

        2

        algo de otro en periplanético
        del carbonífero inferior
        familia de los blátidos, blatélidos, blabéridos, polifágidos,
        criptocércidos, nocticólidos
        cuya unión con lo humano viene de cuando éramos de cuevas,
        nocturnidad y alevosía

        algo de otro
        o caníbales del sentir
        devoran nuestra capacidad de entrar
        y dejarnos pastar cloacas y cepillos de dientes

        algo de otro
        o esa imposibilidad
        está escrita en el adn

y entre menos otro, menos tocadas
más rápidas, más criaturas
reproducción y reproducidas
extendiendo del café su horizontalidad
hasta que no queden piezas
móviles o narrables
cazables en la tierra
y así apaguen el brillo del último desecho

3

if the cockroach is vulva
it is impenetrable vulva
at least I know of no one
wishing to enter
into cockroach

but I know cases
where a cockroach
is allowed to enter a body
maybe there is something in it
some guts we no longer have
which cockroach-ingestion porn
may help us recover

3

si la cucaracha es vulva
es vulva impenetrable
no conozco, al menos
alguien
que quiera entrar en cucaracha

pero conozco casos
en los que se deja entrar
la cucaracha en cuerpo
tal vez hay algo en ella
suerte de entraña que perdimos
que el porno de ingestión de cucarachas
puede recuperar

OF PORN AND SLUGS

there is no porn that can compete
against the mating of slugs

an affirmation sustained
on not enough slime
to make it known to the other
to others
how we long to have our ear nibbled
the tip of a tongue entering us
through orifices where
not even the most
wayward of fungi
would fit

slugs on the other hand
oh, slugs
their phalluses
translucent nordic blue
elongating
squeezing twisting
turning soft fertile
tasting each other the way colour glimmers
heading into the void
a somersault perhaps deadly or perhaps
softened by angels, protectors
of porn and slugs

DEL PORNO Y LAS BABOSAS

no hay porno capaz de igualar
el apareamiento de las babosas

una afirmación sustentada
en no tener babas suficientes
para hacerle saber al otro
a los otros
las ganas que tenemos de que nos muerdan una oreja
que nos metan la punta de la lengua
en orificios donde no cabría
ni el más extraviado de los hongos

las babosas en cambio
ah, las babosas
sus falos
translúcidos nórdicos azules
se alargan
aprietan retuercen
giran blandos fecundos
saboreándose como la luz en el color
se lanzan al vacío
en un salto tal vez mortal
tal vez amortiguado
por los ángeles protectores
del porno y las babosas

from INTERIOR DESIGN / de DISEÑO DE INTERIORES

HOUSE

say house
louder
to the tip
of the nose to the shoelace
sing roar bellow thunder bark
with passion
eeny meeny miny moe catch a tiger in the lime green
take a leap towards the existence of
spintop and the first brick
sweet tooth and a step
american rubber and a veranda on the second floor
parquet and the green carpet nursing dust
that's it, like that, louder
so it's heard

say house
with basement and skin of fear of the little things that may be
awakened in the presence of strangers
yellowing darkness
trails of ants   floor   stone
                 floor mould
where to unwind   this yoyo
where to ride the tricycle we found on the street

say house
and it should be noted that the house enters
through the door and the waiting
shows off its tail
winding it around legs and borders

in a moment of carelessness
beneath the sole of some rubber boots
the house creaks roars howls thunders cracks meows barks
jet black eyes
dilated pupils

I said let it go now

it is no good to be feared
by the place where we dream

LA CASA

digan casa
más duro
hasta la punta
de la nariz al cordón de los zapatos
entonen rujan bramen truenen ladren
con ganas
pico monto un dos tres por mí en el verde limón
salten hasta la existencia de algo
trompo y el primer ladrillo
golosa y un escalón
caucho americano y la baranda del segundo piso
parqués y la alfombra verde amamanta polvo
eso, así, más duro
que se escuche

digan casa
con sótano y pellejo de miedo a las cositas que pueden despertarse
en presencia de extraños
amarillenta oscuridad
trazos de hormigas piso piedra
                              piso moho
donde desenrollar este yoyo
donde montar el triciclo que encontramos en la calle

digan casa
y es de notar que la casa entra

por la puerta y la espera
y desfila su cola
y la enrosca por piernas y bordes

en menos de un descuido
entre la suela de unas botas de caucho
la casa cruje brama aúlla truena maúlla ladra
ojos azabache
pupilas dilatadas

dije suéltenla de una vez

no es bueno ser temido
por el lugar donde soñamos

COMMON PLACE

in the city where I grew up
they call it ñufla
the bit that gets stuck
between your teeth
after a meal
ñufla
sounds horrendous
like a man with a ratty smile
more colour than we bargained for
of dubious origin
wearing no tie
and badly polished shoes

poetry reserves
the right to refuse admission
to that rhyme and to those kinds of individuals
also
to the word soul
and don't even think about
the word life setting foot in here
watch out for tears
that inundate the sirens of the Seventh
and if god appears
– even worse if he turns up with a capital G –

gag him
as soon as possible
stick him in a trunk
may he be terminated by termites
before he is made into word
before
a blind noose
strangles
with the most common of places

LUGAR COMÚN

en la ciudad donde crecí
le dicen ñufla
al mugre que se queda
atascado en el diente
después de comer
ñufla
suena horrible
como un hombre con sonrisa de topo
más color de la cuenta
de dudosa procedencia
sin corbata
y zapatos mal embetunados

la poesía se reserva
el derecho de admisión
para esa rima y esa clase de sujetos
también
para la palabra alma
y ni se le ocurra
que la palabra vida entrará aquí
cuidado con el llanto
que inunda a las sirenas de la Séptima
y si dios aparece
– peor si lo hace con mayúscula –
amordácelo
lo más pronto posible
métalo en un baúl
que se lo coma el comején
antes de que se haga palabra
antes de que
un nudo ciego
ahorque
con el más común de los lugares

SAVING UP

our bread
our daily pavement
should not
waste money
should not
fall in love
should not
say too much

and the mum
        her tragedy as an illegal immigrant in Arizona
and the dad
        his women fifteen large tits Catholic uniform

the stretchmarks
and the hooked-nose revolutions
lard-washing
Jewish surnames
black coffee
no milk or sugar
bamboo groves mules rivers
whirlpools and cousins
landowners in hats
suits and education in London or Paris

death hangs in the balance
between generations
digs around the teeth of the newbies
round about where the drunkards
go out and stare reclining against lampposts

we learn then to love the rats
how brave
risking their lives
for a piece of newspaper
to feed who knows what belly
what rust
and the people besides

telling stories
that a cadaver
three days
that's what they got for smoking crack

although she hasn't seen a cobra
she knows they have its eyes
although she hasn't smelled a skunk
its musk is already among us
the death of the others
is yet to touch her
she hopes not to invoke it
and if it makes a proposal?
her dad would say
she is prostituting herself
because it's either that or washing dishes
when one lives
so far away

soon she'll write him a letter
saying it could be worse
that she has friends who sleep with their editors
that more than once
they have got trapped
in a mole's claws

so, death
what do you think
if he does things to you
and next morning he brings you breakfast
orange juice
and eggs with tomatoes and onions
Colombian-style

will you promise a truce?

how do you like your eggs,
dear death?

AHORRAR

pan nuestro
acera nuestra
no debe
desperdiciar dinero
no debe
enamorarse
no debe
decir de más

y la mamá
        su tragedia de inmigrante ilegal en Arizona
y el papá
        sus mujeres de quince tetas grandes uniforme católico

las estrías
y las revoluciones de nariz aguileña
apellidos de judíos
bañados en grasa de marrano
café negro
sin leche y sin azúcar
guaduales mulas ríos
remolinos y primas
terratenientes de sombrero
trajes y educación en Londres o París

la muerte se abalanza
entre generaciones
escarba en las muelas de los nuevos
por ahí cuando los borrachos
salen y miran recostados en postes

se aprende entonces a querer a las ratas
qué valientes
arriesgar su vida
por un pedazo de periódico
para alimentar quién sabe qué vientre
qué óxido
y la gente al lado
contando
que un cadáver
tres días
eso le pasó por fumar crack

aunque no ha visto una cobra
sabe que tiene sus ojos
aunque no ha olido un zorrillo

su almizcle ya está aquí
la muerte de los otros
aún no la ha tocado
espera no invocarla
¿y si le hace una propuesta?
diría su papá
que se está prostituyendo
porque eso o lavar platos
es lo único
que se puede hacer
allá tan lejos

pronto le escribirá una carta
le dirá que hay peores
que tiene amigas que se acuestan con sus editores
que más de una vez
han quedado
atascadas en la uña de un topo

entonces
muerte
qué opinas
si te hace cositas
y por la mañana te lleva el desayuno
de jugo de naranja
y huevos con cebolla y tomate
muy a la colombiana

¿prometes una tregua?

¿cómo te gustan los huevos,
muerte querida?

ILLUSTRATION

one of the characters in the book is a piece of toast with eyes and a smile
the boy asks if the humans in the book can see the smile on the toast
the mother says they can't
if they could they wouldn't want to eat it
we don't eat the meat of things that smile

ILUSTRACIÓN

uno de los personajes del libro es una tostada con ojos, sonríe
el niño pregunta si los humanos del libro pueden verle la
                                                sonrisa a la tostada

la madre responde que no
si se la vieran no se la querrían comer
no se come carne de aquello que sonríe

JOSELY VIANNA BAPTISTA (Brazil)

Josely Vianna Baptista (b. Curitiba, Brazil, 1957) is a poet, translator of Hispano-American and Amerindian Literature and author of eight books of poetry. In 1996, she created Cadernos da Ameríndia, *a series of Guaraní and Nivacle texts translated into Portuguese. Her poetry has been published widely in South America and Europe and has been included in a number of anthologies in the US. Her work as a translator of Hispano-American literature covers more than a hundred titles by both established and contemporary authors. She currently lives in Florianópolis, Santa Catarina.*

ENGLISH TRANSLATIONS BY CHRIS DANIELS

from AIR / *de* AR

i, wishing a fight, a chimera, th
e odd rigor the rare rhyme, wi
shing menhir and grit, the take
n back retaken, wishing clover a
nd fierce laughter, calm cozin
g, beautiful plaints, caress of d
ishevelled fells, to cry with o
ne eye and laugh with the oth
er; wishing waiting, not delay,
if the west be dark, then east y
our way, wishing war, chase and
amours, every rose without its t
horn. (neon night. the bright i
nside. neon night. the signs. n
eon night. round) all, now, la
ughter, ritual, deleria, shrieks
: love-me-nots in peril, leapfro
gging buildings and logogriphs

❧

queria entreveros e quimeras, v
ários rigores e rimas raras, q
ueria menires e quireras, que o
que desdera se reouvera. queri
a trevos e risos feros, leros
serenos, querelas belas, relar d
e peles arrepiadas, chorar c
om um olho e rir com o outr
o. queria esperas e não demora
s, se o leste escuro o sul segu
ro, queria guerra, caça e amore
s, e por um prazer, sem dores.
(noite neon. o brilho dentro. n
oite neon. dos letreiros. noit
e neon. redondo) tudo agora e
rindo, ritos, delirios, gritos:
bem-me-queria em perigo, ra
sando prédios e logogrifos

❧

```
i  n     d  a  y  b
r  e  a  k     a  c
u  t     e  a  s     a
d  a  g  g  e     r
d  r  i  p  s     w
a     t     e     r
```

❧

```
n  a     m  a  d     r
u  g  a  d  a     a
g  u  d  a     q  u
a  l     a  d  a     g
a     a     á  g  u
a     p  i  n  g  a
```

it's all just
so past artif
ice: it'd be

a fossil if it

weren't an o
nset, a mo
th if not a
missile

isso tudo já
passa de arti
fício: seri

a fóssil, não

fosse iníci
o, seria traç
a, não fosse
míssil

PESSOA TO PERSON

for Arnaldo and Zaba, Maria and Gui

what feels in me thi
nking is what thinks i
n me passing is *what p*
asses in me lying is w
hat lies in me feigni
ng is *what feigns in m*
e sphinx is what sph
inxes me ciphering i
s *what ciphers in me*
creating is what is c
reated loving is *w h*
at loves in me knowi

n g   i s   w h a t   k n o w s   i n
me   s t a y i n g   i s   *w h a t   s*
t a y s   i n   m e   s t a y i n g   i s

D E   P E S S O A   A   P E S S O A

for Arnaldo and Zaba, Maria and Gui

o q u e e m m i m s e n t e e s t á p
e n s a n d o o q u e e m m i m p e
n s a e s t á p a s s a n d o o q u e e
m m i m p a s s a e s t á m e n t i n d o
o q u e e m m i m m e n t e e s t á
f i n g i n d o *o q u e e m m i m f*
i n g e e s t á e s f i n g e o q u e
me e s f i n g e e s t á c i f r a n a d o
o q u e e m m i m c i f r a e s t á
c r i a n d o o q u e s e c r i a e
s t á a m a n d o *o q u e e m m i*
m a m a e s t á s a b e n d o o q u
e e m m i m s a b e e s t á f i c
a n d o *o q u e e m m i m f i c*
a   e s t á   e s t a n d o

M E N H I R   F O
R   K I E F E R

r e c u r r e n t r i
v e r c u r r e n t s i
r r i g a t i n g a t o
m s a n d e t y m s
, r i v e r t i g r i s
a n d r i v e r e u
p h r a t e s (r e v i
s i t e d b y k i e
f e r) b e c o m e t
o u c h , b e c o m
e s h o c k , l e a
d - b o o k s , t o t
e m - b o o k s , d
o l m e n s o f i
m m o b i l e v e r

s e s ,   l e f t   o v
e r   s c r a p s   f r
o m   h i s t o r y ' s
t r a s h ,   p o l l e
n   f r o m   h i s t o
r y ' s   f l o w e r s
,   b e c o m e   m i
r e ,   b e c o m e   v
i r u s   (s e m i r a
m i s   t e l l i n g   t
i m e   o n   a   s u n
d i a l) ,   d o l m e
n s   o f   i m m o b
i l e   v e r s e s ,   m
o n u m e n t   t o   f o
r g e t t i n g   (r i
v e r   t i g r i s   r i
v e   e u p h r a t e
s)   a n d   t o   t
h i n g s   t h a t   l i
v e   i n   t h e   w i

M E N I R   P A R
A   K I E F E R

r e c o r r e n t e s   r
i o c o r r e n t e s   i
r r i g a n d o   á
t o m o s   e   é t i
m o s ,   r i o   t i g
r e   e   r i o   e u
f r a t e s   (r e v i
s i t a d o s   p o r
k i e f e r)   v i r a m
t o q u e ,   v i r a m
c h o q u e ,   l i v r
o s - c h u m b o
,   l i v r o s - t ó t
e m ,   d ó l m e n s
d e   v e r s o s   i m
ó v e i s ,   r e s t o s
d o   l i x o   d a   h
i s t ó r i a ,   p ó
l e n   d e   f l o r e

s d a h i s t ó r
i a , v i r a m l i
m o , v i r a m v í
r u s (s e m í r a
m i s l e n d o a
s h o r a s n u m
r e l ó g i o d e
s o l) , d ó l m e n
s d e v e r s o s
i m ó v e i s , m o
n u m e n t o a o
e s q u e c i m e n t o
(*n i h i l* t i g r
e e r i o e u f
r a t e s) e a o
q u e s e v a i
c o m o v e n t

from CORPOGRAPHY / *de* CORPOGRAFÍA

n o t h i n g ' s n o t h i n g n o t
e v e n a m i s t o f n o t h i n
g : b l a z e i n b l a c k , s p a
r k i n d a r k , l i n e i n f a
u l t , a n d b e t w e e n b l a c
k a n d b l a z e : d a r k , a n d
b e t w e e n d a r k a n d s p a r
k : b l a z e , a n d b e t w e e n
b l a z e a n d b l a c k : f a u l t
, a n d b e t w e e n f a u l t a
n d i - s h e a r s : u n b a l l a
s t e d e y e s , s p o o r o n p
l a n k t o n , d r i f t i n g i n b
l a z e , n e i t h e r g l o w n o
r o a r i n b e r y l - d a r k , u l
t r a m a r i n e , a n d b l a c k i n b
l a z e a n d d a r k i n s p a r k ,
o n l y y o u r s m i l e i n t h e
m i d s t o f n o t h i n g , b l a c k c

loud drawing a blank,
blade-glow and fog-chip, *a*
nd i turned back to me an
d i saw a mist of nothing u
nder the sun: in immemor
y's aerial sand, the wor
d light carved on stone

          e nada e nada, nem név
          oa-nada: o prata em
          preto, o brilho em bre
          u, o risco em falha, e
          entre o preto e o pr
          ata: breu, e entre o b
          reu e o brilho: prat
          a, e entre o prata e
          o preto: falha, e entr
          e a falha, o eu – cisalh
          a olhos sem lastro, r
          astro de plâncton, lúz
          io à deriva sem lume o
          u leme no breu-berilo
          , ultramarino, e o pret
          o em prata e o breu e
          m brilho, só teu sorr
          iso em meio ao nada,
          a nuvem negra em bra
          ncas nuvens, o gume-l
          umbre e a bruma-lasc
          a. *e eu me voltei eu e v*
          i névoa-nada sob o so
          l : na areia aérea da d
          esmemória, a palavra l
          uz gravada na pedra

from BAROQUE SILLIONS / *de* ROÇA BARROCA

SWEAT
the dry pond
sound
the hollow stump
sprout
the fruiting bloom
spread
the powdered pollen

(w o m b)

> SUE
> o secor do poço
> soe
> o oco do cepo
> brote
> o bulbo do fruto
> vente
> o pólen poento
>
> (v e n t r e)

NOMAD MANSIONS

voracious dry rot and termite
gnaw the lath-made shack

from stays hang sheaves of wheat,
charms to fill barns:
broad pans milled grain husks crumble
and hammocks do sway their fray
near the ground where a black stain
bespeaks ancient fire

all abandoned, and, the while,
outside, the seeded orchard
for those who cross now

(empty bundles), one
by one, the eleven thousand
guapuruvus

MORADAS NÔMADES

carunchos e cupins roem,
vorazes, a choupana de ripas;
pendem do esteio ramos de trigo,
feito amuleto para celeiros cheios;
tachos esfarelam crostas de grãos moídos
e redes balançam seus esgarços,
perto do chão onde uma nódoa preta
mostra o antigo fogo

tudo abandono, e, no entanto,
lá fora o pomar semeado
para os que agora cruzam
(trouxas vazias), um
por um, os onze mil
guapuruvus

WORD

be
elán
to
stridor
bestow
the
ode
the
silence
the
name

Guapuruvus: *Schizolobium parahyba,* the Brazilian firetree, or Brazilian fern tree, is
a tree species from tropical America, notable for its fast growth (translator's note).

to
despair
tame
the
fear

VERBO

o
verbo
seja
alento

ao
estridor
doe
a
ode
o
silêncio

o
nome
ao
desespero
dome
o
medo

SUSANA ADA VILLALBA (Argentina)

Susana Ada Villalba (b. 1956) is a poet, playwright, theatre critic, cultural manager and teacher. She has published seven books of poetry, has led a radio program for poetry in the National Library and was a member of the editorial board of the magazine and poetry press Último Reino. Her poetry has been included in a variety of Argentinian and international anthologies and she has participated in numerous international festivals. A recipient of a number of prestigious literary awards, she is currently the Artistic Advisor for the Books, Libraries and Reading Department of the City of Buenos Aires.

ENGLISH TRANSLATIONS BY DAN ELTRINGHAM

from SUSY, SECRETS OF THE HEART*/ de SUSY, SECRETOS DEL CORAZÓN

I KNOW MY REQUEST IS RUSHED

i
i & me
my body & i went to that party
i danced
lovely rich & powerful he caressed
my betty boop my barefoot queen
my name is yonimeri mine too
fury flame you smoke? we went to his place
you're wet i don't know we haven't been introduced
submerged sum of nights weave worsted i was petrified
prophet sentinel i sensed a red car the tobacco blonde
his sturdy back scaling my downfall boundless ill-starred coffees
stones for sleeping he walked me home & i forgot to tell him
words are coins driven into the dirt
susy stories i've always known it
how to make you see what calendar might have caught
the next day lost among the platforms my body fell from floor 29
i forgot to say to him that ever no-one & never me the cowardly loves
crying they don't come because men etcetera
he was pitiless a man all burnt-up with beauty
my body called out like a cat & i envied it but i never
get involved in its affairs
your skin he said baby give me i don't know what which hellish key

Susy, Secrets of the Heart was a Mexican women's magazine published by Editorial Novaro from 1960 (translator's note).

i'd have announced unveiled & paraded a boyfriend
i'd have said to my friends going into any old bar
would've would've that wine would be the death of me
would you look at her so young & necking in the square
o heart if you were to run riot
always sorrow between sorrow & nothingness
my broken body fastened to flotsam odd ritual of spoons on the table
on top of the table in the shower he was water & he scrubbed me
belladonna
strike me at the heart of the mirror's old refrain the shadow
of desire it was lacan sitting on my desk
oh for his study ah for his analysis the climax was seeing
my body too late where were you i asked it
o if only you knew my heart to be a whip & to sleep

SÉ QUE MI PETICIÓN ES PRECIPITADA

yo
yo y mí
yo y mi cuerpo fuimos a esa fiesta
yo bailé
hermoso rico y poderoso rozaba mi cuerpo
mi betty boop mi reina mi descalza
mi nombre es yonimeri yo también
fuego furia ¿fumás? fuimos a su casa
estás mojada no sé no hemos sido presentados
sumergidos suma de noches estera estambres estaba aterrorizada
profeta centinela sentí un automóvil rojo rubio el tabaco
su espalda fuerte trepaba mi caída infinitos funestos cafés
piedras para dormir me acompañaba a casa y olvidé decírselo
las palabras son monedas clavadas a la tierra
historias de susy siempre lo he sabido
cómo explicarte hubiese cupido calendario
perdida en los andenes al día siguiente mi cuerpo caía de un piso 29
olvidé decirle que siempre nadie y yo nunca los amores cobardes
lloraba no llegan porque los hombres etcétera
él era despiadado todo un hombre quemado de belleza
mi cuerpo gemía como un gato y lo envidié pero yo nunca
me meto en sus asuntos
dijo tu piel mi nena dame no sé qué cosa qué llave del infierno
yo hubiese declarado desplegado y estrenado un novio
hubiese dicho a mis amigas entrado en cualquier bar
hubiese hubiese vino que me matara
habráse visto tan chiquita y calentando bancos en la plaza
ay corazón si te fueras de madre

siempre la pena entre la pena y la nada
mi cuerpo roto pegado a lo sumido curioso rito de cucharas en
    la mesa
sobre la mesa en la ducha él era el agua y me frotaba
    belladonna
dame en el centro de lo que siempre habla el espejo la
    sombra
del deseo era lacan sentado en mi escritorio
ah para su estudio oh para su análisis acabar era ver
mi cuerpo demasiado tarde dónde estuviste le decía
ay si supieras corazón ser látigo y dormir

AH! MY BEST FRIEND & MY INTENDED

have the pleasure the good taste to invite you to their ménage a trois that has been arranged who knows if you will want to take our dresses off or take up the gauntlet a challenge to single men a blue garter with a rose the pubic hair an angel is just what we need under the atrium greeted by vagrant fanfares tulips & a little hash if you have any an almost deathly scene your androgynous sine qua non will be afraid tremble almost but smile in blue the colour of your eyes & a translucent emerald cheek will trace the spine down to the wax of your thighs begin to blush but don't miss the velvet begin tangling like a real rattle around the ankle ring jangle your branded bracelet surrender under the shower heno de pravia mingling the furious flow of amber sap the vetiver & the accurate lavender in its tile sculpture the back torturing with one foot sculpted in a sandal seeming wisely surprised at suffering lace about to tear strap casually fallen crawl & stretch out languidly a scribble of rouge returning every so often to an imaginary counterpoint drowsy rolling a cherry yielding plaiting golden thread & wallflowers with haughty eyebrows a perfect opal accustomed to the water's courtship armpit smelling of nutmeg a sprig of rosemary in the mouth & then in other lips between bitter & captivated by such aroma by this point barely dominating gold unshadowed by glass the natural odour of torture rising from the sea with plastered robes ripping apart the not-so-bold in a cry of authentic pearl that bears pleasure like a newborn skin formed around its own imperious heart glowing outwards & not to burn & just because

¡OH, MI MEJOR AMIGA Y MI PROMETIDO!

tienen el agrado el buen gusto de invitar a usted a su menage
a trois que se realizará vaya a saber si usted querrá quitarnos
el vestido o recoger el guante un desafío contra solteros una
liga azul con una rosa el vello púbico un ángel es justo lo que
necesitamos bajo el atrio saludarán trompetas de extravío
tulipanes y un poco de hasch si usted aporta un escenario
casi agónico su andrógino sine qua non que sienta miedo casi
tiemble pero sonría de una manera azul el tono de sus ojos
y la mejilla translúcida esmeralda recorrerá la espina hasta
la cera de sus muslos comience a enrojecer pero no pierda el
terciopelo comience a retorcerse como una verdadera cascabel
en el tobillo haga sonar la esclava dejarse arrinconar bajo la
ducha heno de pravia combinando el flujo rabioso de la savia
ambarina el vetiver y la lavanda precisa en su escultura de
mayólica la espalda atormentarnos con un pie tallado a una
sandalia parecer azorada sabiamente padecer encaje a medio
rasgar bretel caído casualmenate andar a gatas y estirarse
perezosamente un garabato de rouge volverse cada tanto a
un contrapunto imaginario amodorrada rodar una cereza
dejase trenzar hebra de oro y alelíes con el gesto de la ceja
soberbia un ópalo perfecto acostumbrada al cortejo del agua
la axila oliendo a nuez moscada un tallo de romero en la
boca y luego en otros labios entre amargo y fascinada de
tanto olor a esas alturas dominando apenas oro sin sombra
de strass el natural aroma de suplicio naciendo del mar con
túnica adherida desgarrando el no rebelde en un gemido
de auténtica perla que lleva el placer como una piel de
nacimiento alrededor de su propio corazón condesendiente
brillando al exterior para no arder y porque sí

INTRIGUE IN HAWAII

Bitter snakehouses split-screen mirrors not a trace of first hot
love against the cedar dresser over an italian scene hands for
working wood beyond myself i looked at him uncertain i reared
up like a mare stripped bare furious to finish in a coma in a dead
stop tidal notes a beer a beach shack petals & knotted hairs a nest
beating like a talisman i walked i waited steam i dipped my feet
warm hands for working wood firm whoever leaves takes codes
seafaring calends their black sail in flight the fumes forsaken
the poison the next adventure in porto cruel the wind & passion
in a tin can spilled over the fleeting ferrous neck sliced dust

smudged over eyebrows with burnt match with nipples to the
south whiter abstracted i walked all that he left alone but i didn't
come back not even for his open zipper leaving behind hair from
working wood my mouth swelled like a vampire ungainly in
new orleans addicted to nothing much comics nunchaku woven
wool hairy chest arms so italian the bar forms of fidelity the
she-wolf of the hood doesn't marry ever breeches lilacs boiling
the crack is hitting hard every two minutes hard working wood
whoever is leaving & i went back taking the highways taking
things that were so seventies impala platinum blonde i went
back belligerent with magazines for him i kneeled ignited drew
a circle drew on the hookah pipe in a shirt beads positions of
the rosary it ends with the head rhythmically drags beasts along
the beach epouvantable libre his mane such a beast his black
hide puffed up before the fire panic in his eyes i'm too still my
style my study my goddam intellectual waif i can't bear you on
magnetic tape magnificent onslaught sicilian sap it burned weak
tall-tale gut katmandu pose pose magnetic counterpose copper
thin so many books make me a mare a heavy stone in your bed
strap me to your heart too long savage too much i went back &
i said marry me pagans in june all in white candles clay tunics
the streets i raised myself dead natural it was raining but i was
never poor & your hands love working the wood they turn me
on more than joyce i swear it i'll stake it on your tarot cards a
watercolour washes away heavy summer storm pulled the roof
off say nothing leave me engulf me rough raw skin philosophic
cave where i see the shadow of your dance & your body is more
is more than i can stand

INTRIGA EN HAWAII

Serpentarios agrios espejos separados en cámara sin vestigio
de primer amor caliente contra el tocador de cedro sobre un
escenario italiano manos de tallar fuera de mí lo miraba sin
saber me hinchaba como una yegua desposeída furiosa de
acabar en coma en punto muerto claves de marea una cerveza
un tugurio en la playa pétalos y pelos nudos un nido latía
como un talismán caminé esperé vapor mojé los pies caliente
manos de tallar fuerte quien se va se lleva códigos calendas
marineras fuga su vela negra el humo abandonado el veneno
la próxima aventura en oporto cruel el viento y la pasión en
un tazón de lata derramado cortado el cuello fugaz ferroso
el polvo sobre cejas con fósforo quemado con pezones al sur

más blanco ausente caminé todo lo que él dejaba solo pero
no vloví ni por su jean abierto dejando pelo de tallar la boca
hinchaba como un vampiro torpe en nueva orleans adicto a
poca cosa historietas nunchaku lana de pelos en el pecho en
los brazos tan italiano la barra formas de fidelidad la loba
del barrio no se casa nunca calzas lilas hirviendo el crack
está pegando fuerte cada dos minutos fuerte talla quien se
va y yo volví por carreteras por cosas muy seventy en impala
en rubia platinada volví en pistola con revistas para él me
arrodillé encendí tracé ciírculo aspiré el narguile en camisa
cuentas posturas del rosario acaba en la cabeza arrastra
cadencioso animales por la playa epouvantable free tan
bestia su crin su cuero negro encabritado ante el fuego sabía
pánico en los ojos demasiado quieta mi estilo mi bachiller
mi guacha intelectual no te soporto en cinta magnetofónica
embestida magnífica savia siciliana me quemaba entraña
flaca de cuento chino postura postura de katmandú
contrapostura magnética flaca de cobre tantos libros una
casa haceme una yegua una pesada piedra en tu cama atame
a tu corazón demasiado tiempo salvaje demasiado volví y
dije casate conmigo paganos en junio todo blanco velas
túnicas de barro las calles yo me críe natural muerta llovía
pero nunca fui pobre y tus manos amor tallando la madera
me calientan más que joyce te lo juro te lo juego con naipes
de tarot se disuelve una acuarela fuerte tormenta de verano
arrancaba el techo no digas nada lasciame abissame áspero
cruda piel caverna filosófica donde veo la sombra de tu baile
y tu cuerpo es más es más de lo que puedo soportar

from KILLING AN ANIMAL / *de* MATAR UN ANIMAL

THE PANTHER

Killing an animal
calls for an animal
without shadow.
You're walking in the hills
or so you think, you don't know where you are;
you think you knew
when you arrived.
That black
could well be a panther
or woman,

you don't realise.
You like its savage gaze,
no, it turns you on.
No, it fixes you
like one who doesn't know
where they are.
You're already lost,
you'd have to take it home
but you know how it ends:
a wounded animal
always attacks.
You'd have to kill it,
now,
before it's too late
or out of pity.
But that gaze is a trap,
if it is a panther
it knows better than you
how to kill.
Here no-one knows
your name
and now he
or woman turns its back on you.
You think about a short-range
light
Remington.
But no-one would hear,
Red Hot distracts them,
and you too.
And one doesn't kill from behind,
you've seen it in movies
or that's something you believe in.
Killing
is another matter.
It looks at you now and you know
you'll take it home.
It is touched by grace,
it is in sight
or that's how you see it, you're unsure,
or there is something about it

you think you understand.
And yet
you know how it ends:
you don't know how
it hurt you while loving you.
You don't want to approach,
it narrows its eyes
and looks at you as cats do.
It leans against the rail
in front of you,
you're both lost.
You think about the Remington,
you never had one.
Killing is different.
No-one seems to understand it,
not even the black panther
but it sees that you're holding a cigarette
in your hand
and another lit
in the ashtray;
it comes over and smokes it.
You're lost,
you think you know how this ends
and you get it wrong again,
it puts out the cigarette
and splits.
Now there is no-one
who resembles your desire.
And yet nor did it.
A panther astray
in its memory
or gaze
or whatever it was
that you'll never know.
You hail a cab thinking
such beauty is not the motive,
it's the alibi.
To kill a panther
you have to shut your eyes.

LA PANTERA

Matar al animal
requiere un animal
sin sombra.
Vas caminando por un monte
o te parece, no sabés dónde estás;
creés que lo sabías
cuando llegaste.
Ese negro
bien puede ser una pantera
o mujer,
no te das cuenta.
La mirada salvaje te gusta,
no, te calienta.
No, te mira
como quien no comprende
dónde está.
Ya estás perdida,
tendrías que llevarla a tu casa
pero sabés cómo termina:
un animal herido
siempre ataca.
Tendrías que matarla,
ahora,
antes de que sea tarde
o por piedad.
Pero esa mirada es una trampa,
si es pantera
sabe matar mejor
que vos.
Nadie sabe tu nombre
aquí
y ahora él
o mujer te da la espalda.
Pensás en un Remington
liviano
de distancia corta.
Pero nadie escucharía,
Red Hot los distrae,
a vos también.
Y no se mata por la espalda,
lo viste en las películas
o creés en eso.
Matar
es otra cosa.
Ahora te mira y ya sabés,

vas a llevarla a tu casa.
Está tocado por la gracia,
está a la vista
o vos lo ves, no estás segura,
o tiene algo
que creés comprender.
Y sin embargo
sabés cómo termina:
no sabés cómo
te hirió si te quería.
No querés acercarte,
te mira como miran los gatos
cerrando los ojos.
Se apoya en la barra
frente a vos,
los dos están perdidos.
Pensás en el Remington,
nunca tuviste uno.
Matar es otra cosa.
Nadie parece comprenderlo,
el negro tampoco pero ve
que tenés un cigarrillo
en la mano
y otro ardiendo
en el cenicero;
se acerca y lo fuma.
Estás perdida,
creés saber cómo termina
y volvés a equivocarte,
apaga el cigarrillo
y se va.
Ahora nadie
se parece a tu deseo.
Y es que no se parecía.
Una pantera perdida
en su memoria
o forma de mirar
o lo que fuera
que no vas a saber.
Tomás un taxi pensando
demasiada belleza no es el móvil,
es la coartada.
Para matar a una pantera
hay que cerrar los ojos.

from PRAYERS / *de* PLEGARIAS

ELECTION SUNDAY AT SHELL SELECT TANGO

It's all a wall on which life flakes away in a single phrase: Happy birthday, hold on Brukman,* fucking Cuervo. All on a single plane, all flat, coal, chalk, aerosol. If you were to play in heaven Charly would die, Damas for free, dirty Rocas. At times a glimmer of words mysterious as rocks, like mica in stones, yellow-leafed lanes, rubble in the street. Made of which rocks in this plain's crushing plainness, the sky dirty lead from the weariness of Sunday rain. A word smudged out drips on the cartridges scattered on the floor, the recent rounds write themselves as holes in the brick. Rainbow Father, crazy old Viejas, thieving Pibes. All one shot, one take. A stain like men round a fire, like thousand-year-night dogs.

By day the city wakes and everyone goes about as though reading an ultraviolet signal, hereditary, score, like flies, as if passing through turnstiles. Fenced towards an opening to wager what they had anyway already lost. A chalkboard life, between a TV and here. Hardly any time since, five centuries, three reflections, a somebody painted this caravan of the blind on the abyss, on the echo of the ravine. Behind that wall against which they smash.

Chaca forever, I love you Sebi, Los Tarijas stones. Maybe not enough blood, more so, that it would credit that custom of filming horizontally imagining it's an inclined plane, vertical life, the earth a swoon of the sky, Lord, it is going to end. I don't hear

Brukman is a textile factory in Buenos Aires, Argentina, which since 18 December 2001 is under the control of the "18 de diciembre" worker cooperative. Founded by the Brukman brothers, the factory suffered during the Argentinian economic crisis in the 1990s, leading to redundancies and wage reductions. From 18 December 2001, Brukman became one of the best-known of Argentina's "recovered factories", when employees – most of them women – occupied the factory in order to negotiate their demands. When the Brukman brothers failed to return, the workers went into production as a cooperative. Attempts to evict the workers have been successfully resisted by popular mobilization (translator's note).

your voice thunder, if it is a voice, I don't see the wall coming apart, the world or someone in some place. Sometime I'd like to see something different, unexpected ending, mysterious words, rebellion that doesn't bite the dust of the tail end to fall one at a time to the bottom. If it were possible in this century. If it were possible in this world.

Ma terre, mother of sorrows. The one that devours its children, bodies hurl themselves like rocks. I understand, Lord, that some things you don't allow us to choose but to never be more than humanity, more than this clay that kneads as it crumbles, like a rib that breaks off from its soul, bread-brain that slips splashing its little paws upwards, its back submerged, looking again at the tip of the whip to see whether it will be rescued in reverse. For the umpteenth century, place, for the umpteenth life, time, same words.

They vote for the gathering packed on the pavement, in the foyer. Grass, gravel, pebble for playing payana, toad counter, chair, line, cent. The blind have it worse, the deaf who can't hear that waltz, that fanfare of courtly chores. Words on a poster that set fire to a stream, a repeating word-weapon. The pavement attorneys file by, managers of little kiosks, little figures clipped together, pinned-down ideas, little heads like sieves with bag and handle, cards already marked.

El Ciclón, Almas Mugrientas, Santa Revuelta, El Bananazo, the Brukman factory to its workers. Hardly any time ago the people looked after it, now they support the eviction. Just as only yesterday it was Carlos V on the throne, sacred empire, Byzantine or British, Roman, majestic. The syntactic empire that trembles now while somewhere it rains, here, at this corner, in front of a wall. Sons of the son, Patria Chuker, Trujamán.

Our tearful mother, the fumes hardly clear. In this corner, Campeón, we're gonna fuck up the chicks. Cocksure in this waste. Soaked little chickens in the cold. They vote for the cage or the chop, conveyor belt through a ravine. Life's hypnotized progress, the first salvation is that of the body, Lord, remind us of the soul every now and then. In brighter, gentler times. If possible, this year. This life, if possible.

DOMINGO DE ELECCIONES EN LA SHELL SELECT TANGO

Todo es una pared en que se ve descascarar la vida en una sola frase: Feliz cumple, aguante Brukman, Cuervo puto. Un solo plano todo, todo plano, carbón, tiza, aerosol. Si tocaras en el cielo moriría Charly, Damas gratis, Rocas sucias. A veces un destello de palabras misteriosas como rocas, como mica en las piedras, veredas de hojas amarillas, cascotes en la calle. De qué rocas en esta planicie de llaneza aplastante, el cielo un plomo sucio del hastío de la lluvia del domingo. Se borronea una palabra, gotea en los cartuchos dispersos en el suelo, los disparos recientes se escriben como huecos del ladrillo. Padre Rainbow, Viejas locas, Pibes chorros. Todo un plano, una toma. Una mancha como hombres alrededor de una fogata, como perros de una noche de mil años.

De día se levanta una ciudad y todos van como leyendo un llamado ultravioleta, hereditario, partitura, como moscas, como entrando en molinetes. Vallados hacia una ventanilla a apostar lo que total ya no tenían. Una vida de pizarra, de una tele para acá. Apenas hace nada, cinco siglos, tres reflejos, un alguien pintó esa caravana de ciegos al abismo, al eco del barranco. Detrás de esa pared en que se estrellan.

Por siempre Chaca, Sebi te amo, Los Tarijas stones. Acaso falta sangre, más aún, que abone esa costumbre de rodar horizontal imaginando que es un plano inclinado, la vida vertical, la tierra un vértigo del cielo, se va a acabar, Señor. No escucho que truene tu voz, si es una voz, no veo quebrarse la pared, el mundo o alguno en parte alguna. Alguna vez quisiera ver algo distinto, final inesperado, palabras misteriosas, rebelión que no se muerda el polvo de la cola para ir a caer de a uno en fondo. Si fuera posible en este siglo. Si fuera posible en este mundo.

Ma terre, mater dolorosa. El que devora a sus hijos, cuerpos se arrojan como rocas. Señor, entiendo que no nos dejes elegir algunas cosas pero nunca ser más que humanidad, más que este barro que amasa como miga, como costilla que se quiebra de su alma, cerebro de pan que se resbala chapoteando las patitas hacia arriba, el lomo hundido, la mirada a la punta del látigo otra vez a ver si lo rescata para atrás. Por enésimo siglo, lugar, por enésima vida, vez, palabras mismas.

Se vota por la fiesta que se mira apiñado en la vereda, en el zaguán. Gramilla, ripio, guijarro de payana, ficha de sapo, silla, fila, centavo. Peor están los ciegos, los sordos que no escuchan ese vals, esa fanfarria de fajina cortesana. Palabras de cartel que prenden un reguero, un arma frase de repetición. Desfilan los fiscales de veredas, gerentes de kiosquitos, figuritas en clips, ideas con alfileres, cabecitas de tacho con palo y a la bolsa, con las cartas marcadas.

El Ciclón, Almas Mugrientas, Santa Revuelta, El Bananazo, la Brukman a sus trabajadores. Apenas hace nada la gente la cuidaba, ahora apoya el desalojo. Apenas hace igual el hombre como ahora asumía Carlos V, imperio sacro, bizantino o británico, romano, mayestático. El imperio sintáctico que ahora titila mientras llueve en algún lado, en este lado, en esta esquina, frente a un muro. Hijos del hijo, Patria Chuker, Trujamán.

Nuestra Mater lacrimosa, apenas los gases se disipan. En esta esquina Campeón, le vamo a hacer el culo a las galli. Gallito de baldío. Pollitos mojados bajo el frío. Se vota entre la barra de la jaula o el deguello, en un desfiladero como a cuerda. La marcha hipnotizada de la vida, la primera salvación es la del cuerpo, Señor, recuérdanos el alma cada tanto. En tiempos más soleados, más amables. En este año si es posible. Si es posible en esta vida.

ÉRICA ZÍNGANO (Brazil)

Érica Zíngano (b. Fortaleza-CE, Brazil, 1980) is a poet with a number of poetry books and an artist's book to her name. In 2019, having lived in Europe for almost 8 years, she decided to go back to Brazil and is currently completing her PhD in Comparative Literature at the Federal University of Ceará, focusing on Brazilian Literature. As well as being a poet, her work also extends to other areas such as visual arts and performance.

ENGLISH TRANSLATIONS BY LOTTA THIESSEN & MARTY HIATT

METAPHYSICAL PROBLEMS / PROBLEMAS METAFÍSICOS

for Heitor Ferraz

1

The Chicken is a step ahead
of the Egg
in the fight over who is leading
the race
of who came first
"The Egg has fallen behind
the Chicken again", an English study
from Sheffield University
announced
a few days ago
Because the shell of the Egg
is composed of a protein
(ovocledidin-17 or OC-17)
found in the ovaries
of Chickens
it has been confirmed
THE CHICKEN CAME FIRST
A supercomputer
dubbed HECToR by its operators
was used to follow
the stages of the
Egg shell's formation:
researchers were then able
to verify the presence of OC-17
right at the beginning of the process

This protein is responsible
for the transformation
of the calcium carbonate
into calcite crystals
– which make up
the egg shell –
Dr. Colin Freeman
of the Department of Materials
Engineering, declared
"It had long been suspected that
the Egg came first,
but now
we have the scientific proof
that shows
in fact
the Chicken came first"

  2

In response
a new version
of the Egg is being launched
as announced in a
half-page newspaper ad
EGG LIGHT®
from white
to barn raised
to free range
to factory farmed
now the Egg
can be diet too
Technology
in service of
consumer health:
Transgenic Egg
Transfigured Egg
Industrialised Egg
genetically
and genuinely

transformed
for you
no more worries
about high
cholesterol
Eat without guilt
no more heart
problems
half as many calories
because now the Egg is another
The flavour is unchanged
e-x-a-c-t-l-y-t-h-e-s-a-m-e
       (INSANE)
Try it yourself
feel your life become
lighter, healthier
and much more
EGG LIGHT®

     ≈

para Heitor Ferraz

     1

A Galinha anda mais em alta
do que o Ovo
na disputa pela liderança
do ranking
de quem veio antes
do quê
"O Ovo voltou a ficar atrás
da Galinha", divulgou
há alguns dias
uma pesquisa inglesa
da Universidade de Sheffield
Como a casca do Ovo
é composta por uma proteína
(ovocledidin-17 ou OC-17)
encontrada nos ovários
das Galinhas
ficou comprovado
AS GALINHAS VIERAM PRIMEIRO
Um super computador
apelidado pelos seus de HECToR

foi utilizado para acompanhar
as etapas de formação
da casca do Ovo:
os pesquisadores puderam, então,
constatar a presença da OC-17
logo no início do processo
Essa proteína é responsável
pela transformação
do carbonato de cálcio
em cristais de calcita
– elementos que compõem
a casa do Ovo –
O Dr. Colin Freeman
do Departamento de Engenharia
de Materiais, declarou
"há muito tempo se suspeitava de que
o Ovo tivesse vindo primeiro
mas agora
temos a prova científica definitiva
de que na verdade
a Galinha foi a precursora"

    2

Em contrapartida
o Ovo é relançado
no mercado
em nova versão
anuncia a propaganda
em meia página
de jornal
OVO LIGHT®
do branco
ao caipira
do pé duro
ao de granja
agora o Ovo
também é light
A tecnologia
a favor
da saúde
do consumidor:
Ovo transgênico
Ovo transfigurado
Ovo industrializado
genético
& genuinamente

transformado
para você
não mais se preocupar
com os altos índices
de colesterol
Coma sem culpa
nada mais de problemas
cardiológicos
as calorias foram reduzidas
a mais da metade
porque agora o Ovo é outro
O sabor não muda nada
c-o-n-t-i-n-u-a-i-g-u-a-l
    (GENIAL)
Experimente você também
e sinta sua vida se tornar
mais leve, mais diet
muito mais
OVO LIGHT®

FIOS DE OVOS TO GO

for my grandmother

my grandmother died before
she could teach me to cook
she also didn't teach
my mother how to cook
my mother is left handed
and there was no way
it would work out in the kitchen
my grandmother would say
and my mother would repeat it
explaining to me why
it took her so long
to learn to cook
(my mother doesn't complain
about my grandmother because these days
my mother knows how to cook
even though she's left handed)
even though she died before
she could teach me to cook

my grandmother tried
to teach me to cook
once when i was around eight
it was a complete disaster
I went to pick up
the hot kettle with a cloth
to add water to the rice
and the cloth caught fire
and there was a little fire
in my grandmother's kitchen
but she had it quickly under control
she was always ready to deal with anything
something my grandmother did
very well was fios de ovos
every Christmas we had fios de ovos
with crystallized fruit and turkey
served with cereser cider
before supper it was a feast
I always remember
her making fios de ovos
in the kitchen sadly
my mother never learned
to make fios de ovos with my grandmother
nor did my grandmother have time
to teach me how to make fios de ovos
which is the hardest thing in the world
and then to make it every Christmas
I always buy them pre-made
I ask for fios de ovos to go
but they never taste quite like
my grandmother's fios de ovos
the longing I have for
my grandmother is a longing
for the fios de ovos of my grandmother
I think my brother longs
for my grandmother differently
but we never talk about that

FIOS DE OVOS PRA VIAGEM

para a minha avó

a minha avó morreu antes
de me ensinar a cozinhar
ela também não ensinou
a minha mãe a cozinhar
a minha mãe é canhota
e não tinha a menor chance
de dar certo na cozinha
dizia a minha avó
repetia a minha mãe
me explicando o porquê
de ter demorado tanto
pra aprender a cozinhar
(a minha mãe não se lamenta
da minha avó porque hoje
a minha mãe já sabe cozinhar
mesmo sendo canhota)
mesmo tendo morrido antes
de me ensinar a cozinhar
a minha avó uma vez tentou
me ensinar a cozinhar
quando eu tinha mais ou menos
oito anos de idade
foi um desastre completo
porque quando eu fui pegar
a chaleira quente com um pano
pra colocar água no arroz
o pano começou a pegar fogo
e fez um pequeno incêndio
na cozinha da minha avó
coisa que ela controlou muito
rápido porque estava ali
por perto administrando tudo
coisa que a minha avó fazia
muito bem era fios de ovos
todo natal tinha fios de ovos
com frutas cristalizadas no peru
pra tomar com sidra cereser
antes da ceia era uma festa
tenho sempre essa lembrança
dela fazendo fios de ovos
na cozinha infelizmente
a minha mãe não aprendeu

a fazer fios de ovos com a minha avó
nem a minha avó teve tempo
de me ensinar a fazer fios de ovos
que são a coisa mais difícil do mundo
de fazer então todo natal
eu sempre compro pronto
peço fios de ovos pra viagem
mas eles nunca têm o sabor
dos fios de ovos da minha avó
as saudades que eu tenho
da minha avó são as saudades
dos fios de ovos da minha avó
acho que o meu irmão tem saudades
diferentes da minha avó
mas nunca conversamos sobre isso

GENDER THEORY

this poem is, how could it not be, dedicated to my mother

Lyrica® is a fibromyalgia medication that my mother takes every night (before going to sleep) when she is having a crisis. Fibromyalgia is a kind of rheumatism, but of the muscles, tendons and ligaments. Among other symptoms it causes pain, fatigue and discomfort. Besides taking Lyrica® (every night) before going to sleep, my mother does three sessions of physiotherapy a week. It reduces the pain significantly, she says assuredly. Lyrica® is produced by Pfizer™, a large pharmaceutical company that is a market leader in cardiac medication: Norvasc®, for example, which my mother also takes (every night before going to sleep), is without doubt the top selling blood-pressure medication. From North America, Pfizer™ became famous around the world for producing Viagra®, which, for reasons of gender incompatibility, my mother of course does not take.

(this poem was written with data taken from Google Inc. and the poet bears no responsibility for the accuracy of the information provided. Unfortunately the poem seems like publicity for Pfizer™. Despite this, she insists that it was not her primary intention to make a publicity poem. She merely wanted to pay homage to her mother's medication regime. If she has failed in this, she offers her apologies and declares that she will keep on trying)

TEORIA DOS GÊNEROS

este poema é, e não haveria como não ser, dedicado à minha mãe

Lyrika® é um remédio contra fibromialgia que a minha mãe toma todas as noites (antes de dormir) quando está em período de crise. A fibromialgia é uma espécie de reumatismo – só que dos músculos, tendões e ligamentos – e causa dor, fadiga, indisposição, dentre outros sintomas. Além de tomar o Lyrika® (todas as noites) antes de dormir, a minha mãe faz três sessões de fisioterapia por semana, o que ajuda a diminuir bastante a dor, afirma convicta. O Lyrika® é fabricado pela Pfizer™, empresa do ramo farmacêutico responsável por arrematar a maior fatia do mercado de medicamentos para o coração: o Norvasc®, por exemplo, que a minha mãe também toma (todas as noites antes de dormir), é, sem dúvida, o mais vendido para pressão alta. De origem norte-americana, a Pfizer™ tornou-se conhecida em todo o mundo pela fabricação do Viagra®, que, por incompatibilidade de gênero, claro, a minha mãe não toma.

(esse poema foi escrito com dados retirados do Google Inc. e a poeta se exime da responsabilidade pela veiculação de quaisquer dessas informações. infelizmente, parece que o poema está fazendo propaganda para a Pfizer™, apesar de parecer, ela garante que a intenção primeira desse poema não era a de fazer propaganda nenhuma, mas a de fazer uma singela homenagem aos hábitos medicamentosos de sua mãe – se falhou em tal empreitada, pede desculpas, e avisa que continuará tentando)

PHILOSOPHICAL ELUCUBRATIONS

for Andréa Catrópa

knorr stock – who knows
if the real truth
is always
an empty dish
that you can't even serve cold
like expired revenge
I ask myself while
the wooden spoon
turns, turns
my hand

on the black
unreflective teflon
beets and potatoes
tomatoes badly cut
into cubes
carrots onions little pumpkins
the smell of old fat
the fan
on my nerves, the range hood
is on – insistent
               saying knorr stock
do you know
if in this seasoning
full of monosodium
glutamate
antioxidants
steam
and the dust of day
I can find
one of my most recent portraits?
little bubbles of oil sinking
ants in the chicken
bone
its own blood
without feathers
clots
to thicken the broth
scarlet reinforcements
paprika
and red peppers
a little salt or a lot
the customer is king
and finally (grand finale)
a sprinkle of parsley, or ashes
from a cigarette
there's no secret to this recipe
but I give up eating – alone

ELUCUBRAÇÕES FILOSÓFICAS

para Andréa Catrópa

caldo knorr – who knows
se a verdade, verdadeira
é sempre um prato
vazio
que nem se come frio
como a vingança vencida
pergunto enquanto
a colher de pau
gira, gira
a minha mão
contra o teflon preto
sem reflexo
beterrabas e batatas tomate
mal cortado
em cubos
cenoura cebolas abobrinhas
cheiro de gordura velha
a ventoinha
nos nervos, exaustor
ligado - insistente
        me diz caldo knorr
do you know
se nesse tempero
cheio de glutamato
monossódico
antioxidantes
vapor
e poeira do dia
eu posso encontrar
um dos meus últimos retratos?
pequenas bolhas d'óleo descem
formigas no osso
da galinha
o próprio sangue
sem penas
coágulos
para engrossar o caldo
mais reforço escarlate
colorau
e pimentões vermelhos
pouco ou muito sal

é o gosto do freguês
por fim (grand finale)
salpico salsinha, são cinzas
de cigarro
não tem segredo essa receita
mas desisto de comer – sozinha

FOR STARTERS

"no, i'm not against autobiographies i have
nothing against anything, nothing against any-
one" when people ask me where i come from
i say i was born in brazil that doesn't explain much
they say they've never been there i answer me nei-
ther they don't understand what i'm saying and
think that i don't speak good english i don't speak
good english but when i say i've never been there
i do i was on the bus with an argentinian friend
and a blond whitey with a walkman in his ears
was looking at us and laughing and saying "jupen"
it took me half a day to understand that he was
calling us "juden" i'd already understood he was
insulting us when we got off the bus he started
hammering on the door i am jewish every day
when i enter my house KZ 3 [ka: ʦɛt draɪ] is
written below the 2 apples it was my new peru-
vian friend who taught me more about politics
every day and also that time with the photos of
the africans at oranienplatz when i leave my house
i am also jewish every day tsvetaeva wants to have
her say and says that all poets are jewish the poems
sign themselves jews slaves mulattos brown muslim
(and so on) i am joaquín hernández rodríguez javier
and i cheer for uruguay si me gustaba el fútbol
pero este mes estoy haciendo dieta, perdón
stick / stick / stone / stone / palestinian / palestinian
– start over start at the bit with national identities
justify /this poem is not merely an illustrative form

PRA COMEÇO DE CONVERSA

"não, não tenho nada contra autobiografias
não tenho nada contra nada, nada contra nin-
guém" quando as pessoas me perguntam de
onde eu venho eu digo que nasci no brasil isso
não explica muito elas dizem que nunca esti-
veram lá eu respondo eu também não elas não
entendem o que eu digo pensam que eu falei
inglês errado eu falo inglês errado mas quando
eu digo que nunca estive lá eu digo corretamen-
te eu estava andando com um amigo argentino
no ônibus e um lôro branquelo com walkman
no ouvido ficava olhando pra gente e rindo e
dizendo „jupen" eu demorei metade de um dia
pra entender que ele tava xingando a gente de
„juden" eu já tinha entendido que ele tava xin-
gando a gente na parte quando a gente desceu
do ônibus ele deu um cotoco na minha porta eu
sou judia todos os dias quando eu entro na mi-
nha porta está escrito KZ 3 [ka: ʦɛt draɪ]
embaixo das 2 maçãs foi a minha nova amiga
peruana que me ensinou mais política todo dia
também na parte as fotos dos africanos na ora-
nienplatz quando eu saio da minha porta eu
também sou judia todos os dias a tsvetaeva
pede a palavra e diz que todos os poetas são
judeus os poemas assinam judeus escravos
mulatos pardos muçulmanos (continua)
eu sou joaquín hernández rodríguez javier e
torço para o uruguay si me gustaba el fútbol
pero este mes estoy haciendo dieta, perdón
pau / pau / pedra / pedra / palestino / palestino
– comece tudo outra vez recomece na parte
identidades nacionais justifique / este poema
não é meramente um formulário ilustrativo

ABOUT THE EDITORS

Juana Adcock is a Mexican poet, translator and editor based in Scotland. Her Spanish-language poetry collection, *Manca*, explores the anatomy of violence in the Mexican drug war. Her English-language collection *Split* (Blue Diode Press, 2019) was a Poetry Book Society Choice and was included in the *Guardian*'s Best Poetry of 2019. She is currently translating the Mè'phàà poet Hubert Matiúwàa's *The Dogs Dreamt* (Flipped Eye, forthcoming, spring 2023) and Laura Wittner's *Translation of the Route* (Poetry Translation Centre, forthcoming autumn 2023).

Jèssica Pujol Duran (Barcelona, 1982) is a poet, translator and researcher, currently working as Assistant Professor at the University of Santiago de Chile. She writes and translates in Catalan, English and Spanish, and edits the magazine *Alba Londres* (www.albalondres.com). She has three chapbooks in English, *Now Worry* (Department, 2012), *Every Bit of Light* (Oystercatcher Press, 2012) and *Mare* (Carnaval Press, 2018); two books in Catalan, *El país pintat* (Pont del petroli, 2015) and *ninó,* (Pont del petroli, 2019), and two in Spanish, *Entrar es tan difícil salir* (Veer Books, 2016), with translations by William Rowe, and *El campo envolvente* (LP5 Editora, 2021).

ABOUT THE TRANSLATORS

JUANA ADCOCK is a Mexican poet, translator and editor based in Scotland… *see* 'About the Editors' *on p. 327*

RAHUL BERY translates from Spanish and Portuguese and is based in Cardiff, Wales. His full-length translations are *Rolling Fields*, by David Trueba and *Kokoschka's Doll*, by Afonso Cruz and his work has appeared in *Granta, The White Review, Words Without Borders, Partisan Hotel*, the *TLS* and elsewhere. In 2018-2019 he was translator in residence at the British Library.

DANIEL BORZUTZKY is a poet and translator who lives in Chicago. His most recent book is *Written After a Massacre in the Year 2018*. His 2016 collection, *The Performance of Becoming Human* won the National Book Award. *Lake Michigan* (2018) was a finalist for the Griffin International Poetry Prize. His translation of Galo Ghigliotto's *Valdivia* won the 2017 National Translation Award, and he has also translated collections by Paula Ilabaca Nuñez, Raúl Zurita, and Jaime Luis Huenún. He teaches at the University of Illinois at Chicago.

DAVID BRUNSON's poems and translations have appeared in or are forthcoming from *Copper Nickel, ANMLY, Mānoa: A Pacific Journal of International Writing, Booth, Washington Square Review, The American Journal of Poetry, On the Seawall, Poetry Online, The Bitter Oleander, Nashville Review, Asymptote, DIAGRAM, Vassar Review, The Inflectionist Review, Journal of Italian Translation, The Literary Review*, and elsewhere. He is the editor and translator of *A Scar Where Goodbyes Are Written: An Anthology of Venezuelan Poets in Chile*.

WENDY CALL is co-editor of the craft anthology *Telling True Stories: A Nonfiction Writers' Guide*, author of the award-winning book *No Word for Welcome: The Mexican Village Faces the Global Economy*, and translator of *In the Belly of Night and Other Poems* by Irma Pineda (Pluralia, 2021). She was a 2018-19 Fulbright Scholar in Colombia and teaches creative writing and interdisciplinary studies at Pacific Lutheran University. She lives in Seattle, on Duwamish land.

CHRIS DANIELS was born in New York City in 1956 and has lived in the San Francisco Bay Area since 1981. He is a prolific translator of Lusophone poetry. His work has appeared in *The San Jose Manual of Style, syllogism, 26, LVNG, -Vert, Prosodia, Antenym, nocturne, Urvox, Chain* and *Kenning.* His translations of Fernando Pessoa were featured in *Crayon 3* and he has also translated the Brazilian modernist poet Murilo Mendes.

DAN ELTRINGHAM is a researcher, poet and translator currently working on a comparative research project, *Translating Resistance.* Recent poetry and (co)translations have appeared in a range of journals and anthologies. His translation of selections from the Canarian modernist Alonso Quesada's *Scattered Ways* was published by Free Poetry (Boise, 2019) and his poetry collection *Cairn Almanac* was published by Hesterglock Press (Bristol, 2017). With Leire Barrera-Medrano, he co-edits Girasol Press, a small publisher that explores handmade poetics and experimental translation.

ADRIAN FISHER (see under LUNA MONTENEGRO)

MARIA ROSE GIMENEZ is a Venezuelan-Canadian poet, translator, and editor working in Spanish, English, and French whose work has received support from the NEA, the Studios at MASS MoCA, the Breadloaf Translators' Conference, Canada Council for the Arts, and the Banff International Literary Translation Centre. Author of the chapbooks *chelated* (Belladonna*) and *entretanto,* and 2019–2021 Poet Laureate of Easthampton, Massachusetts, María José is the co-translator (with Anna Rosenwong) of Mara Pastor's bilingual collection *Deuda Natal,* winner of the 2020 American Academy of Poets Ambroggio Prize. More at mariajosetranslates.com.

SAMUEL GRAY is a poet and translator based in Portland, Oregon. His translations can be found in previous issues of *International Poetry Review, Words Without Borders* and *Washington Square Review..*

MARTY HIATT is a poet and translator from Narrm, Melbourne, now living in Berlin. He works with Artichoke Reading Series (https://artichokereadings.com), and runs Baulk Press (https://baulkpress.tumblr.com). He is the translator of Nathalie Quintane's *Tomatoes* (Kenning Editions, 2022) and his recent poetry books include *Notes Away*, *Paraphrenia* (Materials / Materialien, UK / DE), *Back to Noise*, *The Manifold* and *Hard-line*. (https://anarchive.mooo.com).

ANNIE McDERMOTT is a literary translator working from Spanish and Portuguese into English. Her recent translations include *The Luminous Novel* and *Empty Words* by Mario Levrero, *Brickmakers* and *Dead Girls* by Selva Almada and *The Wind Whistling in the Cranes* by Lídia Jorge (co-translation with Margaret Jull Costa). Her work has been shortlisted for the Premio Valle-Inclán and the Harvill Secker Young Translators' Prize. She has previously lived in Mexico and Brazil and is now based in Hastings, in the UK.

LUNA MONTENEGRO and ADRIAN FISHER are London-based poets, performers and visual artists working under the collective name mmmmm and the pen name montenegrofisher. They collaborate in making text, visual and sonic interventions, films, hybrid-language-actions, installations and curatorial projects. Their work investigates ideas of locality, transformation and ritual, exploring spaces, borders, translations and bridges between the political and the poetic. Since 2000, they have shown their work internationally in art galleries, museums, residences, festivals, site-specific projects, publications, internet and radio.

JÈSSICA PUJOL DURAN is a poet, translator and researcher, currently working as Assistant Professor at the University of Santiago de Chile… *see* 'About the Editors' *on p. 327.*

JD PLUECKER is a language worker who writes, translates, organizes, interprets, and creates. Pluecker's undisciplinary work is informed by non-normative poetics, language justice, radical aesthetics and politics, and cross-border / cross-language cultural production. Translator of numerous books from the Spanish, including most recently Luis Felipe Fabre's *Writing with Caca* (2022) and Sayak Valencia's *Gore Capitalism* (2018), Pluecker's own book of poetry and image, *Ford Over*, was published in 2016. They have exhibited artistic work at various museums and galleries.

ANNA ROSENWONG is a translator, editor, and content strategist. Her work has been honoured with the Best Translated Book

Award and the American Academy of Poets Ambroggio Prize, as well as fellowships from the National Endowment for the Arts, the Banff International Literary Translation Centre, the American Literary Translators Association, the University of Iowa, and the University of California, Irvine.

ALEC SCHUMACHER is an assistant professor at Gonzaga University. His research interests include Chilean poetry, the neo-avant-garde, and translation. He has published several articles on the works of Juan Luis Martínez and has translated works by Jorge Arbeleche, Elvira Hernández and Luis Correa-Díaz. His translation of *The Chilean Flag* (2019) was nominated for the National Translation Award in Poetry 2020 by the American Literary Translators Association.

ANASTATIA SPICER is a writer and handweaver based in Vermont. She holds a B.A. in Critical Social Inquiry from Hampshire College and has studied and taught weaving at Penland School of Craft. In 2023 she will join the Winterthur Masters Program in American Material Culture, as a Lois F. McNeil Fellow.

HONORA SPICER is an experiential educator and writer based in Providence, RI. Her translations have appeared in *Asymptote*, *Latin American Literature Today*, the *Academy of American Poets* and *Cardboard House Press*. She is a Ph.D. candidate in History at Harvard University.

MARTHA SPRACKLAND is an editor, writer and translator from Merseyside. She runs Offord Road Books, and is poetry editor for CHEERIO Publishing. She has translated poetry by Ana Gorría (*Ciclo*, Debacle Ediciones, 2020) and Gladys Mendía (PTC/Ledbury, 2020), and fiction by Sara Mesa (*The White Review*, 2021). In 2021 she was shortlisted for the Peirene–Stevns Translation Prize. Martha's collection, *Citadel* (LUP, 2020) was shortlisted for the Forward Prize for Best First Collection and the Costa Poetry Award.

LOTTE THIESSEN is a poet and translator living in Berlin. Between 2015 and 2022 she organized the reading and publication series artiCHOKE for which she translated contemporary poetry from

Portuguese, German and English into German and English and wrote critical texts contextualising the works. She is a founding member of Gegensatz Translation Collective. Her translation of *This Energy Wasted by Flight* by Lotte L.S. was published by the Halle für Kunst Lüneburg in September 2022.

JAMES WOMACK is a writer, translator and editor. He is the author of three books of poetry: *Misprint* (Carcanet 2012), *On Trust: A Book of Lies* (Carcanet 2017) and *Homunculus* (Carcanet 2020). Carcanet also publish his translations of Vladimir Mayakovsky (2016) and Manuel Vilas (2020), and Smokestack recently published his new translation of Aleksandr Tvardovsky's epic poem *Vasili Tyorkin* (2020). He lives in Cambridge, where he teaches Spanish and Russian translation and study skills.

LIST OF POETS BY COUNTRY

ARGENTINA
Teresa Arijón
Verónica Viola Fisher
Susana Ada Villalba

BOLIVIA
Elvira Espejo
Marcia Mogro

BRAZIL
Virna Teixeira
Jocely Vianna Baptista
Érica Zíngano

CHILE
Elvira Hernández
Paula Ilabaca Núñez
Luna Montenegro
Leonor Olmos

COLOMBIA
Johanna Barraza Tafur
Fátima Vélez

CUBA
Katherine Bisquet

DOMENICAN REPUBLIC
Neronessa

GUATEMALA
Rosa Chávez

MEXICO
Tania Favela Bustillo
Mikeas Sánchez
Sara Uribe

PERU
Victoria Guerrero Peirano

PUERTO RICO
Mara Pastor

VENEZUELA
Gladys Mendía
Marta Sojo